But not all of the NVA on that slope were still alive. By that time, the dead probably outnumbered the living, and the Lurps slipped in the blood, almost tripped over bodies and parts of bodies.

"Lurps!" yelled Tony. "We're Lurps!"

Very briefly, the enemy fire increased, and up on the bloody knoll, Gary Linderer felt something slap him on the thigh and didn't realize that it was a bullet. Someone was hollering down by the LZ, and that fool Walkabout was hollering back.

"Walkabout! You idiot! Shut up!" Linderer wasn't sure if he said it or just thought it, but then the realization hit him that *he* was the fool, not Walkabout. After all this fighting, the enemy already knew exactly where they were. And those were Lurps down there by the LZ—Lurps!—a reaction force of Lurps!

Walkabout began to shout again, and so did Linderer. Lurps! Lurps! When no one else could be bothered, their brother Lurps had come to their rescue and were there at last!

D0040736

**Also in this series**
*Published by Presidio Press*

**SIX SILENT MEN: Book One by Reynel Martinez**
**SIX SILENT MEN: Book Three by Gary A. Linderer**

F LONG RANGE PATROL 58

# SIX SILENT MEN

## 101st LRP/Rangers: Book Two

## Kenn Miller

PRESIDIO PRESS

**BALLANTINE BOOKS • NEW YORK**

A Presidio Press Book
Published by The Random House Publishing Group
Copyright © 1997 by Kenn Miller

Published in the United States by Presidio Press, an imprint of The Random House Publishing Group, a division of Random House, Inc., New York, and simultaneously in Canada by Random House of Canada Limited, Toronto.

Presidio Press and colophon are trademarks of Random House, Inc.

ISBN 978-0-8041-1564-3

Printed in the United States of America

www.presidiopress.com

First Edition: May 1997

# Acknowledgments and Dedication

It would have been impossible to write this book without the help of those who shared their experiences and perspectives with me, and hoping that I have done them justice, I thank them all without mentioning them here by name. You will find their names in the book itself. Without the patience of my wife, Hwei-li, my son, William, and daughter, Suling, I would not have been able to do this book—or much of anything else. This book began as a team effort, and I am indebted to my teammates, Gary Linderer and Rey Martinez, for their invaluable support, advice, help, and friendship. As the authors of the other two books in this series, Gary and Rey join me in dedicating *Six Silent Men: Book Two* to our brother Lurps and Rangers who died in Vietnam:

| | |
|---|---|
| Donvan Jeff Pruett | John T. McChesney |
| Percy W. McClatchy | Thomas John Sturgal |
| Joseph Griffis | Ashton Hayward Prindle |
| David Allen Dixon | Thomas Eugene Riley |
| John Lester Hines | Terry W. Clifton |
| George Buster Sullens | Albert D. Contreros |
| Patrick Lee Henshaw | Arthur J. Herringhausen |

Michael Dean Reiff

Barry Leigh Golden

John James Quick

Dean Julian Dedman

Keith Tait Hammond

Ronald Burns Reynolds

William Lincoln Marcy

Michael Linn Lytle

James William Salter

Ronald Wayne Jones

Rob George McSorley

Gary Paul Baker

Raymond Dean Ellis

Robert Lee O'Conner

George Edward Fogleman

Bryan Theotis Knight

David Munoz

Roger Thomas Lagodzinski

John Thomas Donahue

Jack Moss

Lawrence Elwood Scheib

Harry Thomas Henthorn

Lloyd Harold Grimes

Norman R. Stoddard

Robert George Drapp

Steven Glenn England

James Leroy Smith

Gabriel Trujillo

Richard Lee Martin

David Roy Haywood

Joel Richard Hankins

Leonard James Trumblay

Paul Coburn Sawtelle

James Bruce McLaughlin

Johnnie Ray Sly

Gary Duane Ellis

Steven John Ellis

Charles Anthony Sanchez

Johnny Howard Chapman

Hershel Duane Cude

Harry Jerome Edwards

David Allen Poley

James Albert Champion
(MIA)

A special dedication is also due two Lurp/Rangers who died shortly after returning from Vietnam—Nick Caberra, who survived World War Two, the Korean War, and an extended tour in Vietnam, then was posthumously awarded the Soldier's Medal for sacrificing his life for his fellow soldiers at Fort Bragg; and Raymond Zoschak, who returned home from Vietnam with at least two Silver Stars and no Purple Heart, and gave his own life on a public highway to avoid a traffic accident that would have claimed the lives of innocent civilians.

It is an honor to have served with such men.

# Author's Note

This book was originally intended to be the middle section of a much longer book about the LRRP/LRP/Ranger units that served as the eyes and ears—and sometimes the talons and teeth—of the 101st Airborne Division during the Vietnam War. As originally conceived, Rey Martinez was to write the first section, covering the 1st Brigade 101st Airborne's Long Range Reconnaissance Patrol detachment from 1965 to early 1968. I was to handle the Division LRP company, F Company, 58th Infantry (Long Range Patrol), from the time of its formation at Fort Campbell, Kentucky, in the spring of 1967, until it was redesignated L Company, 75th Rangers at the beginning of 1969. At this point, Gary Linderer was to take over and tell the story up through 1971. Because the resulting manuscript was too long, our publisher decided to split it into three books and publish them separately. This book is the second of the three—and if you read one of them, you should read all three books in the *Six Silent Men* series.

Not every mission pulled by F Company, 58th Infantry (LRP) is covered, or even mentioned, in this book. Part of this is due to my failings as a researcher and interviewer. Part of it is due to the fading memories of the men I interviewed, and part of it is due to the fact that certain activities of the 101st Lurps seem not to have been declassified yet— which is due almost entirely to bureaucratic sloth and not to any sensible considerations of national security. Human memory is fallible, but anyone writing about Vietnam War Lurps and Rangers is better off trusting the memories of the men involved than in trusting official records.

When it comes to the activities of Vietnam War long-range patrol and Ranger units, official Army records are often unreliable and inaccurate. Lurp and Ranger units in Vietnam were bastard units, commanded by officers without the rank to always assure that the men under their command received full credit for their accomplishments. Lurps and Rangers often worked in conjunction with artillery, aviation, intelligence, and infantry formations commanded by field-grade officers, and it was not at all unusual for these officers to give their own men full credit for operations in which Lurps and Rangers actually played the crucial part. Depending primarily on official records, one of the most prominent military historians of the Vietnam War wrote a book about Green Berets at war that seems to have been accepted as an authoritative source by Special Forces veterans. He followed this work with a book about Rangers at war that most Lurp/Ranger veterans who've read it consider an embarrassing failure. The reason for this is clear to me: Special Forces had a measure of command autonomy and record-keeping capability that Lurp and Ranger units sorely lacked. This is not to make excuses for any oversights or mistakes I might have made in this book. There are sure to be some—and I'm sure to hear about them for the rest of my life at unit reunions.

One final note: If you find it strange that the author refers to himself in the third person in this book, it is not because I am modest. It is because this book isn't about me—it's about the 101st Airborne Division's long-range patrol company, in which I had the privilege of serving.

Kenn Miller
September 1996

# Chapter One

In the early summer of 1967, shortly after the cadre of the 101st Airborne Division's famed Recondo School returned to Fort Campbell from training cadets at West Point, Brigadier General Frank B. Clay, the assistant division commander, and Lieutenant Colonel Charles Beckwith, the division G-2, paid an unexpected visit to the school, bearing the news that General Westmoreland had ordered all the divisions and separate brigade-size maneuver units then conducting operations in Vietnam to organize long-range patrol (LRP, pronounced "Lurp") companies. Since the 101st Airborne Division was scheduled to join its 1st Brigade in Vietnam at the end of the year, it was to organize such a company within the division. And though there was no shortage of talent in the division, it seemed only natural that the Recondo School cadre become the nucleus of this new company.

General Clay's visit was brief, but after his departure, Lieutenant Colonel Beckwith remained behind to go over some of the details. Having previously commanded the 5th Special Forces Group's Project Delta, Colonel Beckwith was more than familiar with the organization and duties of a long-range patrol company. And as he was the G-2, such a company, at least in theory, would be working for him. Wasting little time, Beckwith had

1

already made up his mind to put the new company under the command of Captain Peter Fitts. Fitts, a mustang officer with plenty of enlisted time (and an array of tattoos to prove that most of his service had been as an enlisted man), had a prior tour in Vietnam establishing and running long-range recon teams for Special Forces.

Colonel Beckwith knew what he wanted. The Table of Organization and Equipment (TOE) called for a three-platoon company. Two of the platoons would be patrol platoons, each running four to five six-man reconnaissance teams. The third platoon would be a headquarters platoon with a strong communications section. Beckwith made it very clear to the gathered Recondo School cadre that the company was to be a volunteer unit with standards that would exclude all but the most qualified. There was no disagreement.

When Beckwith had taken over Project Delta, it had been with the understanding that he would be given free rein to hire and fire anyone he wanted and that 5th Special Forces Group's entire roster would be open for recruiting his people. In taking over Project Delta, Beckwith had made a lot of enemies, stepped on a lot of toes, and maybe wronged a few good men. But then, Charlie Beckwith had never been the kind of man who worried about stepping on toes.

He couldn't promise the Recondo cadre they'd have carte blanche in putting together the new long-range patrol company, but he did assure them that they'd have the right to reject any volunteer who didn't meet their standards.

When Beckwith had taken over Project Delta, he'd sent notices out to every detachment in the 5th Special Forces Group advertising for volunteers and, as an inducement, promising a medal or a body bag—or both.

He didn't expect such an appeal would be allowed in the 101st Airborne Division—at least not at Fort Campbell. Still, a message of that sort would almost certainly get out to the troops.

The new company was going to need mature, experienced, well-trained team leaders and cadre, and Beckwith was quick to suggest that every officer and NCO of the Recondo School staff should volunteer to go back to Vietnam with the new Lurp company. As Sergeant First Class Harold Beck noted afterward, when "Chargin' Charlie" Beckwith made a suggestion, it usually carried the weight of an order. But this was one time Charlie Beckwith could have saved his breath. Every man listening to him had already made up his mind to do just that. To build up a Screaming Eagle Recondo Lurp company and take it to war? Hell, those men were professional Airborne soldiers—Rangers, paratroopers, Recondo instructors—and this was the opportunity of a lifetime, the sort of prospect that made all the routine, mundane frustration of a military career, and all the sweat, suffering, and apprehension of a paratrooper's life, worthwhile.

At that first meeting, it was assumed that the team leaders in the new company would come from the ranks of the Recondo School cadre, all experienced NCOs with the training and experience required of Lurp team leaders. All but one of them was a graduate of the Fort Benning Ranger School—and the one who wasn't a Ranger School graduate was Tony Bliss, a genuine hero on his first tour in the 101st's 1st Brigade, Division Soldier of the Year at Fort Campbell, and an honor graduate of the Recondo School. Some of the cadre had served as Ranger instructors, and most of them had previous Vietnam tours in Special Forces or as advisers to Vietnamese units. The TOE of a divisional Lurp company was still a tentative text, but the consensus at the time was that the TOE could probably be stretched to allow E-6 staff sergeant and E-7 sergeant first class team leaders.

But as soon as that first meeting with Lieutenant Colonel Beckwith ended, it became clear that the problem wasn't going to be finding men to lead the teams. It was going to be finding men to fill the teams.

Recruiting proved to be a formidable task. As the call was passed around to the various units at Fort Campbell, word also reached Fort Bragg, and soon a number of 82nd Airborne paratroopers, and a few idle Green Berets, began to give serious consideration to trying to get over to the 101st to join the new long-range patrol company. But since there wasn't much guarantee that they wouldn't be sent to a line infantry company instead—or even worse, get stuck in some damn support or headquarters unit—most of them decided at the last minute to stay where they were.

One man from Fort Bragg who decided to take the chance was Sp4 Jim Venable. He had been stuck driving a truck for the 82nd's support command, and he hadn't gone Airborne to drive a deuce and a half. Venable was on his way up to Brigade Headquarters as a candidate for Brigade Soldier of the Month when he was waylaid by a couple of Special Forces NCOs, who told him about a "special" company some friends of theirs were putting together up at Fort Campbell. Venable immediately recognized this as an escape and evasion opportunity. He and a dozen or so other selected 82nd Airborne Division paratroopers, a Special Forces Training Group student medic who'd shown great promise until his dog died in the final, "dog lab," phase of the medical qualification course, and a very small number of other personnel from

Fort Bragg were recruited for the company by friends of the Recondo School cadre.

Word also went out to promising privates at the Fort Benning Jump School, though orders couldn't be cut for them to the company, only to the division. Recent graduates of the Fort Benning Ranger School were already spoken for, but somehow Staff Sergeant Richard Burnell, who was already well on his way to becoming a legendary Ranger instructor, was lured away to the 101st and managed to pull strings to secure a slot in the new Lurp company.

But the main recruiting effort had to go forward within the 101st, and it was not an easy—or an altogether successful—effort. The 101st Airborne Division had no shortage of paratroopers who wanted to be Lurps, but despite Colonel Beckwith's best efforts, the long-range patrol company itself had no special priority in recruiting. The entire 101st Airborne Division was gearing up to join the 1st Brigade in Vietnam. Unit commanders and senior NCOs were not about to let the Lurps stage raids on their best people. In turn, the Lurps weren't about to let anyone dump a bunch of malcontents, misfits, and duds on them. Sergeant First Class Harold Beck, Staff Sergeant Tony Bliss, and Staff Sergeant Donald Randolph made many forays to the division's replacement companies, getting the word out that the division was looking for Lurp volunteers. Despite their best efforts to recruit new arrivals "before" they were assigned to other units, they did not have the power to expedite getting orders cut. If a man was already pending orders assigning him to another unit within the division, there wasn't much an E-7 and two E-6s could do to get those orders changed. And even though the company had *two* captains—Captain Fitts, the commander, and Captain Nation, the executive officer—

there wasn't much they could do about it either, because
they were going against the staffs of majors, colonels
both light and bird, and in some cases even generals, one
star or two. Even Lieutenant Colonel Beckwith was in no
position to compel compliance on the part of officers who
didn't want to lose their best men on the eve of departure
for a combat zone.

One by one, volunteers did drift in. It was a slow and
grueling process, and the long-range patrol company
remained severely understrength. With the entire division making final preparations for war, the Lurp company found that its low-priority status for training was no
better than its low-priority status for recruiting. Fortunately, the new company *did* have the Recondo School,
and it retained the same access to training sites as any
other infantry company, albeit without the support
resources the other companies enjoyed. But the Recondo
School and the normal training sites on post were not
enough to train Lurps, and as summer turned to fall,
Colonel Beckwith called in some markers and arranged
for the new company to move down to the Florida
Ranger camp for a little specialized training.

Charlie Beckwith had commanded the Florida Ranger
camp before coming to the 101st, and he had some real
power there. He laid on some good training—and some
very nasty weather. Rain was constant, and though the
patrolling was usually slow and careful, the pace of
training was relentless. It was soon obvious to everyone
that not all the Recondo School cadre were going to be
team leaders. A couple of them weren't really cutting it
in the field, while a couple of the new recruits had both
the rank and the talent to qualify for the job.

It was a sadly understrength company that made the
trip down to Florida, just a cadre, and enough new

sergeants and Sp4s and PFCs to fill out three or four full six-man teams. There was some talk about reducing team size to four men, but no one wanted to scrap the TOE of a divisional long-range patrol company before it was even completed. Besides, there were still not enough experienced men to go around on the teams, no matter how you split them up and shuffled them around—not if the intention was to field as many teams as a division as large and aggressive as the 101st Airborne was going to need.

In Vietnam, the 1st Brigade of the 101st had been serving as the war zone's fire brigade, on the move continually like nomads, being fed into one combat situation after another. By the summer of 1967, it had fought almost everywhere in South Vietnam except the Mekong Delta. This made the long-range patrol company's training at the Florida Ranger camp appear to be an excellent choice, since nearly everyone in the unit expected the division to be headed for the swamps, reeds, and mangrove thickets of the Mekong Delta.

But there were also those who believed that the division would be heading north and sending the Lurps out into the mountains. They wished that Lieutenant Colonel Beckwith had previously commanded, instead of the Florida Ranger camp, the Mountain Ranger camp at Dahlonega, Georgia. The navy and the 9th Division could handle the Mekong Delta. These men believed that the real war was up north, in I Corps.

Back at Fort Campbell, the company continued to recruit and train new volunteers, discarding about 50 percent of them for one reason or another. The new Lurps were eager to go to Vietnam, and even by Captain Fitts's and First Sergeant Darol Walker's exacting standards, those who were accepted into the company were adequately trained for the job ahead of them.

The long-range patrol company was still understrength as it began its final preparations for deployment to the Republic of Vietnam. Those who had made it through the rigorous training were ready, but the unit was still woefully short of the personnel it would need to perform its mission. When the departure date finally arrived, there were only sixty-five men, including headquarters, commo, and supply. Sixty-five men wasn't even an understrength company. It was a large platoon—a large platoon with two captains, a full complement of somewhat superfluous lieutenants, a first sergeant, almost a dozen E-7s and staff sergeant E-6s, and a rather severe paucity of fully trained buck sergeants, Sp4s, and PFCs. It was definitely a case of too many chiefs and not enough Indians.

But worse than being understrength, the Lurp company had no support laid on—beyond an uncomfortable and mystifyingly unlikely administrative link with the 326th Airborne Engineers. The engineers didn't understand Lurps, and the Lurps didn't understand the engineers. Even among the junior enlisted men, there wasn't any rancor between the Lurps and the engineers—at least not yet, there wasn't. Sure, the Lurps and engineers did share a common love of C-4 plastic explosive. But beyond that, and beyond the fact that they were all members of the Airborne brotherhood, there just wasn't much common ground between the 326th Engineers and the division long-range patrol company. And being so divorced from the tactical link, the administrative link just didn't make sense. What the company was going to need in the way of support was intelligence, communications, helicopters, air and artillery gun support, exploitation forces, and a whole lot of respect for the Lurps as an elite and essential bunch of people. What the company had instead was an administrative link to the 326th Engineers. But at that point, nobody worried about it too much, trusting that everything would work out once the division got to Vietnam.

For the most part, Captain Fitts and First Sergeant Walker were confident that when the company got to Vietnam and began pulling missions, volunteers would come. Both men were veteran paratroopers and knew that Vietnam would be fertile ground for recruiting new men to swell the ranks, especially when the company's reputation began to grow. Scuttlebutt had it that when the division arrived, the 1st Brigade was going to have to disband its long-range reconnaissance patrol (LRRP, also "Lurp") detachment and send the men who wanted to transfer over to the division long-range patrol company. With any luck at all, that would bring in almost a whole patrol platoon of experienced Lurps—at least four operational teams. Neither Captain Fitts nor First Sergeant Walker had any reservations; the 1st Brigade Lurps had been pulling long-range patrols in Vietnam since 1965. They were among the first two non–Special Forces Lurp units that the 5th Special Forces Group's legendary Project Delta had trained and helped to organize in its own image, and after more than two years of operations, the 1st Brigade Lurps had an enormous reputation. There wouldn't be that many leadership positions open for them, but they were sure to be a welcome addition to the company when they arrived.

When the division began assembling in Vietnam, there was a period of time when little was accomplished while the troops got used to the climate, the terrain, and the lifestyle. During this shakedown period, three of the 1st Brigade Lurps, Alan "Teddy Bear" Gaskell, Jay "Jaybird" Magill, and Rey Martinez, went back to the States

on extension leave. In their absence, the 1st Brigade
LRRP platoon moved up to Song Be, near the Cambodian
border. With its fine, red, powdery dust, its abandoned
rubber plantations, and its heavy population of enemy
soldiers, Song Be was not a particularly charming place.
For the first time since its arrival in Vietnam two and a
half years earlier, the 1st Brigade of the 101st seemed to
lose a little of its legendary initiative. The war went on,
and 1st Brigade paratroopers continued to fight it with
courage and skill, but an unaccustomed mood of uncertainty settled on the brigade. The division was already
arriving in-country, and sooner or later the brigade would
once again become part of the division and no longer an
independent maneuver unit. Maybe those in the higher
levels of command understood the effects of merging the
brigade into the division, but down at the troop level there
was doubt, uncertainty, and more than a little downright
skepticism that the marriage was going to work.

Nowhere was this more true than in Brigade Headquarters Company—the parent organization of the Lurp
detachment. Already, many of the best men were
leaving, some to MACV-SOG, some to battalion recon
platoons, some back to the States when their tours or
extensions came to an end. Because the 1st Brigade had
arrived in Vietnam in June 1965—and because the
normal tour was one year and the normal extension six
months—December and June had always been times of
personnel flux in the 101st, even before the division
came over. Even without the division coming over, old
guys would have been leaving the Lurp detachment at the
end of the year on normal rotations. But despite the division's pending arrival, new men were coming into the
detachment, volunteers from other combat units in the
brigade, most of them on extensions. When Martinez,

Gaskell, and Magill left for their leaves, they were among the few remaining men who'd been with the detachment six months before at Duc Pho. But there were some good Lurps, and some very Foul Dudes among the relatively new men. All of them were experienced combat paratroopers before the urge to become Lurps had affected them.

There were men like William "Crash" Clark, a cynical, humorous, well-read New Yorker who probably would have ended up in a foreign war somewhere even if America hadn't supplied one for him. There weren't any men in the detachment exactly *like* Clark's buddy, Nick Caberra, who had served in the Marine Corps in World War Two and Korea and done a previous enlistment in the army during a Berlin Crisis that disappointed him terribly by not turning into a war. But most of the Lurps were like Nick, at least in their hearts. Nick was no lifer, but he was a professional soldier—one who came into the service only for wars. This seemed an eminently sensible way to avoid the Stateside garrison routine and regimentation of peacetime military life. A few of the younger Lurps hoped to emulate Nick, if they managed to live as long as he had and if America could manage a few more interesting wars after this one.

Staff Sergeants Derby Jones and Lawrence Christian were still in the Lurp platoon. Derby was developing a fine "lifer" dignity, while Christian was maybe beginning to go a little bit crazy. But Derby's lifer dignity fit him well, and Christian wasn't so crazy it would be noticed in the Lurp platoon. As far as anyone knew, both NCOs seemed willing to transfer to the division long-range patrol company if the detachment's platoon was broken up.

Staff Sergeants Ron Weems and Lester "Superspade" Hite were still in the platoon, but they were already getting a little restless. If they were cooking up any plans among themselves, they weren't talking much about it—although Superspade did allow that it was going to take this division a painful passage before it could really break on through all that Fort Campbell structured thinking and get to dealing effectively with the problems at hand. And there are those who remember Weems looking off to the west one evening back in the base camp and saying something wistful about how close Cambodia was and how from there it was within easy range of any self-respecting Lurp. . . .

Sergeant Bob McKinnon was sticking around, and so were Mark Thompson and Clay Wentworth. Brian "Doc" Kraft, the Wolfman, was staying on, and so was Doug "Doc" Norton. Alan "Doc" Cornett, the notorious "Lurch," was staying in the platoon for a while yet, still putting off going back to Special Forces until he was sure those crooks running the Mess Association had been replaced. Lieutenant McIsaac, Mother Henshaw, Virgil Pauk, and Top Smith were gone, but there were still plenty of good Lurps in the platoon.

There were also a few questionable characters in the detachment, and they hadn't all been kicked out yet when Martinez, Gaskell, and Magill got back from their extension leaves. It wasn't unusual for an occasional questionable character to volunteer for the Lurps, and if he made it through the probationary period, a few missions, a contact or two, and his peers' assessment, it wasn't unheard of for an otherwise questionable character to find a home in the Lurps. In fact, in the eyes of the legs (soldiers who do not jump out of airplanes) and REMFs ("soldiers" who do not see combat) and civilians who made up the vast majority of the human race at large, just being a Lurp, any Lurp, branded a man a questionable character. But within the Lurp platoon, different and more demanding standards determined who was and wasn't a questionable character.

There was, for example, a certain combat-twisted nineteen-year-old who was keeping body parts in jars in his footlocker, saying he was saving up to make his own gook. He'd come to the platoon from a line infantry company a month or so before Martinez, Gaskell, and Magill went on their leaves, and he was still waiting to be kicked out when they got back. The kid was brave, but he wasn't exactly reliable. He might have been foul, but he didn't have the makings of a Foul Dude. To be a Foul Dude, a man had to have both good sense and a little bit of class. Taking an ear wasn't particularly disgraceful, just as long as you took only one and didn't keep it too long, or make too big a fetish out of it, or flash it around officers and reporters, or send it home as a souvenir. Of course, taking ears wasn't much of a custom among Lurps, being more the sort of thing a cherry in a line company might find himself doing after his first personal body count. But keeping an eyeball and organs in jars in a footlocker in hopes of making a gook from parts? That was downright insane. The whole point of being in Vietnam was to kill Viet Cong and North Vietnamese soldiers, not to make new ones. This was one young paratrooper none of the other Lurps wanted out with them on a long-range patrol mission. Fortunately, he was in the detachment only until another home could be found for him.

There wasn't much in the way of long-range patrol missions coming down at Song Be, at least not on the part of Americans. Brigade Headquarters was proving increasingly nervous and more than a little reluctant to take the initiative against the enemy now that elements of the division were up at Song Be. The proximity of the

Cambodian border—well within the Lurps' accustomed range—promised rich pickings. But there was no way the brigade was going to send Lurps over the fence or even suggest the idea to whatever higher authority it had to answer to. MACV-SOG managed to bend the rules by taking along indigenous troops and going in sterile. The same approach would have worked for the Lurps if the politicians and military leaders mishandling the war by setting rules of engagement only one side obeyed had allowed it. The NVA blatantly denied its own presence—not only in Cambodia and Laos but also in South Vietnam. Everyone in the world knew they were there, but for an American officer to suggest a clandestine border crossing—well, that would look like something between mere incompetence and treason on his efficiency report. Back in the old days, it might have been a different story—at least as far as getting the suggestion passed up the chain of command, if not to the point of getting the mission approved, some proper support laid on, and teams actually launched. But by the end of 1967 and the beginning of 1968, it was the NVA getting the Lurp missions. Over the border from their Cambodian sanctuary, NVA recon teams were coming right up to the wire of the 101st's forward rear area, just as bold and sassy as could be.

It was, of course, the Lurp platoon's job to deal with them. There must have been close to a thousand paratroopers living inside the forward rear area perimeter at Song Be, and some of them were doing their part sweeping outside the perimeter by day and manning the bunker line at night. But when it came to "long-range" patrolling, the job fell to the Lurps. To those looking out from the Song Be perimeter, "long-range" didn't seem to mean much more than a kilometer or two outside the perimeter—and often even closer in than that.

Six-man recon teams and twelve-man heavy teams were going out day and night. And though they were a little offended to be doing the sort of close-in security patrolling that should have been done by the clerks and cooks and MPs and Airborne infantry companies and cav troops on stand-down, the Lurps didn't really mind. Sure, it was short-range patrolling, but they took the little excursions seriously. They were killing the enemy's own recon troops, on an almost daily basis, just a short hump outside the perimeter. They weren't out there to defend the forward rear area. They were out there to catch and kill the enemy, and they did it with regularity and with gusto. So what if these weren't long-range missions? And so what if they weren't getting proper credit for what they were doing? It was better than sitting idle in the rear, getting bored and getting in trouble.

These 1st Brigade Lurps—and in view of the short-range missions at hand, we must even include the somewhat disturbed young soldier who was building his own gook from parts—were a very formidable and impressive bunch of killers. But even the best of them—even Derby Jones in all his fine lifer dignity, or Teddy Bear Gaskell with all his obvious civilization and good sense—would not have presented a very comforting appearance to anyone fresh over from Fort Campbell. The 1st Brigade Lurps were a scruffy crew of cocky scofflaws, and it was obvious to anyone who got to know them that they weren't going to fit smoothly into what was still a Stateside Lurp company working for what was still a Stateside division—a division that was still accustomed to breaking starch and judging a man at least in part by the spit-shine on his boots.

But in the meantime, there were plenty of gooks to be killed, right there outside the wire at the forward rear area, and at that point, the 1st Brigade Lurps weren't spending much time worrying about the division, and tormenting themselves over what the future might hold for them—beyond the very immediate future, of course.

And the immediate future didn't seem too threatening, at least as far as the enemy was concerned. NVA recon teams were out there for the picking, and the Lurps were having their fun with them. It wasn't long-range recon, at least not for the American Lurps. But it was still satisfying work and would do until something more challenging came along.

# Chapter Two

The 101st Airborne Division's long-range patrol company arrived at Bien Hoa Air Base, Republic of Vietnam, in late November 1967, and including the advance party, which had arrived a little earlier, there were fewer than seventy men.

In their distinctive camouflage uniforms and black baseball caps with the 101st Recondo patch and jump wings, the Lurps drew curious, and occasionally even awed, looks from the sort of rear echelon personnel who liked to speculate about the doings of mysterious ground troops. As they went about their duties moving equipment and getting established on the army base adjacent to the airfield, Lurp EM and NCOs were occasionally mistaken for officers and saluted. This was probably due to the fact that, against the white Recondo patches on their caps, their jump wings were almost invisible except when they caught the sun just right. The resulting glint was easily mistaken for the bars of a lieutenant or captain. Being mistaken for officers disgusted the NCOs, all of whom expected people to know that they worked for a living. But the PFCs and Sp4s were delighted to be mistaken for officers, especially when the salutes came from the Air Police and Army MPs who proliferated in the rear areas around Bien Hoa. As serious as any new second

17

lieutenant, Sp4 Al Contreros returned the salutes very smartly when he got them. But most of the other men responded in a fashion more like Major Ryker's convict commandos in the movie *The Dirty Dozen*. Although they had just arrived in-country, they were already beginning to act like Lurps.

Shortly after arriving at Bien Hoa, Sergeants Tony Bliss and Roger Brown and a few other men went off to run patrols with the Australian Special Air Service, which had a base near the coastal city of Vung Tau. By most accounts, the Aussie SAS thought the new Lurps a little too young and jumpy, a little too rash and trigger-happy for their taste. In turn, the Lurps were a little put off by the fact that the Aussies did not always carry enough ammunition and didn't insist on some sort of weapons compatibility on their teams. One guy might be carrying an FN, while the man next to him had an M-16. How were they going to swap parts to keep at least one of them going if both weapons got damaged? And besides, these Aussies wore their wings on their sleeves, like Girl Scouts. They wore berets that seemed to be modeled after the beret the Lurps over at the 173rd Air-borne Brigade wore, with a beret badge that resembled the 17th Cav crest except for a dagger instead of a horse collar. And if that wasn't enough, their unit motto wasn't even in Latin. Still, the Lurps and the SAS got along well enough. Even though the young troopers and junior NCOs of the 101st Lurp company and those of the Aussie SAS troop didn't seem all that outrageously impressed with each other, the cadre NCOs of the Lurp company and the cadre NCOs and warrant officers of the SAS troop hit it off like long-lost cousins.

To the Lurps stuck at Bien Hoa, it became a regular thing to see their cadre NCOs hung over after visiting with the Aussies and to hear them bitching and complaining about how these damn Aussies liked to get drunk and start singing "God Bless America," mocking the Queen of England, and cracking stupid "Tommy the Pommy" jokes about the British Special Air Service. All the bitching was good-natured and friendly, but not everyone was so impressed with the Australian Special Air Service. Platoon Sergeant Brubaker was heard grumbling one day that for people who never had the balls to have a revolution and kick the Limeys out, the Aussies sure did seem to have an attitude case against England. Cool Bru made known his suspicion that those Aussies weren't much more than cheap Third World imitations. When it came to Special Air Services, the only one that counted was the British. And Brubaker had his doubts that *they* were all they were cracked up to be.

Word soon got around Bien Hoa that, compared to the Second Field Force Lurps, in their own compound right down the road, the Aussies weren't seeing much action at all. The Second Field Force Lurps were seeing beaucoup enemy whenever they went outside the wire. Every team they were sending out was finding big masses of enemy, and almost every team seemed to be getting into contact and having to be extracted under fire. When they weren't in the field, the Field Force Lurps lived in a fenced-off compound that neither allowed for casual visitors nor allowed the enlisted Lurps out to roam the rear area as they pleased. But somehow the 101st Lurps and the Field Force Lurps managed to get together, and according to the Field Force Lurps, the shit was building up and headed for the fan—and all the REMFs and legs, clerks and cooks and officers back there were headed for a heavy-duty surprise. The Field Force Lurps were worried, but they seemed to take a certain grim delight in thinking how bad things were going to be for the REMFs. The Field Force Lurps had tried to warn them, and the time was coming when all these rear area poagies were going to wish they'd paid attention. . . .

One of the Field Force Lurps told his Screaming Eagle counterparts that they had a company cemetery because teams were encouraged to bring their kills back with them to be counted and verified—which was incredibly stupid and dangerous. And then the bodies had to be buried—which was a pain in the ass. Field Force didn't trust the Lurps to count their own kills. And worse than that, Field Force didn't seem to care how many live enemy the Lurps saw. Field Force only seemed to care about how many dead ones could be counted. The Second Field Force Lurps were sure that Field Force was headed for a world of shit because of it. And the 101st Lurps were glad they'd be working for the most elite and aggressive division in the United States military, the 101st Airborne, instead of a paper command like the Field Force. Even without the Lurp scroll on their shoulder sleeve, it was easy to wear the Screaming Eagle patch with pride.

As the newly arrived Lurps trained and got organized in Bien Hoa, new volunteers began to filter in and be integrated into the teams. Somehow or other, the Lurps began to collect vehicles. Jeeps, small trucks, and even a field ambulance—none of which was authorized by TOE—began showing up in the Lurp company area. About this same time, other, "lesser," units began to report missing vehicles. This coincidence, though never proven to be anything more than a coincidence, contributed to a division-wide belief that the long-range patrol company was a band of thieves and cutthroats. This belief dismayed the affable Lurps. Sure, they intended to be cutthroats in the field when the opportunity arose. But thieves? They weren't thieves. They were just abnormally gifted with a deep talent pool of field expedient supply specialists. Reappropriating an occasional vehicle from one unit of the United States Army to another wasn't really stealing. Once you repainted the bumper numbers and got someone to make up some paperwork, it was all very proper, and more or less legal.

A short time after the rash of missing vehicle reports, most of the Lurp company moved out to join the division at Song Be, and most of the vehicles were left behind, to be recovered by REMFs who claimed the vehicles had originally belonged to them. Somehow, no one got in trouble for these alleged misappropriations. Rumor had it that Captain Fitts had had a direct hand in covering for his Lurps. And the company didn't lose all of its vehicles. Back at Bien Hoa, one jeep and a field ambulance still provided ground transportation for the few Lurps remaining in the company area.

When the Division Lurps arrived in Song Be, they moved into a wooded area full of fire ants near the perimeter. They soon found themselves doing the same sort of patrols the 1st Brigade Lurps were doing. There were no air assets available to the Lurps, so long-range patrol missions were out of the question. But just as their 1st Brigade brothers found an abundance of enemy right outside the wire, the Division Lurps also found hunting good. They were getting to patrol at last.

Most of the patrols were into a stretch of rubber plantation just southwest of the perimeter, and most of them were uneventful. On one of these early patrols, the Lurps killed some of the first NVA the 101st Airborne Division (not counting the 1st Brigade) accounted for in Vietnam. The team captured an enemy mortar and the helmet the enemy was using as a baseplate. Even though the 1st Brigade—and the 1st Brigade Lurps—had been killing VC and NVA all over Vietnam since 1965, and were still killing them with regularity in Song Be and environs, news that the Division Lurps had captured a mortar and killed the crew caused a brief sensation at Division Headquarters. Morale soared—but only briefly. The long-range patrol company was new to the war, and the war was about to catch up with it.

The first wound didn't prove too serious. Sergeant Jack Gibney, a quiet NCO from Oklahoma and one of the brightest team leaders to come over with the company, was wounded in the leg by a booby trap five or six kilometers outside the perimeter. Gibney couldn't walk all the way back in without turning a minor wound into a potentially major one. He was bleeding rather heavily, and needed a dustoff ship to get him out before things got serious. Word came over the radio that no medevac was available; back in the rear, Tony Bliss and Roger Brown heard the transmission. They promptly hopped in a jeep and headed off to the Song Be airstrip, where they prepared to commandeer a helicopter at gunpoint—only to discover that the pilot and crew of the first chopper they approached didn't really need any such persuading. It wasn't a medevac ship, but the crew was game for a medevac mission. With Bliss and Brown on board, the chopper set off on its unauthorized mission and got Gibney out of there. Tony Bliss stayed on the ground with Gibney's team, and Roger Brown flew back with Gibney to the hospital.

Gibney was back, on limited duty, in a week, and if you only considered his wound, the company would still be way ahead. But this was a busy time all over Vietnam, and the war was catching up to the Division Lurps. Sp4 Jim Walker was wounded so severely he had to be evacuated out of the country. A half dozen other Division Lurps managed to "win" far less costly Purple Hearts in one fashion or another, and there were a few more enemy killed. But then, on the night of January 23, 1968, the Lurp company suffered its first fatality when John McChesney was killed in a firefight right outside the perimeter. A heavy team had gone out on security patrol. It was set up in an ambush position when the NVA started mortaring the perimeter. The enemy's mortars fell short, and one round exploded right in the midst of the Lurps. McChesney was killed instantly. Jim Venable and William "Raider" Laing were knocked on their asses, temporarily deaf from concussion, and a few other Lurps took slight wounds from shrapnel. That was only the beginning. Soon, the Lurps were caught in the middle of a firefight between the perimeter and the enemy. They finally got the Americans on the perimeter to cease fire, but by then the vegetation around the heavy team was on fire and the enemy decided to charge. The Lurps managed to repulse the assault and break contact, taking McChesney's body with them when they made it back through the perimeter. In the morning, the team that went back to the site found Venable's watch still ticking, despite the fact that the band and part of the casing had melted. It hurt to lose a Lurp so close to the perimeter, but losing McChesney really hurt. McChesney was a popular guy and a good Lurp, and even those who had lost friends on previous tours felt particularly bad about losing him.

A few days after McChesney's death, a few of the Division Lurps were down at the shower point, trying to wash some of that powdery Song Be dust and red mud out of their pores. Their tiger-stripe uniforms were hung on pegs outside the showers, when in came an even scruffier crew of Lurps in tiger stripes. These were 1st Brigade LRRP detachment Lurps, and it was the voice of Lester Hite, the Superspade, that the Division Lurps heard first.

"Now who," Superspade wondered aloud, "might *this* be, wearing tiger stripes? It can't be Special Forces, for I do believe that Green Berets always have hot showers at home. So who could it be?"

"We're the Lurps!" came a voice from the shower.

Superspade considered that for a second, then asked exactly whose Lurps they were claiming to be.

"The 101st Airborne Division Lurps!" came the answer in another voice.

"Now lookee here," said Superspade. "You people have been *severely* misinformed. The pure fact of this here matter is that *we're* the 101st Lurps, not you."

There might have been bloodshed at the shower point that day, but there wasn't. Once Superspade got things squared away as to who was who, the Division Lurps invited the 1st Brigade Lurps to visit them at their compound, which wasn't as far from the shower point as the 1st Brigade Lurps had been stuck. When the 1st Brigade Lurps visited the Division Lurps, they had little difficulty seeing why they were trusted so close to what passed for real luxury here in Song Be. These Division Lurps were damn near breaking starch in their tiger fatigues, and even the Sp4s and PFCs had nothing but praise for the lifers—all of the lifers. Praising some of them, or most of them, would have made sense. But this was a whole company, and it was bound to have its share of fools and ass-holes. No one seemed to have much idea what was going to happen, if the units were to remain separate or be united, but the wiser 1st Brigade Lurps could see that there was going to be a little culture clash no matter what happened. A few of them decided to look for another home rather than risk being disbanded or forced into this very Stateside new Lurp company.

When the Vietnamese New Year holiday, Tet, arrived, the enemy went on the offensive all over the country. The Division Lurps stuck back in Bien Hoa got a chance to rack up the body count by helping defend the perimeter at Bien Hoa, and when things heated up at Song Be, some of the Division Lurps there got a chance to help recapture a truck-mounted quad .50 machine gun that some legs had abandoned to the NVA.

When Captain Fitts volunteered to lead his Lurps in the recovery of the American Embassy in Saigon, the division decided a mere captain didn't deserve that public and important a mission, so a conventional Air-borne Infantry company, under temporary command of a major, got the job instead. It didn't hurt Lurp morale not to get this job, because most of the Lurps never knew that Captain Fitts had tried to get it for them and didn't know what they were missing out on until it was already over and smeared across every newspaper in America.

On the other side of the 101st's forward rear at Song Be from the Division Lurps, the 1st Brigade Lurps were still occasionally killing gooks outside the wire, but morale was falling quickly and a feeling of uncertainty was beginning to set in. The good old days were over. The 1st Brigade of the 101st Airborne Division, per-haps the finest maneuver element of its size in the history of the United States Army, was losing its separate identity. The 1st Brigade of the 101st Airborne Division had been on its own for nearly two and a half years. Becoming part of the division again was a hard pill for the hardcore 1st Brigaders to swallow.

Master Sergeant Lloyd "Top" Smith had already rotated back to the States at the end of his tour, and Lieutenant McIsaac was headed off to advisory duty with MAT 16, in the Mekong Delta. There was plenty of leadership still left in the detachment, but it was all team leadership. That wasn't the kind of leadership the 1/101 LRRP detachment needed to survive as an independent unit. The teams were sitting almost idle while the division swallowed up the whole 1st Brigade, treating it like an ill-favored stepchild compared to the other brigades.

Nobody was very surprised when word came down that the long-range reconnaissance patrol detachment was going to be swallowed up by the long-range patrol company. Nobody was very happy about it, either. It wasn't anything you'd read about in *The Screaming Eagle*, but throughout the 1st Brigade the division's arrival brought with it an unaccustomed mood of loss and foreboding. The 1st Brigade of the 101st Airborne Division had been something special, but day by day, the 101st Airborne Division was beginning to look more and more like the 1st Cavalry Division.

# Chapter Three

It was dusk when the C-130 landed at Bien Hoa, and when what was left of the 1st Brigade Lurp platoon unassed the plane and fell out on the tarmac, they found a two-and-a-half-ton truck already waiting to take them to their new rear area and their new Lurp company. There was no mistaking the Lurps for conventional troops. They were dressed in their normal mixture of tiger-stripe cammies and faded OD jungle fatigues, and on their heads they were wearing faded tiger-stripe boonie hats. Their web gear was well worn and hung with canteens, ammo pouches, knives of various kinds, field dressings, serum albumin cans, smoke grenades, compasses, and canteen pouches full of M-16 magazines and hand grenades. Most of them were wearing cloth bandoliers of M-16 magazines, and all of them were carrying bulging rucksacks. The 1st Brigade Lurps hadn't been allowed to bring their full complement of weapons. The M-60s and most of the M-1911 .45 pistols belonged to the brigade, not the detachment, and they'd had to leave them behind. All of the captured weapons had been confiscated for presentation to field grade officers, and there wasn't an AK in sight. But the weapons they did have were spectacular enough. They were taped so that they wouldn't rattle, and some of them were camouflaged with strips of tiger-stripe cloth.

Because M-16s and CAR-15s were prone to jam due to double feeds and extraction problems, all of the Lurps had cleaning rods taped to their weapons where they could be quickly brought into action in case a round had to be dislodged from the chamber. But not all the Lurp weapons were on display. In addition to the M-16s and CAR-15s and the hybrids of the two, there was at least one unauthorized and basically worthless grease gun, two sawed-off M-79 grenade launchers that had the fearsome look of 40-millimeter coach pistols, and Ernie Winston's radically customized M-14, which was now compact enough to carry to the field as a second weapon but which, for lack of a proper flash suppressor, shot a tongue of flame three feet long when it was fired on full automatic and in any practical sense was really more fuss than it was worth. Winston had moved on to the Tiger Force, but he'd left the M-14 behind in the care of Mark Thompson. These weapons were not on display but packed away, partially disassembled in various rucksacks.

The guy driving the recently "borrowed" truck took one look, and he knew these were the people he was there to pick up. Another look told him who was in charge, for only a couple of the 1st Brigade Lurps were wearing stripes or any other insignia of rank, and only one of those wore E-6 stripes. The driver ambled over and introduced himself to Derby Jones, and Derby hollered for the rest of the guys to saddle up and hop on the deuce-and-a-half. "And for godsake, will you animals try to act disciplined?" Derby added, just because somebody had to say it.

With a few good-natured calls for Derby to lighten up and stop acting like such a lifer, the Lurps clambered aboard the truck and made themselves comfortable. This wasn't bad—a whole deuce-and-a-half, and their own driver to meet them at the airstrip. Even the guys who had misgivings about working for a whole chickenshit Stateside division felt a little better about the move.

Crash Clark looked around doubtfully and wondered aloud how many of the NVA and VC commandos who'd hit this place had survived to escape and regroup. Sp4 Thomas, a quiet, soft-spoken, handsome black Lurp from Tennessee, removed the toothbrush he habitually chewed on and said something about how the REMFs must've finally managed to get things under control. Clark said he wasn't worried about that. He was worried about the guys on the other side. He hoped some of them got back alive, since an operation like they pulled there deserved at least a few survivors to tell the story firsthand.

The Tet Offensive was pretty much over in the Saigon/Bien Hoa area, and Bien Hoa really was the rear area once again. All the roads inside the perimeter were supposed to be clear, and the whole vast military reservation was supposed to be secure. When the driver turned on his headlights, most of the Lurps took that as a good sign. They kept their weapons close at hand, as was their habit, but they settled back, prepared to trust the security of the Bien Hoa perimeter—although not too much.

By the time the truck was away from the airfield, a few of the Lurps began loading their pipes. By the time the truck was on the perimeter road, between the air force and the army areas of Bien Hoa, dusk had deepened to darkness and the pipes were being passed around, smoke and laughter dissolving on the slipstream of warm night air.

Before long, they were singing the Lurp song. There was always a little debate about the various verses, what the private said and what the shavetail lieutenant said, but everyone agreed on the verse where the sergeant said, "Oh, bullshit!" And everyone joined in on the chorus, "Merry men are we, bad as we can be. Hey, there's none so fair that they can compare to the Airborne L-R-P!"

Sergeant Craig Vega suggested that they teach the Lurp song to the new guys they were joining, and there wasn't a soul on the truck, not even the cynics, who doubted for a moment that the Lurp song would pass smoothly on to the Fort Campbell cherry Lurps. It was a catchy tune, and it had just the right Lurp attitude.

At a curve in the road, sitting right up close to the perimeter but with quite a perimeter of its own, was a walled Special Forces compound with a big painted green beret and a sign saying THE PROFESSIONALS that faced the perimeter road like a billboard. Someone made a crack about Green Beret typists and radio repairmen, but Sergeant Vega had served as a Lurp in Germany with guys who now worked out of that place, and he made it known that the guys he knew were not, by any stretch of the imagination, REMFs. According to Vega, those guys really were professionals. Somebody said they hoped the same would be true of the Division Lurp company.

Sitting up front with the driver, Derby Jones glanced back occasionally to make sure the Lurps were behaving—which, of course, they weren't. He hadn't planned on being the platoon sergeant on this move, but who else was there? Derby wouldn't have joined in on any of that pipe-passing bullshit, but he really would have been happier sitting back there with the rest of the guys instead of up front, trying to pry a little intell out of the driver.

Derby had heard of some of the NCOs, and they had good reputations. But it was soon clear that this was still, at heart, a Stateside Lurp company working for a very Stateside division. With every glance at the back of the truck, Derby felt the burden of responsibility grow a little heavier.

When the truck finally got to the almost deserted Lurp company rear area at Bien Hoa, Platoon Sergeant Brubaker was there to meet the men from the 1st Brigade Lurp detachment. He showed them into a comparatively luxurious wooden barracks with real bunks, concrete floor, galvanized steel roof, electricity, and wooden walls. The Lurps were impressed. And when Brubaker pointed out the little refrigerator in the corner of the barracks and offered to get them some beer, the Lurps were really impressed.

Brubaker said he knew SSG Weems and was disappointed not to see him. Weems had said something about not being welcome in this new Lurp company, and he had gone off to Long Tan, or House Ten in Saigon, looking for a job with MACV-SOG, where he might be allowed to cross the border from time to time. Nobody said anything about it to Brubaker, for they didn't much discuss it themselves. Going off to SOG was an act of extreme devotion to the Lurp calling, and when someone actually did it, it was not the sort of thing to mention to strangers. For all that he was trying to ingratiate himself, Brubaker was still a stranger to the clannish and somewhat suspicious 1st Brigade Lurps.

Brubaker mentioned that he knew SFC Bozeman, which didn't particularly impress anyone. Then he mentioned that he'd known Top Smith years before at Fort Bragg, and spoke of him with fond respect. Brubaker's stock went up.

Brubaker explained that most of the unit was still at Song Be, so there wasn't anything pressing until they got back. In the meantime, the 1st Brigade Lurps were to make themselves at home. As far as he knew, there wouldn't be any formations they had to stand until the whole company returned, and he promised the Lurps they'd be able to make and fill their own teams, at least initially.

Early the next day, the 1st Brigade Lurps did not bother to fall out for the morning formation. It wasn't much of a formation, with most of the company still up in Song Be, and perhaps it was because the formation was so small that the new arrivals were missed. He seemed to know he was wrong, but Brubaker stormed into the barracks and rousted the sleeping Lurps, then lit into them for having skipped the formation. A few of the Lurps grabbed their toothbrushes and shaving kits and stomped out in disgust, a few of them tried to reason with Brubaker, and old Nick Caberra—a PFC at the moment, but still a three-war veteran—looked up at Brubaker, and asked him where he was in June 1945. Brubaker sputtered, then said he was in elementary school.

With a scowl, Nick said that he'd been killing Japs on Okinawa.

Next, Nick asked where Brubaker was in November 1952. Brubaker admitted he was in high school, and when Nick pressed him, Brubaker admitted he'd been at least old enough to drop out of school and lie about his age to get in the service in time for the war in Korea. When Nick pronounced him a worthless lifer parasite, a peacetime soldier and fairweather patriot used to living fat off the taxpayer's dollar, Brubaker threw up his hands in despair and stomped out of the barracks, muttering darkly all the way.

The 1st Brigade Lurp detachment's integration into the 101st Airborne Division's long-range patrol company was already off to a rather bad start. And when Sp4 Duckett put a few M-16 rounds through the galvanized steel roof of the barracks, that bad start got a little bit worse. By the time the rest of the company returned to the Bien Hoa rear area, the Foul Dudes of the old 1/101 LRRP were already beginning to fit in like one gnarly, splintery, square peg in a smoothly round hole.

To the former 1st Brigade Lurps, this new company seemed to have almost everything. The rear area orderly room was complete with murals of Lurps parachuting, rappelling out of helicopters and down cliffs, paddling rubber boats, sneaking through the jungle, sniping, calling in air strikes, unassing helicopters, riding McQuire rigs, planting demolitions, laying into ambush positions, counting enemy on a trail, and having all sorts of fun. If this was what the new company planned to do, the murals were encouraging. The company had its own parachutes, being held at the riggers, and the company clerk, Sp4 Shugar, said there were even a couple of Fulton Skyhook rigs available—which wasn't exactly encouraging, except as an indication that this cherry Lurp company intended to pull some very interesting missions.

Sp4 Shugar was a muscular, collegiate fellow who looked and talked and acted a little like he should have been at Princeton instead of a Lurp company in Vietnam, but he made it clear that he was a clerk only because he could type and had no intention of staying a clerk—and this was encouraging.

The 1st Brigade Lurps were issued new uniforms—OD jungle fatigues, woodland pattern "flower power" camouflage uniforms, and new tiger suits. This was encouraging. They were told to have all of their patches and tabs and badges and stripes sewn onto their new OD uniforms, and to refrain from wearing tigers around the rear.

This was discouraging, and it was even more discouraging to learn that they'd be expected to get everything sewn on at least one set of their flower power cammies, thereby rendering them unfit for wear to the field. The 1/101 Lurps were issued black baseball caps with the 101st Recondo arrowhead sewn onto the peak, and they were ordered to stop wearing their tiger-striped Lurp hats around the rear, as had been their custom in the 1st Brigade. This was extremely discouraging, and initially, the 1st Brigade Lurps rebelled. Their ratty, camouflaged boonie hats, their "Lurp hats," had been the distinctive Lurp headgear and a source of pride for a long time. Telling them not to wear Lurp hats in the rear was like telling the Special Forces not to wear their green berets. A man might not like the headgear, but as soon as it was forbidden, he was honor-bound to wear it with pride.

The 1st Brigade Lurps resisted, but in a covert fashion. The black caps were sharp, once you styled them right, and the former 1st Brigade Lurps soon wore them with the same cocky pride with which they'd worn their old Lurp hats. Still, they kept their old tiger-stripe floppy hats in the side cargo pockets of their fatigue pants, sticking out where everyone could see them, and the fashion soon caught on. Before long, even Captain Fitts was seen with a Lurp hat sticking out of his thigh pocket.

There was a shortage of gold-and-black Division LRP scrolls, so the old 1st Brigade Lurps continued to wear their red-and-black "1 Long Range Recon 101" scrolls over the Screaming Eagle patch on their left shoulders— or if they got hold of new scrolls, they moved the old scrolls to their right shoulders as combat patches. New rifles were available, and some of the men turned in their old and worn M-16s and CAR-15s for new weapons. Most of the 1st Brigade Lurps needed new boots, and they were available. So were new rucksacks—including gray "indigenous" rucksacks that, according to rumor, were manufactured by the same Hong Kong company that made the brown and green rucksacks of the NVA. There were plenty of nylon ropes for rappelling, Swiss seat ropes, and D-ring snap links for everyone. There were collapsible canteens, and these were much appreciated because they wouldn't slosh noisily when half full, like the standard plastic canteens. Every man who wanted one was issued an air force survival knife in a light tan sheath that had to be darkened with camouflage stick. The sawed-off M-79 grenade launchers had to be kept hidden, but the company had plenty of unaltered grenade launchers, and there were flare rounds and smoke rounds for them, which most of the 1st Brigade Lurps had never seen before. There were pen flares, new compasses for everyone, and not only were there hundreds of cases of Lurp rations, there were also indigenous rations of rice and shrimp, rice and fishheads, rice and squid, and rice and mutton available. When the 1st Brigade Lurps had worked for Special Forces at Dong Tre, the detachment had developed an institutional taste for indigenous rations, and now the Lurps wouldn't have to bargain with Green Berets for them. There were new camouflaged poncho liner jungle blankets for everyone, and jungle sweaters, precut wire antennae, waterproof plastic watches, and all the socks, sundry packs, and weapons-cleaning equipment anyone could desire. Compared to the 1st Brigade, which had been living like nomads since 1965, making do in the face of what seemed like normal shortages, the division was incredibly rich in equipment. This was definitely a morale factor for the old 1st Brigade Lurps.

* * *

There wasn't much in the way of training available at the Bien Hoa rear, but the men did get a chance to zero their weapons, and there were a couple of sessions on a rappelling tower. There was also a McQuire rig demonstration, during which SSG Christian slipped out of his rig and would have fallen if Rey Martinez and Clay Wentworth hadn't grabbed him at the last moment. With Christian hanging on to Wentworth's foot and Martinez trying to hang on to Christian, the helicopter put the Lurps down long enough for them to adjust and get Christian properly seated, then lifted them back up and flew them around the area some more. But when it came to training, that was about it.

Not much of note happened during the short period that the 1st Brigade Lurps were at Bien Hoa with the new company. The "old Foul Dudes" and the Division Lurps who'd returned from Song Be began getting to know each other. Other units of the 101st were also gathering in the new division rear. One of the newly arrived Airborne Infantry battalions briefly went into quarantine behind concertina wire, and there were rumors they were being quarantined in preparation for a combat jump, but the quarantine didn't last and those rumors died out. The intelligence ship USS *Pueblo* was seized off the coast of North Korea, and very briefly, the Lurp company was put on some sort of preliminary alert, and there was wild speculation that the alert might mean an upcoming trip to North Korea. But those hopes dissipated almost as soon as they arose. Some men didn't buy into them from the beginning. The *Pueblo* was being held in some North Korean port, and if America was going to send a division in to get it, it wasn't going to be the 101st Airborne. The ex-Marines in the company, including the 1st Brigade's

Nick Caberra, were convinced that any division-size mission to get back the *Pueblo* and her crew would probably go to the Marines. Any small-unit special operations wouldn't go to the army Lurps, and they probably wouldn't even go to army Special Forces. It would still be the Marines—Recon Marines, along with the Navy UDT and SEALs.

The Lurps soon came to their senses and realized that unless things really went haywire in Korea, their war was still in Vietnam.

Some of the Division Lurps had been back at Bien Hoa when VC sappers and commandos hit the airfield and completely shattered the comfortable security of all the REMFs. Since these Lurps had managed to get in on the fighting and rack up a body count, they might have still thought of Bien Hoa as a combat zone. But the rest of the Lurps just couldn't quite stretch their imaginations that far. The only thing even mildly operational they were doing back at the new division rear area was internal base security, standing palace guard for division brass at night. And from Captain Fitts on down the chain of command to the men who actually stood the incredibly boring palace guard watches, the Lurps had the distinct impression that it wasn't VC sappers and commandos they were guarding against. There were plenty of stories going around about attempts on the life and person of the division commander, Major General Olinto Barsanti, and some of these rumors even went back to Fort Campbell.

General Barsanti had a chestful of medals and all the right schools and staff jobs behind him, but he'd never had an Airborne assignment before he took over the 101st Airborne Division. Even before bringing the division to Vietnam and taking over the 1st Brigade, General

Barsanti had managed to alienate, offend, and piss off thousands of proud Screaming Eagle paratroopers. There wasn't yet an agreed-upon price on the general's head, or any rumors about how a man might go about collecting the money, but there was little doubt among the Lurps that if General Barsanti wasted too many lives on ill-conceived humbugs, *someone* was going to frag the son of a bitch.

It galled the Lurps that General Barsanti wasn't giving them any good training or any missions, and it galled them even more that Barsanti was hiding behind their fierce reputation and using them for palace guards.

One night, on a bunker somewhere in the heart of the division rear, Crash Clark made the observation that General Barsanti was sure going native in a hurry, already worrying about coups after only a few weeks in Vietnam. The next night, Nick Caberra wondered where General Barsanti got the idea he was safe in the daytime. And the next day, somebody came back from somewhere with the word that there was already a set price on Barsanti's head in the 3rd Brigade, though nobody seemed to know how much was being offered or how a man was to collect the money safely if he managed to earn it.

This immediately gave rise to a few idle discussions, at least among the Foul Dudes from the old 1st Brigade Lurps and their new buddies, about various mechanisms that might be used to pay somebody fragging a division commander without exposing him to the Uniform Code of Military Justice, but nobody came up with anything that would work. The most they could do was hope that nobody tried anything while they were on duty. They would have to do their job and protect General Barsanti, even if their hearts weren't really in it.

It was at Bien Hoa that Lieutenant Shepherd made his first brief pass through the Lurp company, impressing everyone with how smug he was about his Special Forces background and how superior he was about being an officer. Shepherd was in the company area for only a few days—just long enough to identify himself with the company TOC while offending the 1st Brigade Lurps. Then he was gone, and the rumor immediately circulated that Captain Fitts had run him off.

A double handful of days dragged by like weeks. But then, one night, there was no palace guard for the Lurps—at least not for the Foul Dudes of the 1st Brigade Lurps. General Barsanti was cranking up this big division he apparently thought of as his, and wherever the hell it was going, the Lurps were going in first.

Unfortunately, it didn't look like they'd be going in first on a respectable Lurp mission. But at least they were getting away from Bien Hoa and back a little closer to the war. Word was they were going north. Not north to North Vietnam or North Korea, but north as far as the Hue–Phu Bai area. And right then, that was just about the epicenter of the whole damn war.

# Chapter Four

To the south and west of the old Vietnamese imperial city of Hue are the imperial graves of the Nguyen dynasty, widely considered, at least among Vietnamese, finer monuments than the famous Ming tombs outside of Beijing, China. The Perfume River, which drains the wild and dangerous mountains to the west, flows slowly through the city, a most leisurely and civilized river, with life and commerce on its waters and along the banks. To the north of the river—and to the west, too, for the Perfume curves to the north—Hue is dominated by the Imperial Citadel, said by some to be modeled after the Forbidden City of Beijing and by others to be modeled after the ancient Tang dynasty Chinese capital of Chang An. It was widely agreed among Vietnamese of all factions, and particularly those who had never visited China and nursed a historical antipathy toward the Chinese, that as a city of monuments and a seat of high culture, Hue outshone both Beijing and Tang dynasty Chang An.

Neither the government in Saigon nor the government in Hanoi was much respected by most of the people of Hue, many of whom had a hard time accepting the legitimacy of any government that did not make its capital there. In 1963 there had been an uprising against the Catholic-dominated Saigon government. This uprising indirectly led to the overthrow of the Diem government. While Hue was hardly a center of Catholic power, there was a large, fine cathedral—and a tradition of mutual tolerance between the Catholics and the Buddhists that had been strained, but not broken, by the 1963 Buddhist uprising. For more than four years after the uprising, the Saigon government had allowed Hue a rather loose leash and granted the city a certain measure of local autonomy. In some ways, Hue City seemed almost immune to the war that raged all around it—although perhaps *aloof* would be a better word than *immune*. Hue was Vietnam's traditional culture center, and this made it a rather haughty city.

But Hue was also a tolerant place, at least by the standards of a country at war with itself. Though most of the stories of enemies meeting peacefully in the marketplace or sharing filtered coffee near the university were probably not true, Hue was one of the few places in Vietnam where the stories did occasionally have the ring of credibility, at least to Americans—some of whom even had a few peaceable encounter stories of their own.

Hue might have been aloof, and it might have been a little too tolerant. But Hue was not indifferent to the war. Hue's sons and daughters had a long tradition of taking sides against each other, and by the end of 1967 and the beginning of 1968, they were fighting on all sides of the war—except, perhaps, on the side of the Montagnards.

Many of the leaders of both major sides in the war, including Ho Chi Minh, Vo Nguyen Giap, and Ngo Dinh Diem, had gone to school in Hue. Hue was, at least in the minds of her citizens, the guardian of Vietnam's national soul, and there was said to have once been a general feeling that the fighting would stay away from the city itself.

But then, on the night of January 30, 1968, during the lunar New Year holiday, the war came to Hue. Two mixed battalions of North Vietnamese and Viet Cong entered the city against only scattered resistance. In their wake came still more North Vietnamese and Viet Cong soldiers. By dawn, they had the run of the city, except for the American MACV advisory compound, south of the river, and 1st ARVN Division Headquarters, by the moat in the northernmost corner of the Citadel. By the morning of the thirty-first, the rest of the city was under the control of the forces of "liberation." And with the forces of "liberation" came the outside political cadres with their hit lists. Local Communist agents and sympathizers who had been dormant in the city until this time now came to the surface with *their* lists of names. And before long, all sorts of vengeful people began to come forward to settle old scores by denouncing their neighbors and the "liberation" of Hue quickly became a murderous reign of terror.

And then came the United States Marines. And in their wake came the 1st ARVN Division—or at least those members who were able to get back to their units after going home on holiday leave. To say the fighting to recover the city was fierce would be to indulge in some extreme understatement. It was worse than merely fierce. It was city fighting, very bloody to both sides, and extremely costly to the city of Hue. In their unpreparedness for the attack and their trust in the holiday truce, the South Vietnamese and American commands had shown themselves almost criminally naive. In the administration of their "liberation" of Hue, the Communists showed a murderous face that should have shocked the world. But in the streets and along the moats and walls and towers of the Citadel, young Americans, and Vietnamese of both sides, fought the long battle with courage and tenacity.

About the time the 1st ARVN Division's Black Panther recon company was preparing to make its final assault on the last NVA positions in the Hue Citadel, two 101st Lurp teams flew north to the Hue–Phu Bai area in company with a gaggle of majors and colonels from the division headquarters staff. When the staff officers flew off in helicopters to scout the area, they left their Lurp bodyguards on the ground back at the Phu Bai airport. There was a navy medical evacuation hospital right off the airstrip at Phu Bai, and under more normal circumstances the Lurps would have headed that way to get some information, maybe do a little trading, and make some friends. But the navy corpsmen and doctors were still busy with wounded from the battle of Hue, and while the other Lurps hung tight by the manifest shed, a medic went off alone to visit and offer his services if needed. He came back shortly, looking depressed and shaking his head. His services were probably needed, he said, but there didn't seem to be anything he could do without getting in the way.

When the staff officers returned, they soon boarded a plane south, back to Bien Hoa. The Lurps boarded a truck and before long found themselves in an area of rolling, grassy, grave-studded hills just south of Hue, where they passed the night in a loose perimeter of two-man positions. On the way out from the airport, they had passed the supersecret MACV-SOG Command and Control North base, FOB 1, without knowing enough to even notice it. They had passed Project Delta's old Firebase Tokyo in the truck, but it looked like Delta had moved on, and the base seemed to be occupied only by rather lax-looking indigenous soldiers in tiger fatigues and their camp followers. Exposed on their grassy hill, with radios but no signal operating instructions or call signs or frequencies, the Lurps felt very alone that first night. They felt a little better the next day, when they were joined by more Lurps from the First Platoon, and then some engineers.

Those first few days and nights, when there were just a few Lurp teams securing it, the Camp Eagle perimeter was so small and lightly guarded that a company-size enemy element could probably have overrun it. When the rest of the Lurp company—and in its wake, advance elements of the division rear—joined the First Platoon, the base camp was already being called Camp Eagle. Even after they moved in General Barsanti's airconditioned trailer and brought up the china for his mess hall, a good NVA battalion with a sapper company and a platoon or two of mortars could have probably wiped Camp Eagle off the map, or at least severely disorganized it.

But the NVA was in no position to do anything about the small detachment of Lurps on their lonely little hill—much less the military city growing up around them. The enemy was hightailing it out of the area. He wasn't looking for a fight at the moment, and now seemed the time to hit him hard and keep on hitting.

Beyond the perimeter of Camp Eagle, the hills gave way to foothills, and the foothills gave way to mountains. Probably all of the Lurps who had ever been on a mission were a little fearful at the prospect of chasing Charlie into those mountains—or, more accurately, they were fearful of Charlie chasing them. But they were Lurps, and there was a war on, so their enthusiasm more than outweighed their fear. That was really Lurp country out there. The enemy was suffering and temporarily on the run, and it was the right time to send out the recon teams. The Lurps could find them and fix them. And when it came to small parties, the Lurps could destroy them, too. It would have been deadly, dangerous, challenging work, but that's exactly the sort of work the Lurps had become Lurps to do. But there they were, pulling bunker guard and palace guard by night, filling sandbags by day, and getting feisty and bored.

As the division rear grew, the Lurps were run off their original hilltop to make way for division headquarters. They no longer had just themselves and a few officers to protect. They had to provide a perimeter for the expanding rear area. They moved into the graves that dotted the hillside and began to fortify them with sandbags. Some engineers came around and dropped off a couple of rolls of concertina wire, but no stakes to anchor the wire. The Lurps did what they could with the concertina wire. They put out claymores every night and took them in every morning. They established interlocking fields of fire; they turned the graves into fighting positions and made themselves at home.

The graves were fine, massive, old structures, with low walls encircling them, oval biers of stone and concrete, and headstones with the names of the deceased carved into them, always in Vietnamese, and sometimes in Chinese characters as well. With a little sandbagging, the graves made fine fighting positions. They were, however, civilian graves, and the Vietnamese are a people who honor the graves of their ancestors and don't much appreciate them being turned into fighting positions. For a couple of weeks, the Lurps continued to live in the graves, but as things returned to normal in the Hue–Phu Bai area—and as Camp Eagle continued to grow—the Lurps were ordered out of the graves and into sandbagged tents in a company area near the northeast gate, between the 326th Engineer Battalion's rear and the officers club, and over a small rise from the place the Lurps called "the Leech Pond."

Within a week of moving north, the Recondo School cadre began earnestly looking for excuses to administer Article 15 company punishments to 1st Brigade Lurps. None of the offenses were serious, but the cadre seemed to delight in reducing 1st Brigade Lurps in rank, and before long almost half of the men who had come to the company from the old 1/101 LRRP detachment had been busted at least one pay grade.

One of the most outrageous of these Article 15 punishments was given to Jaybird Magill. While on detail painting the new company outhouse, he noticed the company operations NCO—who was considered perhaps the most hostile of the cadre NCOs—pitching horseshoes not far away, and in a burst of editorial inspiration, he painted "Lifers Suck" on the side of the shithouse. He immediately painted over his comment, but not before it was seen. Shortly thereafter, Magill was called into the orderly room, where a smiling First Sergeant Walker first presented him with orders promoting him to sergeant E-5—a long-overdue promotion. And then, smiling even more broadly, the first sergeant presented him with an Article 15 busting him two pay grades, down to PFC. Maybe it was a good joke, but Jaybird and the rest of the 1st Brigade Lurps did not see the humor in it.

Ever since the first Lurps arrived at Phu Bai, they'd been running short local security patrols as well as filling sandbags and standing perimeter guard. By Lurp standards, this was galling idleness—and this idleness continued as Camp Eagle grew. For all its many helicopters, the 101st Airborne Division didn't have aircraft to spare for long-range patrol missions. And for all the emphasis that Airborne units traditionally place on training, the division did nothing to help the Lurps mount a training program, leaving the company no opportunity to do anything beyond holding classes in the company area. Ironically, most of the training sessions were held down by the Leech Pond, which had become something of a refuge for the Lurps who wanted to get away from the company cadre while they passed the pipe and talked about war.

Consigned to palace guard, perimeter guard, and local patrols, Lurp morale deteriorated—and so did Lurp behavior. Lurps are Lurps, and they can't help "lurping," even back in the rear.

First Sergeant Walker and the general's cook were old friends, dating back to before the general's cook became a cook. The general's cook offered to slip some of the general's excess steak and ice cream to Walker for his Lurps, but he wasn't able to follow through on his offer, for the day after making the offer, he discovered that all of the general's steaks and ice cream were missing. The Lurps had already mounted a raid and helped themselves.

The Lurps feasted openly, and First Sergeant Walker and Captain Fitts helped dispose of the evidence, but there were those at the nearby division headquarters who were definitely not amused. Additional MPs were placed on guard around the general's quarters and his mess hall, but this only inspired the Lurps to greater efforts. These men were, after all, commandos—and dangerously idle commandos, at that. Until the Lurps finally lost interest, there was almost nothing the MPs or General Barsanti's aides and staff and lackeys could do to thwart the raids. It became a game on the part of the Lurps, and before long it also became a game on the part of the MPs. The object was not so much to reappropriate the general's luxuries as it was just to penetrate his security. Only once was a Lurp captured on one of these raids, and by that time the MPs were so involved in the game for its own sake that they let the Lurp go. It was about then that the Lurps lost interest. But the raids on General Barsanti's area did have one positive effect—the Lurps were no longer to be trusted as palace guards, and division headquarters was forced to think of other ways to employ them.

In some important ways, the company was beginning to come together. Captain Fitts was heard referring fondly to his Lurps as his "hoodlums." First Sergeant Walker covered for three 1st Brigade Lurps who were accused of instigating a brawl at the tent the 326th Engineers were using as a club—even though the engineers were adamant that one of the troublemakers was old Nick Caberra and had pretty solid descriptions of the other two. And word was that even the operations NCO stuck up for the company, and the men in it, against outsiders. But inside the company, there was still a lot of mutual distrust and misunderstanding.

The Old Foul Dudes felt like unwanted orphans. All of the 1st Brigade Lurps who had joined the company were on teams—all of them except Staff Sergeant Derby Jones, who was their only ombudsman at the company TOC. Yet despite his reasonable manner and fine lifer dignity, Derby Jones had not served on the Recondo School cadre, so he didn't fit in closely with the rest of the NCOs and officers at the TOC. They worked with Derby, and some of them listened to him, but he wasn't one of them, and before too long he started looking for another home. Most of the Old Foul Dudes were already serving on extensions, and they had not extended in order to play palace guard—or to get busted. They felt that their experience was unappreciated, and they resented what they saw as the Stateside chickenshit of this new company—and even more than that, of this new division. There was a war on, and the Lurps were supposed to be out there winning it for America. And when they were back in the rear, they were either supposed to be training or living it up. That's what they'd extended for, but that wasn't what they were getting.

The company cadre was appalled at the customs, bearing, attitude, and rear area behavior of the 1st Brigade Lurps. For more than two years, the 1st Brigade had been, in effect, a separate unit from the 101st Airborne Division, and now that the whole division was in Vietnam, and the 1st Brigade was once again part of that division, the 1st Brigade's accomplishments—and its separate identity—were being degraded and denied. The esprit de corps the division was operating on was the esprit de corps it had brought over from Fort Campbell and not the esprit de corps the 1st Brigade had established in Vietnam. This was true not just of the division but also of the Lurp company. The old Recondo School cadre knew almost nothing about the 1st Brigade Lurps and was not much impressed with what it saw of them. The fact that the division was not giving the new Lurp company any challenging missions or any opportunity for serious training made it difficult for the Old Foul Dudes to show what they could do. And it was true that the Old Foul Dudes weren't exactly the best garrison troops—but then again, neither were the Lurps who had come over from Fort Campbell. Keeping such men idle was a potentially disastrous piece of command stupidity. And while the Old Foul Dudes who'd been among the 1st Brigade Lurps tended to blame the cadre of their own

company, this inactivity was not really their fault. If the
blame has to fall on anyone, it should fall on General
Barsanti, who did not seem to have a clue about the
employment of Lurps and who was already well on his
way to becoming the most widely hated division commander in the U.S. Army in Vietnam.

The idleness at Camp Eagle was terribly frustrating.
But still, the Lurps were not entirely idle. Within three
weeks of arriving at Phu Bai, the platoon sergeant of
Second Platoon, Staff Sergeant Owen "Rocky" Bigelon,
led two heavy team missions consisting of men from
both platoons. On the first mission, the team found two
downed helicopters, the wreckage side by side. The team
also found an unoccupied NVA ambush site near the
wreckage. Apparently, the enemy had set up to ambush
any recovery effort, but there was no recovery effort until
the Lurps found the helicopters, some days after they
went down. It was hard to tell whether or not the NVA
had done anything to the bodies of the crews, but some
sort of animals—probably either tigers, leopards, or wild
pigs—had sure done a job on them, and there were body
parts scattered everywhere. Rocky's heavy team secured
the site while a graves registration team was inserted to
bag up and remove what they could of the bodies. When
the graves registration team flew back to Camp Eagle
with the bodies, Rocky's team moved on to patrol to the
west, finding many signs of recent enemy passage. They
were extracted two days later, and then, almost immediately after being extracted, Rocky's heavy team was
again inserted, far to the west of the crash site.

This was a long mission—almost three weeks—so
long that the team had to be resupplied twice. On the
second day of the mission, the team found and destroyed
a cache of 20mm rounds. Destroying the cache of 20mm

rounds entailed a little more excitement than anyone had bargained for. Charges were set, and then the team moved what should have been a safe distance and set up in security wheel to wait for the explosion. The explosion went off right on schedule—but then, ten or twenty seconds after the initial explosion, 20mm rounds began to rain down around the team, some of them exploding on impact with the treetops and others impacting on the ground. It was, everyone on the team agreed, both a real fuckup and a real miracle. The way the charges had been set was certainly fucked up, and it was a miracle that no one was hurt.

That night, the team set up around a large tree. In the middle of the night, some sort of large animal, probably a big cat, jumped out of the tree and hit the ground running in circles among the Lurps before breaking away and disappearing into the blackness. The team was spooked, but discipline held, and no one opened up or called out.

The next day, Rocky's team found sleeping positions, abandoned fighting positions, bloody bandages crawling with insects, and trails with fresh signs of passage. Moving on, they came across some blue commo wire. They followed it to both ends, but the wire was not attached to anything. A little later, next to a trail, they found a hastily buried NVA body in the first stage of decomposition. The weird thing was that the body had been buried head down, with the feet exposed. There was no identification on the body, and it had been stripped of gear. There was no telling what had killed this particular NVA—the body was already decomposing, and none of the Lurps had been trained as pathologists. But the manner of burial seemed to indicate that this NVA's comrades had been hard-pressed to keep on moving— either that or they hadn't liked the guy very much. Rocky was of the opinion that the man had been buried in such an undignified position on purpose and had probably been done in by his comrades for cowardice, treason, or some other transgression.

A few days later, the team moved into an area that they knew was hot even before they saw any sign of the enemy. Rocky had the feeling that they were being watched, and when they came to a small river, he could feel the hair stand on the back of his neck. The team quickly went to ground, listening all around, and after hearing nothing unusual, Rocky sent out two- and three-man point recon elements. Everyone was tense, everyone alert. But the point recons found no enemy—just signs of their passage. Rocky briefly considered waiting until dark to cross the river but then decided against it. The river was two to three feet deep, twenty meters wide, and curved enough to limit visibility up- and downstream. Setting out security to cover the crossing, the Lurps quickly made it across at the best ford the point recons had been able to find. This was apparently also the best fording point the enemy had been able to find, for when the team was on the far bank, they found themselves on a trail that flanked the river—and on the trail were footprints with water still seeping into them. The team set up to monitor that trail and river crossing for the rest of the day and that night, but to everyone's surprise—and perhaps as much to their relief as their disappointment—no one came along.

The next day, the team found another NVA cache. This time, it was fuel drums and artillery rounds. This time, however, they were a little more careful about planting their charges, putting them on top of the artillery rounds and fuel drums. The explosion was spectacular—so spectacular there was a mushroom cloud and a shock wave that singed the eyebrows of some of the men. Moving away with a hillside burning behind them, the Lurps continued to patrol and continued to find signs of recent enemy movement. Among these signs was a handful of trucks that had been shot up from the air and abandoned. Russell Rowe was so incensed that the letters stamped on the tires were in the Roman alphabet—not the Cyrillic alphabet used by the Russians, nor Chinese characters, nor even the Roman alphabet with diacritical marks used by the Vietnamese—that he cut a section off a tire to bring back for G-2 to check out, suspecting that the tires had probably been supplied by peace creeps back home, even though the trucks themselves were of Soviet origin.

When this mission was over, the team was not extracted by helicopter. Instead, Rocky's heavy team walked out to a firebase, and this is probably why this mission isn't recorded as a "real" long-range patrol mission. It was, however, a long-range patrol—and a very good one. There was no contact, but then, it was a reconnaissance mission, and on recon missions it is not necessary—or usually even wise—to get into firefights when there are enemy positions, enemy caches, trails, trucks, and enemy bodies to be found. It is interesting to note that during these missions, Rocky's heavy team was operating without any dedicated helicopter support laid on, no fastmovers on call, and that they were outside of any allied artillery net for most of the mission. It is also interesting to note that almost every man on Rocky's heavy team returned from that last mission even more convinced than before that the Tet Offensive had gone so seriously awry for the enemy that the poor bastards were pulling back to Laos to lick their wounds, and now was the time to hit them in *their* rear area and finish them off.

That didn't happen—at least not on a large enough scale to make any difference. But on a smaller scale, something good did come out of this mission, for when Rocky's heavy team was finally lifted back to Camp Eagle, Rocky's promotion orders were waiting for him. He was a sergeant first class and had the pay grade to go with his responsibilities in the company.

Most of the Lurps were still stuck idly back at Camp Eagle, but by the end of March there was always at least one team working off one or another of the division's newly established firebases. Most of these operations weren't long-range patrols, and they were usually of short duration. But four-, six-, and twelve-man teams of Lurps were still patrolling enemy areas with very minimal support, sometimes consisting of artillery and sometimes 4.2-inch mortars, but almost never helicopters or TAC Air.

On one of these patrols, a heavy team made up of Teddy Bear Gaskell's team and Jack Gibney's team skirted along a trail overlooking a tributary of the Perfume River—the Song Bo. They were looking for river landings and hoping to find some sampans hidden from aerial observation along the bank. They didn't see any boats, but they did see plenty of places that looked suitable for a sampan landing and plenty of trails leading down to the tributary from the high ground. After checking out one of these trails for a few hundred meters and then working back down toward the river they came upon a very foul smell, so strong and localized it seemed to hit them like they were walking into some sort of invisible wall. Following their noses, they found first a scattering of body parts and then a large, square, open pit containing a jumble of bodies in scraps and remnants of civilian clothes. It was hard to look down at the grave without being driven back by the stench, and it was even harder to determine how many people were in it. But the Lurps had to try. The pit was about ten feet deep, and one side was gouged where a tiger had apparently jumped in and then scrambled out with a meal, the scraps of which still littered the trail. Jaybird Magill looked around and noticed that Kenn Miller was the smallest man on either team, then, smiling evilly, he suggested that Miller be lowered into the grave to count the bodies and search them for anything that might identify them. If the rope broke, he could get out the same way the tiger did. This suggestion was quickly seconded by a smiling Crash Clark, but was just as quickly overruled by Gaskell and Gibney—much to Miller's relief. Still, it was Miller's job to stand on the edge of the pit and count the skulls. Everyone else except Steve "Little John" LeGendre backed off to stand security and try to catch a breath of relatively fresh air. Miller was grateful that LeGendre had stood with him to share the ordeal, even if "Little John" didn't go right up to the edge and do any of the counting.

After more than a month of exposure to the elements, insects, and animals, the bodies were in terrible condition, but there was still a thin, brownish parchment of withered flesh and shrunken skin clinging to some of the bones, and there were still strands of hair visible on some of the skulls. Some of the hair was blond hair, longer than military standards, and the rags clinging to the bones appeared to be remnants of civilian clothing. Miller counted the eight skulls he could see and told Gibney and Gaskell there might be four or five more he couldn't see. And, of course, there was the body the tiger had dragged out.

The Lurps called in their find, and everyone expected to be told to secure the area until a graves registration team could be brought in. Instead, the team was told to continue its mission—which at that point pretty much consisted of patrolling back toward the firebase from which the team had launched. Teddy Bear Gaskell was glad to be getting away from the stench, but Miller and Jaybird and Crash Clark were disgruntled, assuming that once again the Lurps had done their job and there would be no follow-up. They'd found the grave and reported its location, and if the rear didn't want to do anything about it, it wasn't the fault of the Lurps.

Apparently, however, the rear did respond to the Lurps' find. Accompanied by an infantry platoon, a graves registration team was eventually sent in and the bodies were recovered. A few days later, about the time the two teams got back to Camp Eagle, word leaked back to the Lurp company that at least some of the bodies were those of German faculty members from Hue University medical school. During its murderous occupation of Hue, the NVA had apparently arrested them, moved them up the Perfume River, then down this tributary for execution. Word didn't come down officially, and no formal report was ever sent back to the Lurp company, for in Vietnam, American intelligence tended to flow upward from the troop level and almost never back down to the troops who needed it most. Maybe the word that came down was not the word sent up the chain of command. But the Lurps had seen blond hair clinging to some of the skulls, and it was by now common knowledge that the Communists had outdone themselves when it came to the atrocities they'd pulled in Hue, so everything about the story made sense—except maybe for the bit about Germans teaching at the university. That made sense only to the few Lurps who knew enough about Hue to figure the place might have actually had a university good enough to lure German professors, and those Lurps were in the minority.

Not all of the missions during this period were without contact. On two consecutive walk-in missions, off two different firebases, SSG "Contact" Johnson's team got into brief firefights with enemy troops, and Johnson's team continued to make contact on subsequent missions inserted by helicopter. It was only natural that the men on his team became objects of envy to some of the other Lurps.

And then there was Task Force Fitts, in which the entire company was inserted by helicopter to perform a conventional infantry sweep through an area thought to contain at least a company of main force Viet Cong. There were no enemy to be found, and no sign of any. The Lurps grumbled and bitched, but performed about as well as an infantry company organized and trained to work as a company. Division was pleased with their performance, if not with the fact that they hadn't found the enemy. Captain Fitts, however, did not seem to be pleased. He seemed to be embarrassed by having the "task force" named after him, and he was clearly unhappy at seeing his company of Lurps misused as conventional infantry. When the "task force" returned to Camp Eagle after its little walk in the sun, Captain Fitts went up to division headquarters to raise a little hell about getting his "hoodlums" helicopter support and some real Lurp missions. Captain Fitts seemed to be doing this more and more, and every time he went up to division headquarters, word soon filtered down to the men on the teams.

Though none of them idolized him to the extent some of the Lurps who'd come over from Fort Campbell seemed to, Captain Fitts was an impressive man and obviously a real soldier, and most of the 1st Brigade Lurps were willing to concede that if Fitts had had

someone like Top Smith for a first sergeant, sobered up
SFC Brubaker, and got rid of the operations NCO, he
would have been a hell of a fine commanding officer—
even if he couldn't get this unwieldy Stateside division to
make proper use of its Lurps.

The real problem, according to Nick Caberra, wasn't
Captain Fitts, and it wasn't even the senior NCOs, most of
whom Nick considered peacetime Army lifer parasites.
The problem was General Barsanti. This was Nick
Caberra's third war, and even when he was sober, he
stuck to his prediction that sooner or later General
Barsanti was going to have to start making better use of
the Lurps. Army generals were turning out to be pretty
much the same as Marine generals, and Nick was of the
opinion that throughout American history no general with
more than one star had ever shown much good sense in
employing the special operations assets at his command.

"They usually come around in the end, though," Nick
allowed glumly. "And when they do, they usually end up
trying to run the show themselves. If your chain of command doesn't skip from a lieutenant or captain to a bird
colonel, or at most a brigadier general, then skip up to at
least a full four stars, you've got to deal with all sorts of
chickenshit meddling in between. That's why a brigade
is better than a division. And that's why if Captain Fitts
has half a brain, he's going back to Special Forces."

Nick might not have put it in those exact words, but
that's the gist of what he said, and the Lurps sitting with
him in the rear, sharing the canteen cup of Pernod with
him and Crash Clark, all nodded respectfully at old
Nick's wisdom.

# Chapter Five

Not long after moving up to Phu Bai, while the Lurps were still living in graves, a nineteen-year-old soldier named Tony Tercero came to the company out of the hospital. He'd come to Vietnam with one of the division's Airborne infantry companies, leaving a wife even younger than him back at Fort Campbell, and since he'd come over as pretty much a standard-issue, MOS 11-B bullet-stopper, i.e., a rifleman, within a few weeks of arriving in-country he found himself in the hospital, trying to figure out a way to survive the ten months or so left in his tour. The solution that he hit on was to bribe the medics into giving him a profile that would keep him out of the field, and to con the clerks into reassigning him to some relatively safe rear-echelon job. Having already volunteered for the army, and then for Airborne, he didn't think there was anything unusual when the clerks told him that he'd have to specifically volunteer for his new assignment, which was to be a truck driver for a company that was based right there at Camp Eagle. The clerks had mentioned something about this being a Lurp company, but that didn't mean anything to Tony. What he volunteered for was to drive a truck back in the rear. It was, he figured, the perfect job for a man of his talents and experience.

Tony had grown up in Arizona, pretty much dividing his time between the streets of Phoenix and various reform schools and youth ranches, and his talents did not necessarily lie in the field of truck driving and motor pool arts. Tony was an accomplished con artist, entrepreneur, and hustler, and he tried to live by the philosophy that the ethical hustler never left a victim—which meant that he tried to never leave a mark feeling like a mark, never leave a victim feeling like a victim. Long before the term became a cliché among businesspeople, Tony was an exponent of the "win-win" deal. He was a good talker in both English and Spanish, and after all the time he'd spent in reform schools and working on youth ranches as a kid, he was an expert at getting around unrealistic rules and working under regimented conditions. Except for his newfound aversion to getting killed in the infantry, he felt right at home in the army. A good rear area truck-driving job was just what he needed to get to know people and find out where his opportunities lay.

Volunteering to be a truck driver for the Lurp company seemed like a very good idea to Tony. But when he got to the Lurps and made a few friends, he could understand why all the lifers had seemed a little put out when he reported to the TOC with his orders. There weren't any slots for truck drivers in the Lurp company. And except for that purloined field ambulance back at the rear area at Bien Hoa, and a jeep that a couple of the men had found sitting up on blocks, tireless, and then outfitted with spare tires off five other jeeps before taking it back to the company to have the bumper numbers repainted, there weren't any vehicles at all.

But while the first sergeant was figuring out what to do with him, Tony was doing some figuring of his own. He was, after all, an Airborne infantryman, even if he had done some heavy negotiating for a profile to keep him out of the field. He hadn't gone Airborne just to strut around in the jump boots and wings. He'd gone Airborne so that he could get out there and do some hard-core soldiering, and that ambition was not entirely dead. There'd been plenty of hard-core soldiering back in his old company, but too much of it had been stupid, dangerous, and dispiriting. These Lurps were different. They were his kind of people, and what they did for a living sounded like fun. After only a couple of days in the company, Tony approached Rey Martinez about joining his team— on a probationary status, if need be.

In what was either an effort to split up the former 1st Brigade Lurps or an effort to get him away from SFC Brubaker, who had taken an unreasonable dislike to him, Sergeant Martinez had been moved out of SFC Brubaker's First Platoon to SFC Rocky Bigelon's Second Platoon. At that stage, the teams were still numbered without reference to platoon, and Martinez was the team leader of "Terrible Team Ten." He had been training his team even when the company provided little opportunity to do so, and "Marty" was fond of telling his buddies in First Platoon that his team might be full of cherries but these were very good cherries. At that time, "Terrible Team Ten" consisted of Sergeant Martinez, Sp4 Jim Venable, Sp4 Jerry Prouty, PFC Paneck, PFC Barry "Goldy" Golden, and PFC William "Raider" Laing. When Prouty went home, Tony took his place. Sergeant Martinez had talked to Tony in English and he'd talked to him in Spanish, and in either language, Tony sounded like he had the makings of a very good Lurp. He took to the training and proved a quick learner, and went on to prove himself a very good Lurp.

\* \* \*

By the time the company moved in next to the Leech Pond, Tony was doing everything with his team, including ambushes and short missions off various firebases. He had found a home among the Lurps, and as he was now himself a Lurp, Tony figured it was time to do something for his brother Lurps. Morale back in the rear was low for a number of reasons, but Tony focused in on the only morale factor he could do anything to improve—the paucity of good soda and beer. Since the Lurps were pretty much banned from all the little NCO and EM clubs that were springing up in tents all over Camp Eagle, the only soda they could get without pulling raids on the nearby officers club was warm Canada Dry ginger ale, and the only beer was warm Falstaff. Tony figured he could do something about that without having to make the company any new enemies at Camp Eagle. All he needed was a pass and travel orders down to Da Nang, where there was plenty of beer and soda.

Tony went to Sergeant Martinez with his idea, and Sergeant Martinez approached Staff Sergeant Richard Burnell. "Burny" didn't think there was any reason to bother SFC Bigelon with this. He said he'd talk to First Sergeant Walker himself. Sergeant Martinez didn't trust the first sergeant, but he did trust Burnell. To everyone's amazement except Burnell's, First Sergeant Walker okayed a three-day pass to Da Nang for Tony Tercero and two confederates of his choosing.

Tony immediately chose Russell Rowe and Ashton Prindle, both of them experienced freebooters even before they became Lurps. The three-man team set off for Da Nang in the early afternoon of April 21, catching a flight at the Phu Bai airstrip.

They had a three-day pass but no specific instructions, and were pretty much on their own, as long as they didn't get caught. But there was a Cinderella clause on the three-day pass, for Prindle and Rowe had to be back by late afternoon of the third day. They had an ambush patrol scheduled that night, and though there would be plenty of men willing to fill in for them, they didn't want to miss it.

When they deplaned at Da Nang, Tony looked around this land of opportunity with a smile, and he asked Rowe and Prindle if they were ready to go forth and accomplish great deeds. Rowe guffawed and Prindle snickered cynically, but they were ready.

What this three-man Lurp team did accomplish almost immediately took on the patina of legend, and since none of it was exactly legal, you'd have to ask the two surviving participants themselves if you want all the details of how this whole thing was accomplished. But the basic story can be told without verging off into legend. Da Nang was the *rear* rear area, second in riches only to the Saigon–Long Binh–Bien Hoa area, down south. Da Nang was also heavily patrolled by military police, heavily populated by officers and fat REMF lifer NCOs, and heavily dependent on paperwork. After enjoying themselves in the clubs and snack bars, visiting a PX, making a few friends, and wandering around checking things out, Tercero, Prindle, and Rowe crashed out in a transit barracks. In the morning, they had a hot mess hall breakfast and got to work.

To the extent that rear echelon troops are often the natural enemies of combat troops, this three-man team was now operating behind enemy lines. Down in Da Nang, about all they had on their side was their own wit, guile, charm, and daring. Somehow, these three Lurp PFCs soon managed to "reappropriate" a three-quarter-ton truck. Making use of the trade goods they'd brought along, they got the bumper numbers repainted, but this small truck wasn't enough. Sitting at the China Beach PX, thinking over their next move, the three Lurps saw opportunity, in the form of a fully loaded two-and-a-half-ton truck, pull up and park outside. As soon as the two men on the truck went into the PX, the Lurps sprang into action. They cut the chain securing the truck with the bolt cutters they'd brought along and quickly made their get-away. When they inventoried the goods on the back of the deuce-and-a-half, the Lurps realized they'd struck a real bonanza. Already loaded and ready to go, they had two shipping pallets of beer, two pallets of soda, twelve cases of scotch whisky, and various and sundry other luxuries. It was now time to get out of Dodge.

It was dusk when the three Lurps left Da Nang in their two reappropriated trucks. After examining their orders, the final American gate guard warned them that they were going to get killed, but Tony and Prindle just laughed, and Russell Rowe glowered and scowled, so the gate guard shrugged and let them through. Prindle and Rowe were in a hurry to get back for their ambush patrol, and Tony was in a hurry to get back to the company and improve everyone's morale.

Highway One between Da Nang and Hue was not always a secure highway, and no stretch of it was ever reliably secure at night. Even in peacetime, it would have been a dangerous stretch of highway, particularly where it snakes along the seaside mountains—and this wasn't peacetime. Tercero, Prindle, and Rowe were fortunate in picking up a few riders. There was a guy in old unmarked fatigues who might have been army and might have been a Marine, and didn't much care that he was AWOL from wherever he belonged. There was a REMF from Da Nang who'd stayed at the whorehouse too long and fig-

ured he'd be safer trucking up to Phu Bai, then flying
back to Da Nang in the morning, than he would be trying
to get past the gate guards and ending up with another
Article 15 punishment. Before he was even out of the
city of Da Nang, Rowe picked up a couple of stranded
Marines who were trying to get back to their units and
who hopped aboard the truck and settled in, looking out
with rifles ready, leaning back against the cases of premium scotch. Russell Rowe was confident that he could
handle things himself if he had to, but he was still glad to
have Marines along. And the South Vietnamese soldier
who soon hitched a ride with Tercero had his rifle and
web gear, and seemed like a pretty righteous dude for
an ARVN.

Thus armed and manned, the two-truck convoy set out
on the road to Phu Bai just as darkness was falling and
the roads really started to get dangerous.

A good part of the road between Da Nang and Phu Bai
was along the side of mountains, with a drop to the ocean
on the right. The Lurp convoy drove without lights, but
the trucks weren't exactly invisible, and they weren't
exactly silent. Every now and then, a few sniper rounds
would crack overhead. Twice, where the road dipped
down into more level ground, the trucks pulled over and
everyone but the drivers dismounted to perform a brief
on-line assault against enemy snipers rash enough to
have opened up on them. The on-line assaults were
mainly just for the fun of it, but they were effective. No
one objected when the ARVN, who was apparently an
officer, took command and started barking orders in
Vietnamese—which none of the Americans could understand—for the man had balls.

As combat went, it wasn't much, even though it could

have gotten a man killed. No one except the REMF who'd stayed too long at the whorehouse took it all that seriously, and even he took it with a touch of humor, wondering aloud if there was any way he could get a Combat Infantry Badge out of it.

From what Tony could pick out of the Vietnamese officer's rather shaky English, these snipers were apparently typical Viet Cong amateurs who really couldn't shoot and never stuck around longer than it took to get off a few rounds as a political statement. The officer grinned, showing gold caps, and allowed that it was fun going after the VC amateurs, and since they almost certainly got away, the VC amateurs had probably had a good time, too.

Here and there along the way, the small convoy stopped at positions manned by local militia troops. Here they would have a drink or a snack and inquire about conditions ahead, which always drew frowns of foreboding and much gesticulating from the militia troops.

Shortly after dawn, the two trucks descended into an area of rice paddies. A few minutes later, they encountered their first traffic going the other way. It was a five-ton truck with a winch on the front, and the driver was so nervous at being out before the road could be swept for mines that he was barreling along, half out of control, and hit the deuce-and-a-half Tony was driving, bashing in the bumper and the left fender and sending Tony's heavily laden truck into the paddy mud. Tony sent the three-quarter after the five-ton truck, and after a lot of persuasion that included Russell Rowe's locking and loading his M-16, even though it was already locked and loaded, the big truck returned and winched Tony's deuce-and-a-half back onto the road. Tony's truck was somewhat crippled when it came to turns, but it still ran, and the Lurp convoy drove on.

By the time the two-truck convoy limped into the MACV-SOG Command and Control North launch site, FOB 1, Phu Bai, with its cargo, the three Lurps had dropped off their passengers and Tony was ready to do a little dealing. Talking his way past the Nung Chinese mercenary guarding the gate was impossible, even for Tony. But Tony was a good talker, and the Nung called for an American Green Beret, who let the Lurps in, then headed off to find someone to assess the cargo. Tony told Prindle this was going to be easy. The Green Berets were outlaws, just like Lurps, and these MACV-SOG Green Berets were outlaws even by Special Forces standards. There were going to be no victims here. This was going to be a good deal for everyone.

Later that afternoon, Tony Tercero, Russell Rowe, and Ashton Prindle led an amazing convoy back to the Lurp Company area. Tony, Rowe, and Prindle led the procession in their new three-quarter ton truck. Following the triumphant three-quarter was an SF deuce-and-a-half, with two pallets of beer and soda and a case of scotch, and towing a front-end loader. The deuce-and-a-half was driven by Green Berets and manned by indigenous strike force troops in tiger fatigues, but Tony was definitely, and splendidly, in charge.

As Lurps came boiling up out of their gravesite hootches and the company cadre came pouring out of the TOC, amazement on their faces, Tony waved grandly, then turned to the Special Forces NCO in the truck behind him and told him where to have his strikers start unloading the goods. Among the goods Tony was bringing back to the company were two somewhat obsolete, but still serviceable, "silenced" Sten guns and a couple of boxes of subsonic ammunition. Among the goods Tony was leaving at FOB 1 were all but one case of scotch and the slightly damaged deuce-and-a-half, which, ironically—and unfortunately for the Green Berets—later turned out to have been originally registered not to some unit down in Da Nang but rather to the radio research unit right across the road from FOB 1. When the radio research unit eventually recognized their old truck, FOB 1 had to give it back. But at this point Tony didn't know that he and Rowe and Prindle had gone all the way down to Da Nang only to steal a local truck, and he was proud to proclaim that he had struck a perfect deal with the Green Berets because there was no victim—at least not up in the Hue–Phu Bai area—at least not among respectable special operation types. Maybe there was a victim or two down in Da Nang. But there was so much whiskey and beer, so many trucks just lying around down there, Tony couldn't think of them as victims. And besides, the trucks and everything else belonged to the United States military, and if the Lurps and Green Berets weren't part of the U.S. military, then nobody deserved that title.

While the unloading went on, Tony smiled benevolently at his brother Lurps, and all the lifers from the TOC stood scratching their heads in wonder. Russell Rowe and Ashton Prindle went back to the graves to get ready for their ambush patrol. With everyone crowding around them asking for details of their adventure, they were walking on air and grinning like tomcats, and it seemed at the time that the ambush patrol was going to be a continuation of the fun.

Later that evening, Sergeant Rey Martinez was sitting back, relaxing with a beer, enjoying the star-filled night sky, and listening to Tony talk about what cool customers Rowe and Prindle were, when all of a sudden a single shot rang out from the direction in which the ambush patrol had gone. Shortly thereafter, Platoon Sergeants Bigelon and Brubaker came running over to Rey's position and yelled for him to grab a medic bag, they were going out. Rey wasn't a medic, except by cross-training, but there was a medic bag handy and Rey grabbed it. They jumped into the new three-quarter with a stretcher and radio, and headed out the Camp Eagle gate and down the road a piece, where they left the truck under guard of the Sp4 from Commo Platoon who was driving it and set out on foot for the patrol's location.

Ashton Prindle had been shot in the head by "friendly fire," and the rest of the team seemed almost unable to deal with it. Even the normally unflappable Russell Rowe was shaken. Rey Martinez placed a sterile four-by-four bandage on his exit and entry wounds, then tied a triangular bandage around his entire head to cover and contain the wounds. Twice, he tried to start a serum albumin IV drip, but Prindle's veins were flat from shock and blood loss. Still, Prindle was not dead. He flinched from the poke of the needles, but it was almost an unconscious reflex. Despite Rey's best efforts, there seemed to be no saving him. He was taken to the division aid station, then evacuated, and was still clinging to a pulse when he arrived at the navy hospital ship off the coast, but died soon after.

It was a fuckup—a terrible fuckup. Prindle and the patrol leader had sent word down the line that they were going to scout out the ambush position and its back approach before moving the team into it. This was normal procedure. Unfortunately, word hadn't been passed down the line. Someone had fucked up badly, and the last man in the ambush position had not been told what was going on. When he looked up and saw an armed man approaching him in the darkness, he'd fired—just one round, but a well-aimed round—and he'd killed his best friend.

It was not the fault of the man who fired, and it was not Prindle's fault. Neither was it the patrol leader's fault. He had passed the word down to make sure that every man knew what was going on. Unfortunately, someone had not passed the word. The men on the ambush did not blame the patrol leader, nor did the other Lurps who knew what had happened. Still, he was a responsible soldier, and he blamed himself. Feeling that he couldn't stay in the Lurp company, he voluntarily transferred to a line infantry company, where he was later killed in action. The dickbrain who had failed to pass the word down never came forward and admitted it, and for some reason, he was not thrown out of the unit, though most of the other Lurps knew who he was and never trusted him again.

As for the man who shot Prindle, it wasn't his fault, but he was devastated. Russell Rowe tried to console him. Martinez tried to console him. Tony tried to console him. All sorts of people tried to console him, but he was too stricken with guilt and grief for consolation. For a while, it looked like he would no longer be able to serve effectively as a Lurp.

But then the oldest and most experienced man in the company, old Nick Caberra, took the young Lurp under his wing, and somehow Nick managed to help him deal with what had happened. The young Lurp went on to serve well for the rest of his tour, and though the story of what had happened to Prindle was not passed on as a lesson to new arrivals in the company—at least not with any names attached to it—the old guys knew what had happened, and they respected and admired the unfortunate young Lurp who had killed his best friend, for the man bore his burden bravely. They also shunned the Lurp who had failed to pass the word down until the day he left the company.

Ashton Prindle's death was the saddest tragedy to hit the company since its formation, and probably the saddest tragedy to hit the 101st Lurps since 1965. Maybe some of the other deaths could have been avoided if people hadn't made mistakes, but no one else had been killed by another Lurp. It was a sobering lesson, and a very sad loss. Prindle was one hell of a Lurp, and he would be missed.

People were drinking to his memory long after the beer and soda he brought back from Da Nang were gone. Even today, when old Lurps from F Company, 58th Infantry (Long Range Patrol) get together, they still have a drink in Prindle's memory.

# Chapter Six

F Company, 58th Infantry (Long Range Patrol)...
none of the men on the teams were too sure when that
had become the company's official designation, and most
of them continued to use "Division LRP" as a return
address on their letters home until they were warned that
mail would no longer be forwarded to that address. Only
then did the 101st Lurps begin to think of themselves as
members of F Company, 58th Infantry (Long Range
Patrol). The designation did not have much of a ring to it.

No one had ever heard of the 58th Infantry, but the
senior NCOs were wise to the game. The 58th Infantry
was a paper regiment, used to designate off-the-wall
orphan units. In the modern army, where battalions rarely
have more than four or five companies, there wasn't
much place in the regular order of battle for an F Company. And so the Lurps became F Company of the 58th
Infantry Regiment. They were still a bastard unit, but
now at least they had a proper unit designation. The part
that made it proper in the eyes of the Lurps themselves was the part in parentheses—Long Range Patrol.
The army could have designated them Z Company,
10,000,000th Infantry and it would have been all right
with most of the Lurps, just as long as it had that Lurp
designation tacked on in parentheses.

It was shortly after the Lurps were ordered to include the new address when writing home that Riley Cox, "the Bulldozer," was joined in the company by his old buddy from AIT and jump school, Joe Bielesch. One evening they were sitting around trying to figure out how to celebrate Cox's recently passed twenty-first birthday, when they came up with an idea that showed how bored and desperate for action the Lurps were getting. After altering the detonator of an M-26 fragmentation grenade, then testing it to make sure it wouldn't ignite, they screwed it back into the grenade and went off to one of the REMF clubs, where the Lurps were not welcome. When the bartender gave them the expected ration of shit, Cox calmly took the grenade out of the cargo pocket of his fatigue pants, pulled the pin, let fly the handle, then set it on the bar. The club cleared out in a mass panic, leaving Cox and Bielesch free to grab a few six-packs and scoop up their inert grenade before booking on out of the club. They didn't get far before they were set upon by a furious mob of REMFs and about a platoon of MPs. It was quite a chase, but the two Lurps managed to elude their pursuers and find a safe spot to drink their beers in peace. In the morning, when they awoke and realized that they were outside the perimeter, Cox shook his head and looked around, then asked Bielesch how the hell they got there and exactly where the hell they were. Bielesch smiled and took a look around of his own. "I don't know how we got here," he said. "But I'd say that we're still in Vietnam."

About the time the Lurps began getting mail addressed to F/58 LRP, they finally began to receive their fair share of real Lurp missions.

Ralph Timmons was one of F/58 Lurp's six or seven

ex-Marines who had improved themselves by becoming army paratroopers, and then improved themselves still more by becoming Lurps. Timmons had come to Vietnam on orders for the 5th Special Forces Group, and had only volunteered for the Lurps because in a post-Tet panic, the idiot REMFs at 90th Replacement had sent him to the 101st, along with every other Airborne-qualified soldier they could get their hands on. It looked like the 101st was preparing for something big and important, and Timmons didn't much mind becoming a Screaming Eagle instead of a Green Beret. And when he heard about F Company, 58th Infantry (LRP), he figured he'd found his sort of unit.

Timmons had been put in the First Platoon, under SFC Brubaker, and that meant he'd been crowded in with the remaining Old Foul Dudes of the 1st Brigade Lurps. That was fine with him, for he was on Sergeant Bob McKinnon's team, and Timmons was fairly confident that McKinnon was the best team leader in the company. Besides, despite the fact that they weren't that old, and weren't all that foul, the Old Foul Dudes were not particularly dull characters to hang around with. The only trouble was, what good was it being on McKinnon's team—what good was it being a Lurp—if you didn't go out on any Lurp missions?

But things were beginning to look up. Timmons had gone to Recondo School in March and come back in April, with the knife awarded the honor grad, and the company was finally beginning to get a few proper long-range recon missions. Of course, most of them were not particularly *long-range* long-range recon missions—only out into the rocket belt, the mountains within a well-launched 122mm missile's range of the city of Hue, Phu Bai airport, and other allied installations and civilian areas along Highway One. A 122mm rocket had a range of twelve miles, although some said twenty if the rocket was the latest model and was launched properly by a trained crew. The rocket belt wasn't long-range enough to qualify as the enemy's rear area—that was another twelve or twenty miles on, in the Ashau Valley and over the fence in Laos. But the rocket belt was definitely hot enough to qualify as enemy territory.

Despite the fact that he was an ex-Marine, Ralph Timmons was an intellectual, a reader and thinker, and something of a cynical right-wing political wit, with a fine collection of malicious old Eleanor Roosevelt jokes he'd picked up somewhere. He was an intellectual, but he was not fooled for a minute by all this liberal nonsense that said Communists were not as bad as Nazis. They were as bad, and the proof of it was that for every two 122mm rockets the NVA launched against Camp Eagle or the airport, or the ARVN training center, or any other allied military area, they launched three against the civilian population in Hue and along Highway One. Sure, it seemed a little defensive, going no farther out than the rocket belt, when now was the time for America and South Vietnam to take the offensive, doing damage to the enemy instead of just trying to cut down the damage the enemy was doing to them. But going into the rocket belt was a real mission. And stopping the rockets seemed a worthwhile cause, even to a cynic like Timmons.

As far as the Lurps were concerned, army-issue insect repellent was wonderful stuff. There were said to be occasional fanatics in some Special Forces recon units who didn't use insect repellent for fear of the odor and didn't allow the men on their teams the use of it, either. But there wasn't anyone that masochistic in the 101st Airborne Division's long-range patrol company. The

Green Berets were notorious bleeding-heart liberals, and no doubt they were worried that the leeches and insects weren't getting a proper diet, but the Lurps weren't that bighearted. They were perfectly willing to let the insects and leeches feed on the enemy, but not on themselves.

Sergeant McKinnon was certainly no fanatic about insect repellent, and he didn't stop the men of his team from making full use of it. Without insect repellent, a Lurp in the field was in trouble. If he was in grass, he'd have to deal with mosquitoes, and if he was in trees, even on the highest mountain—even on a *defoliated* hillside— he'd have to deal with leeches. If he was in the swamps or rice paddies, or along a woodline looking out on grass, then he'd have to deal with both at the same time. Insect repellent didn't keep them all away, but it kept some of them away, and a quick squirt from the little plastic bottle was enough to send most leeches writhing off into their death throes, the slime boiling up out of them. Insect repellent was good for softening camouflage stick, too, and it had a thousand other reputed uses. It was a miracle fluid, this bug juice out of the little plastic bottles, and Sergeant McKinnon had no objection to men soaking their boots and tiger fatigues in it the night before a mission, just as long as they understood that it would wear off in those first few hours on the ground and wouldn't offer much protection against the creatures out there that really meant to kill them. Sergeant McKinnon was not particularly worried that the enemy would find them by the smell of their bug juice. If the enemy got to sniffing around that close, they'd be too close for rifles, so close you'd have to kill them with knives.

McKinnon's team was short one man, but as long as they didn't get into real trouble and have to fight and maybe carry out wounded, there was little a six-man team could accomplish that a five-man team couldn't do as well—and with any luck and skill, they could do it more quietly. The patrol order was to conduct an area reconnaissance of a suspected NVA regimental area of operations for the purposes of updating intelligence, locating base camps, and verifying enemy units. Since the NVA wasn't big on wearing distinctive unit insignia, the best way to verify units was to kill someone carrying documents or to snatch a prisoner. But there was another, secondary mission to the pure reconnaissance mission, and that was to interdict and destroy any rocket teams or rocket sites they might find—either with the team's organic weapons or by calling in gunships or artillery. This was a standard secondary mission in the rocket belt.

McKinnon and his assistant team leader (ATL), Sergeant Gray, came back from the overflight saying the area seemed relatively flat for the rocket belt, but with double and triple canopy jungle. The primary landing zone (LZ) was to be a large, grassy area, and this was to be a first-light insertion.

The team completed the usual premission rituals. There were rehearsals, immediate action drills, and load checks. There was weapons firing to make sure everything worked, and there were commo preparations, map study, and briefings. There was no special, mission-specific, equipment to be carried for this mission, but each man on the team carried four or five fragmentation grenades, smoke grenades, a white phosphorus grenade, a claymore mine, as many as forty magazines of M-16 rounds, cleaning equipment, rations, at least two gallons of water, a poncho liner, pen flare, signal mirror, camouflage stick, pill kit, morphine syrettes, knife, map, protractor, and compass. Being one of the radio men,

Timmons was also carrying a radio; short, long, and wire antennas; an extra handset; spare batteries; and of course, the codebook containing call signs, frequencies, and brevity codes.

The night before the mission, Timmons soaked his boots and pant legs in insect repellent, and as the team gathered at the chopper pad in the dark morning hours, he shot a few more jets of bug juice at his boot tops.

The insertion went perfectly. The team flew in the lead ship, followed by a chase ship rigged for emergency extractions, with the command-and-control ship bringing up the rear. The three ships flew nap of the earth, skimming valleys and hills at treetop level, racing the predawn shadows. At the LZ, the lead ship flared briefly, and the Lurps unassed it in seconds, then all three ships continued on. It had been so fast and smooth an insertion, any enemy would have had to be right on the LZ to know a team had been inserted.

The team moved quickly about twenty meters into the woodline and set up a hasty perimeter with every man facing outward from a tight circle. They listened intently for any sound or movement that would indicate that their insertion had been compromised, and then after ten minutes or so of silence, they moved another hundred meters from the LZ and set up another perimeter, where they lay dog, waiting for daylight to filter down through the jungle canopy. The vegetation was still very wet with dew, and only a few birds were calling in the treetops. After ten or fifteen minutes, first Timmons, then Gray, and then everyone else on the team became aware of a soft rustling sound. At first it sounded a little like someone walking slowly and carefully through the rather sparse undergrowth, and everyone tensed. But then, very suddenly, and seemingly all at once, everyone noticed the leeches. They were everywhere, more of them than anyone had ever seen before. They were inching along the ground, on blades of grass, leaves, small branches— thousands of leeches, coming from every direction, converging on the team. As they inched along, they would pause and rear up the front part of their bodies, then weave back and forth, as though sniffing the air, then they would go back down, inch a little farther, and rise up again. It was easy to see the sucker pads with which they attach themselves to feed on their victim's blood, and there were so many of them, the jungle floor seemed to writhe with them.

Timmons was disgusted, but he wasn't overly concerned. It was early enough in the mission for some of the bug juice he'd soaked into his boots and uniform to still be effective, but even so, he fished a plastic bottle of insect repellent out of his pocket in the hope of killing at least a few of those who managed to breach his defenses. As far as he knew, no one had ever had his blood supply completely depleted by leeches, but if such a thing was possible, there were probably enough leeches here to do the job.

Everyone was more than happy when there was enough light to see clearly, and they moved out of that lay dog position.

Before long, the team came across a trail. It appeared to have been well used at one time, as it was cleared and fairly wide, but there were no signs of recent passage. The team monitored this trail for a short spell, then quickly and cautiously crossed it and moved on. Almost immediately, they came across another trail. They skirted along this trail for a while and soon found themselves in the middle of a complex of NVA fighting positions. There were foxholes, sleeping positions, and even vines stretched between the trees as clotheslines. There was none of the litter such as cans and wrappers an American troop unit might leave behind it, but there were leaves in the holes, and it was clear that these positions had not been used in the last couple of days. It was equally clear, however, that the former occupants might choose to return and set up housekeeping at any time.

After calling in a brief spot report, the team moved on—very slowly and very cautiously.

At approximately 1100 hours, the team came upon another trail, this one even wider than the other two. Sergeant McKinnon and Sergeant Gray were somewhat more expert at this sort of thing than Timmons and the other men on the team, and they were sure the trail had been used recently. After a very quick but very cautious crossing, the team halted perpendicular to and about ten meters from the trail. The undergrowth was fairly open there, with only a thin screen of vegetation between the team's position and the trail, and anything closer than ten meters or so would have been too close. Word was passed around in whispers. The team was going to monitor this trail for a while, and everyone was to make himself as comfortable as possible to minimize the need to shift around, and as inconspicuous as possible to avoid being seen. It wasn't too hard to be inconspicuous, considering how well each man was camouflaged, but comfort was a different story. The day was beginning to heat up, the air was steamy with moisture burning off the vegetation, and there were almost as many leeches as at the first lay dog position.

Finally, Sergeant McKinnon passed word that the men could begin to eat, one at a time, in turns. When it was Timmons's turn to eat, he took an already prepared Lurp ration from inside his shirt. He'd mixed the water into the ration packet before insertion, then resealed the packet and let his body heat warm the ration. Heat and fatigue being wonderful appetite suppressants, Timmons usually ate only a few spoonfuls, then resealed the ration for later, and in that way, one ration could last him a couple of days.

He unsealed his ration package and had taken a couple of bites when he sensed a presence near him and had the spooky feeling that someone was watching him. He looked up, and there it was—a very big and very black leopard. The leopard stepped around the man next to Timmons and moved closer. It was amazing how silently the big cat could move—and it was amazing how close it was. Had he been so inclined, Timmons could have reached up and patted the leopard's nose. He was definitely *not* so inclined. He froze, his spoon poised between his ration package and his mouth, debating with himself whether or not to offer the big cat a bite.

But the leopard obviously had better taste in haute cuisine than Timmons did. It seemed more interested in Timmons than in what Timmons was eating. The tip of its tail twitching, the big cat sniffed Timmons's foot and then his leg, then it snorted softly, shook its head, and walked slowly past the rest of the team members, showing little interest in them. As suddenly and silently as it had come, it was gone. After exchanging amazed glances with his teammates, Timmons resealed his ration and put it away. He wasn't hungry anymore.

Moments later, the team heard a noise on the trail. Everyone froze and watched intently as a squad of eight NVA soldiers with SKS rifles slung on their backs and shovels in their hands came down the trail past them. The NVA were very relaxed and nonchalant, talking among themselves and not paying much attention to their surroundings. They were obviously a work party of some sort, and it was obvious that there were more of their comrades around.

The NVA passed the team's position and continued down the trail. Timmons himself could not follow them with his eyes because his back was against a tree and he could not move without making too much noise. Other men on the team could see the NVA more clearly. Presently, word was whispered through the team that the NVA had entered an encampment farther down the trail—an encampment the team had somehow missed earlier. Very slowly—very, *very* slowly and carefully— the team edged a little closer. NVA could be seen stacking ammunition and crates big enough to contain 122mm rockets. Timmons himself couldn't see them, for he was the next-to-last man in the route of march, but the men in front of him could see the NVA encampment clearly.

The team eased away, stepping very cautiously, ready for all hell to break loose. When they were far enough away from the NVA encampment, they paused, and word of what had been seen was passed in whispers through the team. It was essential that every man on the team know everything that was going on, because in the event that part of the team did not make it back alive, those who did would have to be able to report everything that had been seen, everything that had happened. McKinnon called in the sighting, and soon word was passed that the team was to move back to the LZ as quickly as possible for extraction.

The team got up and turned around. Aware that any out-of-place noise could bring a horde of NVA down on them, they moved very quickly but very warily. They moved back through the complex of fighting positions and across the maze of trails toward the LZ. It took only thirty or forty minutes to cover the same ground that had taken the team hours before. They moved to the edge of the LZ and set up in a tight perimeter. Because the open area was so big, and the extraction helicopters approaching so rapidly, there was no time to recon and secure the LZ. Word came over the radio requesting smoke to mark the team's position. McKinnon popped smoke and asked the pilot to identify the color. This was a normal precaution, and this time it proved very necessary. The pilot radioed back that he had three smokes in sight. McKinnon identified the color he'd tossed, and the pilot acknowledged, then came in on his short final approach.

The extraction ship came in fast and low, the door gunners firing up the woodline on either side with their M-60s. The team broke cover and dashed for the bird, then clambered aboard, and the bird nosed out, banked to the left, and picked up airspeed. Within minutes, the ship had gained altitude and the team was on its way back to Camp Eagle.

Once on the ground back at Camp Eagle, the team was rushed into the debriefing tent, where members of the Division G-2 intelligence section were waiting. When the team had finished the formal debriefing, each team member was individually questioned as to what he had seen and heard on the mission. Almost before the debriefing was over, word came back that an air strike had gone into the area and two large secondary explosions had been triggered by the bombing. This pleased the Lurps. Too often, teams came back with information and there would be no apparent follow-up. This time was different.

Back in the team hootches, the men stripped off their camouflage suits and searched themselves for leeches.

The insect repellent had worked as well as could be expected, but many had still gotten through. They were no longer the thin little one- to two-inch worms they had been. Bloated with blood, they were now as fat as banana slugs, and it was with some disgust—and a great deal of malicious pleasure—that the Lurps doused them with bug juice and watched them die.

Ralph Timmons couldn't help being grateful that the only creatures to feed on his blood this time were leeches. His encounter with the leopard now seemed downright surreal. The big cat hadn't found him appetizing, which didn't really hurt Timmons's feelings. It had apparently not found the Lurp ration all that appetizing, either, which was fine with Timmons, since he hadn't wanted to share it. What struck Timmons as strange was the way the leopard had just appeared there, nonchalantly sniffed him, then continued on its way, as though it was an everyday occurrence to come across small teams of strangely dressed and painted, heavily armed men in its jungle. The leopard had not seemed in the least bit impressed.

With the NVA so close, it was a good thing that the leopard hadn't attacked, and a good thing, too, that none of the Lurps had panicked when it appeared. If that had happened, this successful mission would have had a very different outcome.

Shortly after Timmons went back to the States, bug juice was augmented with bug spray, as the company received case after case of DDT in aerosol cans. Lurps still soaked the strategically important boot laces, pant cuffs and waistbands, shirt cuffs, collars, and sweat rags with bug juice, but it also became the fashion to spray the pant legs, the back of the rucksacks, and anything else an individual Lurp wanted to protect from the leeches and mosquitoes those first few hours in the field. If anyone knew anything of the health hazards of DDT to humans or the environmental harm arising from the use of aerosol sprays, it was just passed off as more peacenik Communist propaganda, like all that stuff some girl sent Miller about defoliants.

It was after Timmons, McKinnon, Gray, and the other men on the team had gone home, and shortly after the arrival of DDT aerosol cans, that the story of this particular mission changed. The enemy soldiers the team had found were forgotten, but the big cat wasn't. Occasionally, as Lurps sprayed their trousers with DDT the night before a mission, some voice of caution would speak up and remind everyone of the time a tiger hopped out from behind a dead tree, sniffed old Timmons up the leg, then sneezed a line of snot on his crotch before bounding off into the jungle.

It was only natural that the story had grown some with distance, the leopard becoming a tiger, and the tiger sneezing snot onto Timmons's crotch. But the point was still valid: Bug juice wasn't just an insect repellent, it also discouraged big cats. The DDT spray, however, was as yet unproven. When men sprayed down the night before a mission, some voice of caution or another would usually speak out and remind the foolhardy sprayers that for all anyone knew, a hungry cat just might take the spray for a spice and bite a man's balls off.

# Chapter Seven

Of all the senior NCOs who'd come over together from Fort Campbell, SFC John Brubaker had initially been one of the few Rey Martinez had much reason to respect. Brubaker had seemed a good guy at first, and there was no denying that he was, at least at heart, a real field soldier. According to the Lurps who'd known him at Campbell, he'd been expecting to serve as both a platoon sergeant and a team leader. But shortly after the company moved up to Phu Bai, it became clear that the two patrol platoon sergeants might be allowed to take out heavy teams occasionally but wouldn't be allowed to have recon teams of their own. This seemed to have affected Brubaker's morale. He started drinking heavily and looking for enemies in his own company. For some reason that no one on the teams could figure out, Brubaker zeroed in on Martinez and began bad-mouthing him behind his back. Article 15 company punishments were still coming out of the TOC like bats out of a cave, and it was easier to count the former 1st Brigade Lurps who *hadn't* been busted at least one pay grade than it was those who had. But by the end of May 1968, it was Brubaker's strange grudge against Martinez that was becoming the focus of tension in the company.

Things finally came to a head at a company party where everyone was feasting on stolen steaks and drinking cold beer. Rey Martinez was standing around, relaxing with a bunch of guys, when Brubaker suddenly materialized right in front of him and proceeded to badmouth him to his face—which was a welcome change from his usual habit of badmouthing him behind his back. Brubaker accused Martinez of thinking he was hot shit when, in fact, he was nothing. Martinez tried to ignore him. Brubaker said that Martinez wasn't a real Lurp and had no idea what a real Lurp was. Martinez said nothing. He knew that Brubaker was egging him on, but he was determined not to bite. With Brubaker still badmouthing him, he turned and walked away without saying anything in reply.

Martinez knew it wouldn't be wise to let Brubaker get to him. Brubaker outranked him by two pay grades, and striking a senior NCO was a serious offense. Even though it probably embarrassed them, the company cadre were behind Brubaker, and Martinez knew that if he didn't handle this problem wisely he was almost certain to face a court-martial.

Martinez got another cold beer and found a different group of guys to hang with. But before long, Brubaker came over to him again. He told Martinez that he had killed better men than him. He said that he knew what recon was all about because he'd had men killed under him on recon missions. Martinez was getting fed up, and he couldn't resist saying that if Brubaker had men killed under him on recon missions, it had to be because he'd fucked up. Martinez knew that wasn't necessarily true, but he figured it was time to step back on Brubaker's toes— and it worked. Brubaker turned red with anger, and there might have been a fight right there if Raider Laing and Tony Tercero hadn't led Martinez away to get another beer. On the way, Tony observed that striking a senior NCO was a serious offense but defending yourself wasn't. The only hitch was that you needed a witness. He pointed out that Martinez didn't have just one witness—if he handled things intelligently, he would have the whole company. After getting his beer, Tony split off from Martinez, advising him to think things over, then make his move.

About ten minutes later, Martinez spied Tony sitting on the ground with Lieutenant Guy, Rocky Bigelon, and Brubaker. Rocky was Marty's platoon sergeant and a good man, and Martinez figured that if there was any chance he'd be able to fight back without getting busted, this was it. He started walking in their direction, but Tony got up and intercepted him. Speaking softly in Spanish, Tony told Martinez that Bru was telling everyone that he was going to sucker punch him and knock him cold. This sounded good to Rey. If he was alert, Bru couldn't sucker punch him. And if Bru tried, Martinez had no intention of letting Brubaker knock him cold.

Martinez eased on over and squatted down right in front of Brubaker, letting him stew in his juices. Under his breath, Rocky told Martinez that Bru was planning to hit him, and Rey thanked him with a nod. As soon as Martinez took his eyes off Brubaker to look at Lieutenant Guy, Brubaker launched himself at him. Still squatting, Martinez speared Brubaker with his fist, twisted, and slammed him to the ground. They squirmed around for a few seconds, wrestling for advantage. Bru was a little bigger than Martinez, and about as strong, and it was a good match while it lasted, but Captain Fitts saw the fight and ordered them to break it up.

The operations NCO, who was the one company NCO who seemed to have the most against the 1st Brigade Lurps, and whom almost all of the field Lurps in the company considered a truculent parasite, grabbed Martinez from behind and tried to muscle him around. Martinez was sorely tempted to punch him in the nose, but Captain Fitts was already there, putting a stop to it.

Captain Fitts looked at Martinez and Brubaker and told them that if they had a problem to take it over the hill. The whole company got up to go watch the entertainment, but Captain Fitts said, "No, just the two of them."

With Martinez leading the way, they both walked over the hill to the Leech Pond. As soon as they got over the hill, Brubaker rushed Martinez and grabbed him by the neck. He ripped off the AK round that Martinez wore around his neck on a parachute cord, choking him in the process, and trying to punch him with his right hand. Martinez replied with some heavy body punches that brought Brubaker's hands down, and then he started to work on Brubaker's face. Brubaker got in a few good licks, then Martinez tagged him with a right, and Brubaker slipped and fell. Martinez immediately pounced on him, and got in a few more good punches. He was wearing his Airborne ring, and every time he hit Brubaker, the ring cut him. Brubaker was bleeding from his right eyebrow and his lip. Martinez paused, his fist still cocked, and asked Bru if he'd had enough. Brubaker said that he had, and Martinez let him get up. He asked Brubaker why they were fighting, and shaking his head to clear it, Brubaker said he didn't know. Martinez said he was sick and tired of Brubaker's abuse, and Bru apologized manfully. They didn't bother shaking hands, but they both knew it was over.

While Martinez looked for his AK round, Brubaker went back over the hill. When the rest of the Lurps saw Brubaker stumbling back, bloodied, they figured Martinez must have been in even worse shape. Doc Proctor was already suturing up Brubaker's eyebrow when Martinez came back over the hill, almost unmarked. It was important to Martinez that Rocky Bigelon seemed glad that he'd prevailed, and though the operations NCO didn't seem too happy, most of the other Lurps were. Martinez and Brubaker shook hands in front of the whole company and told each other they had no hard feelings, then Brubaker turned around and told whoever cared to listen that Martinez had kicked his ass fair and square and that he'd had it coming.

It was the beginning of the end of the friction between the Fort Campbell Recondo School cadre and the Foul Dudes of the 1st Brigade Lurps, and with that out of the way, the party could continue.

The party was just beginning to pick up again when Doc Norton and Jaybird Magill came running up to Captain Fitts with word that the mail truck had just been hit by an RPG (rocket-propelled grenade) outside the gate and a mile down the road. There was a wounded, disoriented, gore-spattered officer up in the TOC. He'd stumbled in, half in shock, and Doc had done what he could for him, but there were apparently more wounded out on the road. While Jaybird and Doc Norton were talking to Captain Fitts, three Lurps who'd been coming back from the Phu Bai airstrip in a jeep behind the mail truck returned to the company area. They had seen the whole thing, and they assaulted the woodline from which the RPG had come, but didn't think they got anyone and didn't know there were still wounded on the truck.

Captain Fitts ordered everyone to saddle up and fall out with radios, weapons, and all their other ass-kicking gear, and the Lurps went running off for their tents. A few minutes later, everyone was falling into formation. Captain Fitts looked around for a second, then allowed himself a slight smile and looked at Tony Tercero.

"We'll take Tony's truck," he said, and the Lurps ran for the deuce-and-a-half and clambered aboard, overloading it severely. If there was any one moment that the company jelled and became a unit, it was then.

The company moved out and secured the burning mail

truck and began to sweep the surrounding area. Everyone was wound a little tight. At one point, Rey Martinez came upon an earthen bunker and hollered in Vietnamese for everyone to come out. He knew people were inside, but there was no answer. His knees shaking, he pulled the pin of a grenade and yelled down to the bunker that he was about to toss in a live egg. All of a sudden, three terrified women and a bunch of kids came scrambling out. As he fitted the pin back into his grenade, Marty's knees were shaking even worse than before. He'd been *that close* to killing a bunch of women and kids, and it scared him.

The driver of the mail truck was still alive—just barely alive—when the Lurps got to him. The truck was burning, and any second the gas tank was going to blow. Doc Norton and Jay Magill and some of the other Lurps got the man out of the truck, and Doc started to work on him. Just then, the general's helicopter landed right there on the road and all sorts of officers started gathering around, offering a fat target to any enemy who might still be in the area. The general offered the use of his helicopter as a medevac, but while Doc was preparing to move him, the driver died, so the general took off.

By the time the Lurps got back to the company area, everyone was sweat-soaked and exhausted, and though the party resumed, it was a good deal more subdued than it had been before this interruption. SFC Brubaker seemed more tired than anyone else, but he wasn't too tired to tell everyone who came near him that he'd been wrong about Martinez and had deserved to get his ass kicked.

Nobody argued with him about that—except maybe the operations NCO; half the company suspected him of putting Brubaker up to all this bullshit in the first place.

# Chapter Eight

A week after the attack on the mail truck, the Lurps were back in the little hamlet between Camp Eagle and Highway One. Some of the villagers had alerted a Vietnamese soldier attached to the 101st that there were two or three VC in the area, and they wanted the soldier to get his American friends out there to do something about it. Four or five months earlier, the villagers might have paid their "liberation" taxes and been cajoled into spying on the American base and maybe even helping the Communists with acts of minor espionage. But after the Communists had shown their true face in the "liberation" of Hue, the Viet Cong were not too welcome anymore. The people of this little hamlet next to the large and growing American base camp had not willingly helped the VC who attacked the mail truck, and now the VC were back, making trouble again, straining relations with the villagers' powerful new American neighbors. So the villagers alerted the ARVN soldier, and he immediately alerted someone up at Division Headquarters. And since the Lurps were right there by the gate, and apparently idle, the job went to them.

Searching a hamlet next to the perimeter was not really a job for Lurps. It was a job for the Military Police and their attached ARVN interpreters, and as the Lurps saddled up and trudged down to the gate, there was at least the normal share of bitching. Security patrols and ambushes a few klicks outside the wire were at least relevant training, with the chance to maybe kill a few enemy. But this? The VC were probably long gone, and this was going to be just another futile bearfuck. And if the VC weren't long gone, then they were suicidally stupid—and suicidally stupid VC could be dangerous in unexpected ways.

Among the most unhappy Lurps was Doug "Doc" Norton, who was still ruefully marveling at the clusterfuck he got caught up in when the general's chopper landed on the road after he and Jaybird and some other Lurps pulled that guy from the burning mail truck and tried to save him. Doc sure hoped there weren't any enemy lurking around the hamlet outside the gate. The general would probably come swooping down in his helicopter, try to take command, and turn this into a clusterfuck, too.

Just outside the gate, the Lurps paused to check out the bridge and sweep the banks of the little river, and then they moved out. The Lurps hadn't really been trained for village searches, and they hadn't really been trained to operate as a company. But Lurps are flexible, and Task Force Fitts had, unfortunately, proven that the long-range patrol company could fill the role of a conventional infantry company if need be.

The Lurps cordoned and searched the hamlet the way an infantry company would have searched it. They were invited guests this time, and though Lurps were, by mission and tradition, a good deal less sympathetic to the indigenous people than the Special Forces—and also a good deal more ignorant about the indigenous people than the Green Berets were—this was a surprisingly friendly bunch of people next to Camp Eagle, and except to the most suspicious Lurps, the friendliness seemed genuine.

Sergeant Gray and the recently demoted Sp4 Mark Thompson poked their flash suppressors and suspicious noses in on a family just sitting down to a midday meal, and had to beg off, half bowing and making an embarrassed exit, when the people started jabbering Vietnamese at them and motioning for them to sit down and eat with them. Doc Norton and Kenn Miller were standing security for Thompson and Gray, and Doc Norton said something to Miller about how there were supposed to be some interpreters around but he hadn't seen any. It just didn't make sense not to have interpreters along on something like this.

The Lurps swept and searched the hamlet for an hour without finding the VC. Doc Norton was moving to the southwest, with the river on his right, when he heard automatic weapons fire off to the left. Being a medic, Norton was carrying his medical bag, and with Miller for security, he headed toward the sound of firing. One of the other Lurps shouted over, telling them that the firing hadn't been due to an enemy contact. It was a water buffalo, and the excitement was already over.

It wasn't clear at the time, at least not to Doc Norton and the guys with him, but some of the Lurps had apparently spooked a water buffalo, and it had started chasing one of the local kids, so the Lurps had opened up on it, putting it down. SFC Brubaker came over and told Miller that the water buffalo was down and no one was hurt, but maybe Doc ought to go check out the kid he'd chased. There was an interpreter around somewhere, Bru said, and as soon as he found the sonofabitch, he'd send him up to Doc. This struck Norton and Miller as somewhat strange because water buffalo were normally docile creatures, at least around the kids who tended them. If one of them had to freak out, it should have gone after the Americans, not some local kid.

Curious, Doc and Miller moved forward. The little river was to the right of them, and in front of them was a shed and a hedge-and-bamboo fence, then an open area, and beyond that, two houses with a threshing yard between them. Before crossing the open area, Doc Norton paused, wary about crossing the stretch of open area while exposed to the tree line along the river. It was definitely beginning to seem that the VC were not in the area, but there was no sense in taking any stupid chances. Bent over to present a smaller target, Doc edged away from the bamboo fence and then froze. Something was moving to his left.

Doc turned slowly, and as he turned there was a flurry of movement. Before he could react, a thousand pounds of pain-enraged water buffalo hit him. The firing earlier hadn't put the damn thing down, at least not for good. All it had done was tear up its nose and *really* piss it off.

The buffalo hit Doc in the small of the back and drove him forward forty feet or so, through the wall and into one of the houses. The next thing Doc knew, he was on the packed dirt floor of what passed for a living room around there. Well, I'm inside and safe now, he thought as he got up on one knee, and prepared to stand if he could. There was a water buffalo around somewhere, but Doc was sure it couldn't be there in the house with him.

Of course, he was wrong. The buffalo was right there in the house with him, and just as soon as Doc got painfully to his feet, it attacked him again. Hooking right and left, it drove one of its horns up between his anus and his scrotum, then lifted him, and with the painfully surprised Lurp medic impaled on one horn and holding on to the other to keep from sliding down any farther, the bloody buffalo pranced around the living room, tossing his head and jolting Doc terribly.

Doc could feel the horn inside him, trying to poke out from the front, then from the back. Somehow, he managed to hit the quick release on his aid bag, and dumped it because the extra weight was driving him farther down the horn. He didn't know where his weapon was, and he didn't much care, since his weapon wasn't going to do him any good. As the buffalo finished prancing and charged out the open front of the house and into the threshing yard, Doc managed to get his feet up in an attempt to put some of his weight on his attacker's shoulder. Trying to scramble onto the shoulder of a raging buffalo while impaled on one horn and clinging to the other made about as much sense as Jackie Kennedy's crawling out onto the trunk of that Lincoln, but Doc had no idea what else he could do, and it hurt so much he had to do *something*.

After trampling, kicking over, and spraying blood into half the wicker baskets of rice and fish drying in the threshing yard, the buffalo paused for a moment, with Doc still impaled on one horn, still clinging to the other horn. The buffalo looked horrible, and Doc didn't look so good, either.

"Would you please kill this fucker?" Doc asked Miller, very politely and calmly, considering the circumstances.

Miller nodded and stepped in front of the buffalo. The buffalo's eyes were unreadable, but definitely malevolent, and blood hung like tree moss from its nose.

Doc's eyes were plaintive, but his voice was very cool. "Just kill him," he said. "Try not to hit me."

Miller tried. The flash suppressor of his weapon an

inch from the beast, he drained a full magazine into the buffalo's head, firing up that bloody, mangled nose, wishing that buffalo had brains as big as elephants so he'd be sure to hit something vital with at least one round.

Miller had seen what M-16 rounds could do to mere human beings, but the water buffalo didn't seem all that impressed. With one toss of its head, it threw Doc off and charged Miller, hitting him in the upper abdomen with the hard ridge between the horns. Miller tumbled over the buffalo's head and shoulders, bounced on the animal's back, then hit the ground just in time for the damn thing to spin around and try to gore him.

Rolling on the ground, desperately trying to stay between the hooking horns, even if the buffalo crushed him with its head, Miller was not all that alarmed when he noticed little puffs of dust hitting all around him. His brother Lurps were coming to the rescue, and he assumed they were aiming at his antagonist, not at him.

Someone yelled "Cease fire!" and for another couple of seconds the buffalo tried to get Miller with its horns. It stepped on Miller's leg and drove its head into his side, but Miller managed to stay between the horns. And then, suddenly, the buffalo was gone.

As Miller got to his knees, he saw that the buffalo wasn't dead and wasn't honoring the cease-fire. It was back on Doc, and once again it had Doc over its head. But this time, Doc was hanging down, head first, between the buffalo's horns, and the buffalo was plowing the ground in front of it with his face.

Bad as things had been when he was impaled, Doc couldn't help thinking that this was worse. Dirt was going into his eyes, his mouth, and his nose. He couldn't breathe, and he was sure he was being blinded. He wasn't thinking too clearly at the moment, but in one instant of clarity he was sure that if he somehow survived, he would be a man without a face—just a blind, living skull with a guide dog and white cane.

Doc was sure he was dead, or at least blind, because the human face did not hold up well when used as a plow. But suddenly the buffalo lost interest in him and turned away. The buffalo lifted its head, and Miller was sure it was coming back for him. But instead the beast charged the other Lurps—who quite appropriately opened up on it with M-16 and M-60 machine gun fire. The buffalo staggered and raged, and seemed confused for a second. Then it made one last charge into the bullets and fell dead right at the feet of SFC Brubaker, Sergeant Martinez, Sergeant McKinnon, Bob Lindvedt, and three or four other Lurps.

Before the sound of firing had died away, three or four men were rushing to Doc Norton. Miller was up searching for his M-16 and the M-79 grenade launcher he'd been carrying slung on his back. He'd spent summers as a kid on his grandfather's cattle ranch, but he never wanted to get this close again to anything bovine unless it was already dead, butchered, and served on a bun with mustard and onions.

Doc somehow managed to get to one of his canteens. He poured water on his face and was delighted to learn that he could still see—but his delight was very short-lived, for then the pain swept over him. Insisting on treating himself, he managed to get a field dressing onto his wound, and then he tried to stand but couldn't because the buffalo had crushed his knee. It was probably a good thing that he couldn't stand just then, because the wound between his legs was a wide one and a deep one. The horn had stirred up his insides, and chances are one field dressing wouldn't have been enough to keep everything inside.

Doc Norton was a cool one. He had the help of concerned brother Lurps if he needed it, but he was the medic. He was conscious, and even if they wouldn't give him the aid bag he'd dropped when the buffalo impaled him, he still had his morphine Syrettes. After getting Rey Martinez to fill out the tag for him, he shot himself up, and felt a little better while he waited for the medevac. When the first flush of morphine euphoria swept over him, he didn't feel all that euphoric, but he still managed to joke with Martinez and some of the other guys, saying something about how he should have just shot up with morphine in the first place and skipped the part with the water buffalo.

Doc Proctor insisted on looking Miller over before letting him hobble over to Doc and try to apologize for not having successfully killed the water buffalo. According to Doc Proctor's hasty diagnosis, Miller had a couple of cracked ribs and some big bruises, but nothing too bad—particularly compared to Doc, who even as he waited for medevac knew that he wouldn't be coming back to the unit and would be very lucky to recover with only minor disabilities. The medevac chopper was already landing for him before Miller could get over to Doc.

As for the water buffalo—it was very torn up, and now, at last, it was dead. It had taken hundreds of rounds, and looking at its body afterward, the Lurps couldn't help noticing how many rounds hadn't really penetrated but had only torn up a little skin before vectoring off the slope of its back or belly. When Miller mentioned the rounds hitting near him when he was on the ground under that thing's head, someone said they had to be ricochets, and looking at the dead buffalo, he believed that at least some of them probably were.

The dead buffalo had been a big beast, a good tractor to the villagers, and before it went crazy, maybe even a gentle friend to the kid it had chased. But the Lurps couldn't help thinking of it as a monster—a vicious and very stupid monster, but a brave one even so.

And, as things turned out, it was also an expensive monster. Because these people were living right outside the Camp Eagle perimeter, and because the 101st Airborne Division was trying to keep them friendly, the Lurp company had to pay for the damn buffalo—which somehow didn't seem quite right, at least not to the Lurps, who were pissed off about losing Doc Norton on a humbug, and also a little disgruntled that they had to pay for a buffalo that someone else was getting to barbecue.

# Chapter Nine

The second week of May 1968, Rey Martinez and his Terrible Team Ten received a warning order for a mission into the dread Ashau Valley. They'd be going into a section of the 1st Cavalry Division's tactical area of responsibility that was now outside the range of allied artillery due to the closing of Fire Base Vicki, and their primary mission was to monitor the junction of three high-speed trails that had been spotted from the air. Their secondary mission was to look for the base camp of the 325C NVA regiment, which intelligence suspected was somewhere in the general area, although not necessarily within Team Ten's assigned recon zone. It was to be a five-day, six-night mission, which meant last-light insertion. It was becoming the standard practice to insert Lurp teams at first light—which usually meant early to mid-morning instead of first light—and Martinez was glad that this was to be a last-light insertion. Martinez knew that the enemy soldiers were not the masters of the night that some people credited them with being. At night, hearing was the dominant sense, and it had been Rey's experience that a six-man Lurp team could move much more quietly than the NVA out beating the bush for them could.

There was one thing slightly strange about this

mission—they were supposed to see to the secondary mission first, spend a day or two looking for signs of the base camp, and only then move on to monitor the trail junction. It made sense, after a fashion. If there was a base camp in the area, one of those trails would surely be leading to it, and it might be a good thing to know which trail it was.

Martinez had a full team, and it was an intact team, a team that had worked together and trained together and relaxed together. That was the way things should have been, and that was the way things had been, most of the time, back in the 1st Brigade Lurp detachment. In this division Lurp company, however, team integrity was hardly honored in concept, much less in practice—particularly now. Ever since the 1st Brigade came to Vietnam in June 1965, June and December were always times of personnel flux in the 101st Airborne, and that was bound to have its effect on team integrity in a company-size Lurp detachment where about a third of the men were on extensions, and those extensions were beginning to come due. Sergeant Martinez hadn't seen much good luck in it when he, alone of the 1st Brigade Lurps, had been sent over to Second Platoon and given a team of cherries, but he figured he was lucky now. The Lurps on his team weren't complete cherries anymore, and all of them still had a lot more time left in-country than he did. He had an intact team, and it was a good one.

Rey, of course, was team leader, and Sp4 Barry Golden was his assistant team leader. "Goldy" was a little light in rank and experience to be an ATL, but he was a good Lurp and could handle the job—just as long as Rey didn't suddenly dump it all on him at a bad moment by letting himself get killed. Rey had no intention of doing such a thing. But if it happened anyway, he figured that Goldy would probably be up to the job. Goldy wasn't just the assistant team leader; he was also the point man, and for that job he had a natural talent.

Walking Goldy's slack was Tony Tercero. Having Tony Tercero walk your slack was an honor and a real confidence builder. Tony was a scoundrel, but he was a brave, stand-up sort of scoundrel, a man who liked to expound philosophically about brotherhood and honor, and as a young delinquent in Phoenix, then a guest of the juvenile courts at reform schools and youth ranches a good part of his formative teen years, Tony had not only learned to talk the talk but also how to walk the walk. Tony was cool and quick thinking under pressure, a man you could trust, and having him on slack was enough to make any point man feel a good deal safer, if not completely safe.

Sp4 William "Raider" Laing was senior RTO. It was Tony Tercero who had pronounced Raider a Foul Dude at a set of pipe-passing down by the Leech Pond, after Raider declined the pipe and stood up, saying, "You Foul Dudes are too foul for me!" Raider was an extremely fit, intelligent, well-read, well-spoken, thoughtful young Lurp from Louisiana, but Tony was right. Raider was a very Foul Dude, in the laudatory sense of the term. Tony once said something about how Raider might have become a hippie if he'd stayed home and gone to college and shirked his duty to America—and Raider at least looked the part of an Airborne hippie, with his raffishly customized Lurp hat and the gas mask granny spectacles he wore instead of more normal eyeglasses. Raider himself didn't look at all like John Lennon, but John Lennon would have looked right at home in Raider's gas mask granny glasses.

Junior RTO was Eric "Sugar Bear" Shugar. Shugar

had come over with the company from Fort Campbell, but he'd come over as company clerk. That was against his wishes, but he was an expert typist, at least by Lurp standards, and so he'd been stuck with the job. Being an intelligent fellow, Shugar had made good use of the powers a company clerk could wield, and he had arranged for himself to be among the first group of newly arrived Lurps to attend the MACV Recondo School in Nha Trang. Returning to the company with the honor grad's dagger assured him a place on a team.

Walking rear security was Sp4 Jim Venable. Venable was a quiet, competent Lurp, a very steady man, meticulous in his duties and therefore a perfect "tail gunner." With him on rear security, the team was not going to leave much of a spoor behind for the enemy to track, and no one was likely to sneak up on the team from the rear. No one had ever seen Venable get excited. He stayed calm and sensible, no matter what, and he was enormously respected by the men on his team.

The recon zone was mountainous and thickly forested, with a fairly large stream running down the middle of the main valley. On the overflight, Sergeant Martinez had selected a primary LZ just a little bit out of the recon zone and separated from it by a good-size ridgeline. Going in on this LZ meant the team would have some humping to do before getting into the area of operations (AO), but Martinez reasoned that it was the only possible LZ in the area that offered any hope of getting in without being seen.

During the overflight, and then again during the pre-mission briefback, no one raised any questions about the choice of a primary insertion LZ, but on the way out to the recon zone for insertion, Martinez noticed that the pilot did not seem to be taking them to the LZ he'd chosen. He tried to tell the pilot he was off course, but the pilot was nervous and pretended not to know what Rey was complaining about. It was a long way from Camp Eagle to the recon zone, but the pilot had chosen to fly most of the way contouring along at treetop level, and so Rey didn't dare to argue too vociferously for fear the pilot would get even more rattled than he already was and fly them into a hillside or a tree.

When they got to the general area where the mission was going in, the pilot suddenly flared out over a prominent hilltop on a ridge that overlooked the valley in the center of the recon zone. Sergeant Martinez had considered and rejected this LZ on the overflight, but now there was no choice. The team unassed the insertion ship and ran for the bush. Right there on the LZ, Tony Tercero almost collided with two NVA who seemed a good deal more surprised than he was. The NVA fled down the steep side of the hill, and Tony joined his teammates in their security wheel, whispering the bad news that they were already compromised.

While this was going on, the pilot of the insertion ship was taking the exact wrong course away from the insertion, flying over the southeast corner of the recon zone, as if to advertise the fact that he'd just put a Lurp team on that ridge overlooking the valley.

Raider Laing got his commo check and advised the insertion chopper to go a little way off station and then go into a holding pattern, because the team had probably been compromised. The insertion pilot's reply was not exactly a morale booster. He didn't roger the transmission in the affirmative, nor in the negative. He just didn't seem to know what the fuss was all about.

Almost immediately, the Lurps heard the plop of mortars being fired down in the valley, and a couple of seconds later a round exploded thirty meters to the team's northwest. Raider called the relay team and reported that the team was being mortared. Seconds later, another round impacted twenty meters to the north, then three more hit just to the east of the team's position. In between the explosions, the Lurps could hear enemy shouting back and forth in the valley, and then, after the last round exploded, there was silence.

The relay team called back with the word that the fire had been friendly artillery. Raider passed the horn to Martinez, and when Martinez had them repeat the message, he was amazed. The team was outside the range of friendly artillery—and what the hell was friendly artillery doing firing on them anyway?

Still, this was no time to start arguing over the radio. Martinez considered calling in the gunships that had accompanied the insertion, but he didn't have a visual sighting on the mortar tubes and wouldn't be able to direct fire. He had an azimuth on the sound, but that wasn't enough.

The Lurps heard voices again. These were loud voices, not too close, but they sounded remarkably—ominously—relaxed. Martinez figured the enemy had to be confident to be talking like that—confident, but not sure exactly where the team was.

Martinez quickly assessed the situation, then he sighed and called in to release the choppers. Now the team was committed. They were going to continue the mission.

Terrible Team Ten moved out. They had gone only twenty-five meters down the west side of the ridge when Tercero motioned Martinez forward. Goldy had found an ant trail with footprints in the loose dirt around it and freshly disturbed ants running every which way. It was not a good sign.

Adding things up quickly—the two NVA Tony had almost bumped into on the LZ, the mortars, the voices, and now this sign of very recent enemy presence—Martinez came to the inescapable conclusion that the team was indeed compromised. Maybe the enemy didn't know exactly where they were, but he sure knew their general location, and he almost certainly knew how many Lurps there were on the ground.

After moving a little farther, Martinez called a halt. It was dusk, and the Lurps wanted to make use of what little light remained. On the last transmission, Control had ordered the team to move three hundred meters down the ridge before laying up and hiding for the night. There wasn't time for that, and besides, it just wasn't a good idea. There were no emergency extraction LZs on the side of the ridge, but there were plenty of NVA in the area. Control might order the team to move that three hundred meters, but Control wasn't down on the ground with them, and had no real business dictating the on-the-ground conduct of the team's movement. Martinez set the team up in a defensive position, then took Goldy and Tercero on a short recon of the little knoll they were on. Less than fifty meters from their LZ, they found a temporarily empty system of fighting positions and bunkers. They couldn't help reflecting that if those positions had been manned when they inserted, they would probably be dead.

Still, the bunkers and fighting positions did offer the Lurps something they needed at the moment—good defensive positions. Just after dark, the team moved into the bunker system, set out claymores, and called in their situation report.

There had obviously been a command breakdown of some sort. It seemed to Sergeant Martinez that Control did not trust him to conduct his mission according to his own good judgment, and he certainly didn't much trust Control anymore. It is always dangerous—and usually very stupid—to call in a false position, but after some consideration that's what Rey had Raider Laing do. As far as Control was concerned, they had moved that three hundred meters off the ridge. To have actually done so, under the circumstances, would probably have been suicidal. Under normal circumstances, to call in a false position was maybe a little unethical, but the team had been compromised right on the LZ, Control didn't seem to believe anything the team reported, and so these were not normal circumstances. The team had good defensive positions and fairly quick access to an LZ. Three hundred meters off the ridge, they would very likely not even have had good communications with which to call in their last, final, situation report if—or more likely, when—the enemy hit them.

Around 2200 hours, the team heard voices again. The enemy had a better idea where the team was than Control did—but the team had a better idea where these particular enemy were than the enemy did of them. Silently, tensely, the Lurps listened to the enemy party searching for them. The terrain was tough and the vegetation thick, and the NVA were not practicing the best noise discipline. They got within ten meters of the team and then backed off. Martinez couldn't help wondering if the enemy might know exactly where they were but not want to push matters unless the team tried descending into the valley. Then the NVA would chop them up.

The Lurps stayed on alert all night. By 0430 hours, the NVA soldiers who had been beating the bush around them could no longer be heard. Sergeant Martinez figured the enemy would either hit them at first light or wait for them to move off the ridge.

Shortly before 0500, Martinez sent Goldy and Tercero out to pull a 360-degree security check around the team's position. They were back shortly with news that Goldy had spotted three NVA just off the LZ. He was reasonably sure the enemy had not spotted him.

This was just about as compromised as Martinez had ever been without actually making contact. There was, he reasoned, no way the team was going to be able to get off that ridge and down into the valley to perform its mission. They could reinsert at their original primary LZ and start the mission all over, but if they continued it now, about all they were likely to accomplish was getting themselves killed. Martinez called in for extraction.

Again, Control wanted to know if they were positive they had been compromised. Raider replied in the affirmative. It was then that Sergeant Martinez noticed that Raider didn't look quite right. Raider didn't want to say anything about it, but he admitted that he was running a fever. Martinez decided to relieve him of the radio. Raider was still doing a good job of communication, but the radio was heavy, and it was best to relieve him of the burden.

Control came back on the horn and verified the extraction, but announced that it would be an hour before a chopper could get out to them. While they were waiting, the Lurps heard more voices to the north and down in the valley. Finally, they got word that two slicks and two gunships were five minutes out. The Lurps pulled in their claymores, moved cautiously back to the edge of the LZ, and set up in their security wheel, each man on his belly, facing out, with weapons at the ready.

It was a long five minutes—a very long five minutes.

In fact, it was more than ten minutes after the first "zero five mikes" transmission that the extraction ship came over the net, saying it was ten minutes out.

A couple of minutes passed in silence, and then Jim Venable touched Martinez and slid over to whisper in his ear. "Hey, look at this," he whispered, and pointed off to the northwest. Six 122mm rockets were rising out of the jungle and heading toward LZ Goodman and Signal Hill, where the relay team was. It was an awesome sight.

Martinez got the gunships on the horn and told them he had a mission for them. The gunships were still five minutes out, which gave Martinez more than enough time to plot the map coordinates of his target and call them in to the gunships.

Two more rockets rose out of the jungle valley and headed off in the same direction. Then there was another one. The gunships arrived on target just as a tenth rocket lifted off. This time, the gunship pilots had seen the rocket, and they called back to Martinez that they were going in hot.

The gunships went into their run just north of Team Ten's position, flying straight up the valley. They put their own rockets right on target, and the whole valley seemed to open up on them with small arms and at least two .51-caliber heavy machine guns. One of the gunships finished its rocket run and pulled away. The other began hosing down the slopes of the ridge and started taking hits.

Circling overhead in the C&C ship, Captain Fitts had seen everything. He called for jets, and a flight of Marine Corps F-4s was diverted from another target. Coming in two at a time, the fastmovers blasted the valley with bombs and rockets—and to their credit as soldiers, the

NVA fired back bravely as the jets screamed down on their positions. One of the jets came out of its run trailing smoke and had to break off and return to base.

While the Marine Corps jets were blasting the valley, and diverting the NVA's attention in such a spectacular and deadly fashion, the extraction ship slipped into the LZ and extracted Terrible Team Ten without mishap. Shortly after, a platoon of "Blues" from the 2/17 Cav tried to come in on a combat assault atop the ridge where Team Ten had spent the night and was shot out of the LZ and forced to turn back.

Had the team moved down, as ordered by a Control element that didn't seem to quite believe they were as severely compromised as they were, the chances are the team would have been wiped out.

As things worked out, the mission could be judged a success. Team Ten did not get to monitor the trail junction or search the valley for the suspected base camp. They did, however, help put one hell of a dent in the enemy's ability to rocket allied installations. And they did help answer one of the basic questions intelligence had about that valley. There were beaucoup enemy down there—and an uncounted but certainly sizable number of those enemy soldiers were now dead enemy soldiers.

It took a few days for the complete story of Terrible Team Ten's mission to get out to the other Lurps, and then it was passed along as sort of a moral lesson in command responsibility. A team leader's first responsibility was to the mission, and his second was to the men on his team—or maybe it was the other way around. Either way, a Lurp team leader was under no great obligation to put his own judgment aside and let someone in the air or back in the rear start telling him when to move, where to move, how fast to move, and how far. In fact, if such meddling might endanger the men or the mission, a good team leader was obligated to ignore it.

The men who had been on this mission were unanimous in their judgment that Sergeant Rey Martinez had done the right thing and saved their lives by calling in that false position and sticking to the high ground, close to the LZ. According to the Lurp doctrine Rey Martinez had worked under in the 1st Brigade Lurp detachment, and been taught at the 5th Special Forces Group's MACV Recondo School, once a long-range reconnaissance patrol team was on the ground, it was supposed to be the team leader calling the shots and making the judgments about where to move, and when, and how far. That order to move three hundred meters down from the ridge before laying up and hiding might have been a legal order under the Uniform Code of Military Justice, but by the Lurp doctrine Rey Martinez had lived by, he was under a far greater obligation to ignore it than he was to obey it. He was the one leading the team on the ground, not Control, and Control should have believed his reports and trusted his judgment. By Lurp doctrine, Control should have extracted the team as soon as it was compromised and reinserted it the next day—on the right goddamn LZ.

But then, on the other hand, if things had gone the way they should have gone, Team Ten would never have spotted those rockets.

A couple of weeks after this mission, Martinez joined Lurch Cornett down at the division rear area in Bien Hoa, where both of them had prestigious, but somewhat dull, jobs training new arrivals coming into the 101st Airborne Division. Lurch was just waiting to go back to Special

Forces, and Rey was just waiting for his extension to come to an end so he could go home and get out of the army.

When SSG Lester "Superspade" Hite and SSG Ronald Weems came around, trying to talk him into staying in the army on the grounds that you can't have yourself this much fun in the civilian world, Rey listened with interest and was tempted. Weems and Hite weren't too forthcoming about what they'd been doing the past four or five months, but Weems was headed for MACV-SOG Command and Control Central, and Hite was either going to go with him to SOG or was going to take a job he'd been offered in the Hawk Recon Platoon. He hadn't made up his mind yet.

Weems and Hite were persuasive. They were wearing very faded jungle fatigues with nothing sewn on them, tiger-stripe Lurp hats, and real field boots that hadn't seen polish since they left the factory. The Superspade was wearing about a pound of bracelets of Montagnard brass and Hong Kong gold on each wrist, and Weems's eyes were flashing with excitement as he talked of the opportunities still available in the Republic of Vietnam. Sergeant Martinez had a hard time imagining leaving a life like this and brothers like these for the dull routine and petty frustrations of civilian life. It was particularly hard to imagine leaving Vietnam when Superspade thoughtfully rubbed the scar under his eye and asked him where he expected to have this much fun in the civilian world.

Martinez thought it over very quickly, and since he thought of all the fun he could have in the civilian world instead of all the fun he could keep having for a while more—maybe a very short while more—in Vietnam, he told Weems and Superspade that he was getting out of the army. He was going to break on through to the other side, just as Superspade encouraged, but the way Rey looked on it, the other side he was going to break on through to was civilian life.

Although he was down in the rear, training new arrivals, and had only a week or so left in the army, Rey Martinez was not yet through with the war. One evening it was his job to meet a group of new arrivals coming into the division, most of them right out of training in the States. This group arrived at night, by bus along the secure road from the replacement depot at Long Binh. All of them were still in the khaki uniforms they'd worn from the States, and all of them were hungry and unhappy to find the mess halls at the 101st rear area already closed. Sergeant Martinez welcomed the new arrivals to the 101st Airborne Division— noting with silent dismay that about half of them weren't wearing parachute wings—then he gave them a brief introduction to what they'd be learning in replacement training. That done, he took them off to their assigned barracks, warned them about the early formation in the morning, and pointed out the bunkers and the immediate action drill in case of a rocket or mortar attack. He put the senior man of them in charge and went off to find Lurch, Mark "Wolverine" Thompson, his old high school buddy Vic Cisneros, and a new friend, a black sergeant stationed back in the *rear* rear area, who loved to box and was thinking about volunteering for Lurps in order to get away from the rear echelon doldrums. Wolverine was going home the following day, and it was his going-home party.

Martinez and the others went to the NCO club, where they had a bunch of beers. Closing the NCO club, they were happily driving along in Lurch's jeep-based field ambulance, past the transient barracks and the barracks where Rey had taken the new replacements, when suddenly he and his companions were jolted by the impact of a couple of 122mm rockets similiar to those he'd seen rising out of that jungle valley. Rey had been sitting high in the back of the field ambulance, protected only by the sides of the canvas top, and as soon as he realized the area was under rocket attack, he threw himself out the back of the vehicle and hit the ground.

Almost immediately, he heard a commotion in front of the barracks where he'd taken the new guys, and he scrambled to his feet. The black sergeant jumped out as Lurch roared off in his ambulance, yelling back over his shoulder that he was going to get some aid bags and medical supplies.

The two paratroopers raced for the barracks. One of the rockets had hit right in front of the entrance, and the other one had hit close enough to do some damage. The place was a mess, and all around there were dead men, dying men, wounded men, and men who were too freaked out to function. The first wounded man Rey came to looked like a goner. His chest had been ripped open, his ribs laid to the side, and even in the dim wash of his penlight, Rey could see there wasn't anything he could do for the man. He was dead. Feeling he was standing in something mushy, Rey looked down and saw he was standing in the intestines of the man he'd just tried to help. The next man had half his right knee gone and multiple shrapnel wounds in both legs. The third person was still alive, but unconscious, and having trouble breathing. Rey began to give him mouth-to-mouth resuscitation when something broke inside the man, and blood and vomit flooded into Rey's mouth. Swallowing most of it, he started gagging and spitting. Rey checked for a pulse, and he tried to keep this man from going into shock. He began shouting orders at the unwounded replacements, hoping to shake them back into a functional condition of some sort and to keep the wounded man's weak pulse going.

Martinez and the other sergeant were soon joined by Lurch with a field ambulance full of medical supplies and stretchers—and they were soon joined by a dozen other 101st troopers, all of whom, except a few of the officers, pitched in to help. Lurch stayed with Martinez, trying to keep his man alive.

When the wounded and dead had been evacuated to the hospital at Long Binh, one of the officers, a major who had just stood around "supervising," spoke up with the opinion that these rockets hadn't really been intended for the 101st Airborne's rear area. They were just short rounds, the major said, intended for Bien Hoa Air Base. For some reason this set Rey off, and he told the major he was full of shit—you didn't get two short rounds falling in the same place, and Charlie didn't have rockets to waste just firing them at unaimed random. Someone among the indigenous personnel working in the area during the day had paced off the area for the enemy, and Rey was not hesitant about letting the major know that he suspected it was either one of the goddamn hootch maids or that goddamn barber with all the gold teeth. The major was about to gather up his commissioned dignity and lock young Sergeant Martinez's heels when Lurch pulled Rey away. Going back to Lurch's hootch, they found Wolverine and Cisneros and continued celebrating Wolverine's going-away party.

The next morning, Rey and Lurch went by the barracks and found the one survivor who knew most of the men who'd been killed. This poor fellow was an eighteen-year-old private who had been in Vietnam less than twelve hours when he saw half a dozen or so of his

Advanced Individual Training buddies killed, and it was the sad duty of Sergeants Martinez and Cornett to take him over to the morgue at Long Binh to identify the dead. They were all so new to Vietnam, so new to the division, there was no one else who knew them.

Although Lurch strolled in just as calm as he could be, munching on a carrot, this was Rey's first visit to a morgue, and he wasn't much enjoying it. The poor private they'd brought along was having a far worse time of it, struggling not to vomit every time the morgue attendant unzipped one of the body bags and the stench rose up. By the time they left the morgue, the poor private was a basket case.

Lurch was a firm believer in shock introductions as the best way to get someone's attention. He liked to start his medical classes by drawing a syringe of blood from his own arm, then tossing the syringe, like a dart, at a wall map of Vietnam. But this klu had had a little too real a shock introduction during his first twelve hours incountry, and he wasn't likely to make it through the next twelve months unless someone took an immediate interest in his psychological health. Being a compassionate fellow, Rey Martinez agreed with Doc Cornett's diagnosis, and so they spent the rest of that day administering to the poor fellow's traumas and trying to boost his morale.

They took him into Saigon, got him laid, and got him drunk. When they got back to Bien Hoa, they took him away from everyone, got him high on his first taste of marijuana, talked to him like a couple of older brothers, listened to him like a couple of Viennese shrinks, and did nothing at all to stop him from getting even drunker than he already was.

By the time they got him back to the replacement

barracks, the young private had already pissed on himself and was too drunk to walk, but Sergeants Martinez and Cornett were sure that he was squared away now, his morale improved, his confidence restored, and his outlook a whole lot more positive than it had ever been before. Rey and Lurch were sure of this because, while he could still talk somewhat coherently, the young private had so assured them himself.

Rey had the man excused from the morning formation, and Lurch left word to let him sleep in, but by the next afternoon the young private was back in training with the rest of his somewhat depleted replacement class. For the rest of the young private's stay in replacement training—which just about exactly coincided with the rest of Rey's time in Vietnam and Lurch's time in the 101st—Sergeant Martinez and Sergeant Cornett kept an eye on him and offered him an occasional encouraging word, and when the time came for the kid to report to his unit, he was already turning into a suprisingly stable and competent soldier.

Rey Martinez might not have noticed it at the time, so consumed was he with fighting the temptation to stay in Vietnam for at least one more extension, but among that class of new arrivals who had been so harshly welcomed to Vietnam were a big, athletic young paratrooper from Chicago by the name of Dave Biedron, and a thin, wiry paratrooper from Chicago named Jim Schwartz, who must have come to the somewhat questionable conclusion that it was safer and more fun to be sneaking around out where the enemy was launching rockets than it was to be hanging around back in the rear waiting for the rockets to impact. They volunteered for Lurps right out of replacement training, and had little trouble being accepted and finding slots on the best teams.

# Chapter Ten

In mid-May 1968, the company was visited by a couple of strange characters, one of them dressed in fatigue trousers, a loud Hawaiian shirt, and a goofy little straw hat, and the other man wearing unmarked fatigues so fresh they still smelled of mothballs to anyone who got close. The general assumption among the Lurps was that these men were either CIA, military intelligence, or techno-wizards from some army research lab back in the States—and judging by the ridiculously eye-catching getup of that cowboy in the straw hat and Hawaiian shirt, Lurp money was on the CIA. Whether art imitated life or life imitated art wasn't usually a major topic of discussion among the Lurps, but the guy in the colorful hat was obviously trying to look like Felix Leiter, James Bond's CIA buddy. He wasn't carrying it quite to the extent of having a hook in place of one of his hands, like the "real" Felix Leiter, but he did have the clothes down.

Whoever these guys were, they had with them some highly classified new devices that they seemed to think would hasten the end of the war by halting the flow of supplies and soldiers coming down the Ho Chi Minh trail network into the South. The devices they so proudly introduced to the Lurps were black plastic boxes about the size of a shoe box, with thin little antennas disguised

**119**

to look like twigs. Once in place along infiltration routes, they were supposed to pick up the vibrations of passing traffic and send off radio signals that would bring on artillery or air strikes, and win the war on the quick-and-easy with a nice technological fix. No one was much impressed with these black boxes—no one except the men who brought the damn things. Of course, the men who brought the black boxes obviously weren't going to be the men who planted the devices out along the infiltration routes. That was going to be a job for the Lurps. The man in the unmarked fatigues was obviously somewhat leery of turning the boxes over to them, and kept stressing how expensive and fragile and highly classified the devices were. The guy in the straw hat and Hawaiian shirt didn't seem quite so nervous and didn't take much part in the instructions, preferring instead to hang back and pretend he was being inconspicuous.

The Lurps listened attentively, if not exactly respectfully, as the pale, nervous man in unmarked fatigues conducted a short class on how to plant the devices. The older NCOs tried to look grave and dutiful and professionally respectful, but it was obvious that they were not particularly impressed with the black boxes—or with the men who had brought them. The enlisted swine paid attention too, but they made no visible effort to look dutiful or respectful.

At the end of the class, one of the civilian types turned to Captain Fitts and told him to choose his best team for the first mission. Captain Fitts then turned and said something to SFC Brubaker.

After the class was over, Magill, Clark, and Thomas headed back to the team tents. Clark said something about how those legs in the unmarked fatigues had probably gone to FOB 1 first and been run off because the SFers had more balls than these Fort Campbell lifers running the Lurps, and had probably told them where to shove their electronic warfare "black boxes." Thomas looked at Jaybird and Crash Clark, and if Jaybird remembers correctly, Thomas shook his head and smiled that gentle, friendly smile of his, then took the toothbrush out of his shirt pocket and started idly brushing his teeth as he cast around, looking for their team leader, Teddy Bear Gaskell.

Teddy Bear was over by the TOC tent, locked in earnest conversation with SFC Brubaker. Teddy Bear looked serious—very serious. Of course, Teddy Bear always looked serious, even when he wasn't. This time, however, he *really* looked serious.

SFC Brubaker asked Teddy Bear if he felt his team was ready for the first black box mission. Teddy Bear shrugged. He would have felt a lot better about this sort of mission if he'd been with one of the old 1st Brigade Lurp teams on which *he'd* been the cherry, but he figured his team was as ready as any team in the company. Of course, he had a lot of questions, but he had only three questions that grew out of real misgivings.

The first question was where they were going to plant these things. Probably somewhere around the Ashau, said Brubaker. He didn't have any details himself yet, and he was straight enough to admit it to Teddy Bear.

Steve LeGendre was already back in the rear, on his way back to the States, Kenn Miller was on R&R, and the team was a little short. When Teddy Bear asked who he was going to get to take Miller's place, Brubaker frowned at the stupidity of the question and said he'd find someone. Miller wouldn't be hard to replace.

Those were the two questions Teddy Bear asked, but there was another one he didn't ask—and that was, just why was the division Lurp company sending the last basically intact 1st Brigade Lurp team out on the first of these black box missions? Were they finally acknowledging the 1st Brigade Lurp as the more reliable, experienced component of the company? After all, these civilian types had asked Captain Fitts for the best team.

Teddy Bear was glad to be getting the mission. The Ashau was about the scariest place in South Vietnam, but he figured his team could probably get in and plant the sensors and get out undiscovered if they took it slow and sneaky and had any luck running for them at all. He was proud, very proud, to have been chosen, and he called for his team to come up to the Operations tent.

Outside the Operations tent, SFC Brubaker warned the Lurps to be on their best behavior around the spooks—be on their best behavior or else! Ever since Rey Martinez cleaned his clock, Bru had not much engaged in bluster, particularly to former 1/101 Lurps, and so he was taken seriously.

Inside the tent, Captain Fitts had the men sit down, and without any introductions, the dude in the straw hat gave them a quick rehash of the earlier class and put a very stern note in his voice when he warned the Lurps that they were, under no circumstances, to allow the devices to fall into enemy hands. The only reason the Lurps didn't snicker was out of respect for Captain Fitts, and because they'd grudgingly promised Brubaker they'd behave.

After the black box briefing, Captain Fitts and the Operations NCO took over, rolled down a large map, then a large acetate overlay, and launched into a premission briefing that was really little more than a premission warning order at this point. There were still a few details to work out involving linkups with line infantry companies—and that was an unpleasant surprise. Lurps had a very reasonable fear of linkups with anyone but their own people, and were a little leery of that, too. It was easy to get shot on a linkup, and by the Lurp table of values, if a Lurp had to get shot, it was better to get shot by the enemy than it was to get shot by other Americans. What was surprising—and alarming—about this was that there seemed to be a whole series of linkups planned for the team, and they would apparently have no say about it, even if they came up with a more workable plan to get out there and plant the boxes where these people wanted them planted.

The area in which these people wanted the black boxes planted wasn't really much of a surprise. It was the Ashau Valley, one of the two or three scariest, most challenging areas of operations (AO) anywhere in South Vietnam. The only thing surprising about the mission being into the Ashau was the presence of line companies in the area. None of the Lurps had had any idea that division had any line companies out near the Ashau.

On the way back to the team tent to begin their preparations, and to find out who Brubaker was going to send out with them in Miller's place, Jaybird Magill asked Teddy Bear what he thought of the mission.

Sergeant Gaskell was already into his third year as a Lurp in Vietnam and was planning to outgrow this nonsense soon, get out of the army, and go to college. But he was still a Lurp, a team leader, and in experience he was clearly the senior field Lurp in the whole company, so he played it calm and philosophical.

"Sounds like a pork chop to me," said the Teddy Bear cheerfully. "Sounds like a real pork chop to me."

\* \* \*

The night before Teddy Bear's team was to go out, Camp Eagle was rocketed again—and this time one of the rockets hit the Lurp area. No one was seriously hurt, but among those who picked up scratches and bruises from shrapnel and debris was Jaybird Magill. Teddy Bear was very relieved when Jaybird said he wasn't hurt badly enough to stay back. His face was cut and bruised, and if he'd gone to the medics, he could have had himself an easy Purple Heart. But if he'd done that, he wouldn't have been able to go out with the team the next day. So he decided to ignore his "wounds." The team was already taking a replacement for Miller, and Magill damn sure didn't want his team to go to the Ashau with two last-minute replacements.

In a final briefing by the visitors, Teddy Bear was told that the team was supposed to plant one relay of three boxes at one end of a valley leading into the Ashau, and another three-box relay at the other end. The 1st Battalion, 327th Airborne Infantry was operating in the area, and the civilian types promised Teddy Bear that his team would have "full support" from that battalion. Teddy Bear wondered how they could make such a promise, but the 1/327 was a 1st Brigade unit, and he figured that if he had to be out there depending on a line battalion, 1/327 was about the best you could ask for.

There wasn't much time to prepare for the mission, and there wasn't going to be much planning left to the team. There wasn't even any time for the Lurps on Teddy Bear Gaskell's team to get to know the man taking Miller's place any better than they already knew him, which wasn't very well at all. That very afternoon, the team was flown out to 1/327th's forward area.

It was immediately clear that the battalion commander did not appreciate the presence of the Lurps and wasn't too happy about having to give their mission any priority when his own companies were taking a thrashing. The last thing he needed was a team of Lurps, working for the CIA or whoever, getting in the way and adding to his troubles. He showed Teddy Bear his map and told him where he definitely *did not* want him taking his team.

Unfortunately, this just happened to be one end of the valley where the team had been ordered to plant a relay of boxes.

The battalion commander said there had been sightings of tanks, artillery, trucks, and beaucoup NVA. There were even said to be reports of Caucasian advisers to the NVA, and Teddy Bear knew enough to take these reports seriously. Being a consummate diplomat when the need arose, he did not tell the battalion commander that the forbidden area was one of the places where he was supposed to plant his boxes. Nor did he tell the battalion commander that he considered his orders from the CIA types a little more binding than the wishes of a battalion commander. That would have been hard to say anyway, because he liked and respected any Airborne infantry battalion commander one hell of a lot more than he liked and respected the REMFs and civilians who'd apparently come up with this mission.

When the battalion commander was through with Teddy Bear, the Lurps got aboard a heavily laden helicopter and flew out on an evening resupply flight to join one of the infantry companies and the battalion's Tiger Force recon platoon. It was a secured LZ, and the Lurps paused to exchange greetings with the walking wounded and other men who were waiting to get out on the flight that brought them in, then they hurried off to link up with Tiger Force.

The 1st Brigade Lurps and Tiger Force went way back.

Though their jobs were different, and though the two platoons had been rival elite formations in the 1st Brigade for two years, the Lurps and Tigers were old friends. Ernie Winston, who had been a Lurp and was now with the Tigers—and who had less than a week to live—had pulled the front seat out of an NVA truck and was using it as a bed for the night. Winston had been a true Foul Dude as a Lurp, and Jaybird had been with him when he got his third and fourth Purple Hearts. Teddy Bear's team set up around Winston and passed a night of rare luxury, not having to pull guard despite the fact they were out in the field. In theory at least, there was safety in numbers, and a night with a line company, or even just a full platoon, was a welcome break for a Lurp team—welcome, at least, for the first night. On this night, the Lurps had both a line company and a recon platoon, and they slept well because whenever they woke to check, there was always someone else on guard.

The next day, the team moved out with the Tigers, spent the day patrolling with them, and then, that night, based up with them near a creek. All was quiet in the immediate area, but there was fighting not far away, and the combined recon element stayed alert, monitoring the creek bed and keeping good security all around. No one had any trouble staying awake and alert—not with the sounds of fighting so close.

Early the next morning, the team split off from the Tigers and moved out on its own. They proceeded up the valley with their boxes, moving slowly, cautiously, and quietly. At one point, the team crossed a creek and emerged into a clearing that had to be crossed in order to reach the place where they were to plant their first relay of black boxes. Halfway across, Teddy Bear noticed that the grass was tied back in places and immediately real-

ized that they were moving through a prepared ambush
site. Although he had already determined that the immediate area was temporarily free of enemy soldiers, the
tied-back grass still shook him. Once the team was safely
across the clearing and into thicker vegetation, Teddy
Bear called a brief halt and sat there silently berating
himself for not having found a way around the clearing.
They'd been lucky, but if they had moved a little more
intelligently, they wouldn't have been so dependent on
luck. They could have found a way around the clearing.
It would have thrown them off their schedule—and
because they were supposed to be linking up with
another line company after planting that first relay, they
did have a schedule of sorts to keep—but Teddy Bear
knew he'd taken a risk he should have avoided, and
being a cautious, experienced, and responsible team
leader, he should have known better.

The Lurps planted their first relay of boxes without
incident and began working back up the valley toward
their rally point with the next line company. There was a
road running down the valley, and they paralleled it for a
way. They were very alert, very aware that the enemy
was supposed to have both wheeled and tracked vehicles
in this area. Eventually, the concealing vegetation along
the road thinned out and the Lurps had to move along a
creek bed where the vegetation was thick enough to
conceal them but so tangled it slowed their movement
considerably.

Finally they reached the general area where they were
supposed to link up with the infantry company. They
halted in a security wheel while Teddy Bear made radio
contact with the company they were supposed to link up
with. There was fighting in the vicinity—fighting in
almost all directions—and Teddy Bear wanted to make

sure that the line troops were aware of the linkup. Linking up with friendly troops in the field was always dangerous, but it was particularly dangerous in a situation like this.

Fortunately, the linkup went smoothly and none of the line troopers mistook the Lurps for NVA.

After spending most of his adult post–high school life skulking around on Lurp teams, Teddy Bear felt surprisingly safe moving with a whole infantry company. It wasn't particularly safe, and intellectually Teddy Bear knew it. But there was a certain instinctive comfort in numbers, and Teddy Bear couldn't help at least *feeling* somewhat safer than usual.

Again that night, the Lurps did not have to pull guard—but that didn't stop them from maintaining a watch rotation of their own inside the company perimeter. It was a spooky night. Every so often, one or another sleeping 1/327th paratrooper would go into a nightmare and have to be woken. Life in the line companies of the 101st was tough and harrowing, and it was a normal part of the job for those on guard duty to wake those with nightmares.

The next day, the company commander told Teddy Bear that his company wasn't due to be resupplied soon but that he would do what he could if the Lurps needed anything. It was a polite offer, but Teddy Bear was pretty sure the company commander knew that the Lurps were conserving their food and water, and that if they needed anything, they would be able to get it from those who were killed or wounded and evacuated without taking anything from those who would need it later. The CO seemed to want the Lurps to cause him as little trouble as possible, and as long as they were moving with him, he wanted to think of the team as just another of his infantry squads. Teddy Bear agreed, although his team was more a fire team than a squad, and shortly after he returned to the team from the company CP, the company saddled up and moved out.

That morning, the company came across an NVA burial detail, and a short firefight ensued. The Lurps spent a leisurely hour or so while the line troopers took care of the burial party, then dug up the graves to search for weapons caches. The company commander was content to ignore the Lurps, and as long as matters didn't get desperate, the Lurps were perfectly willing to let him ignore them and keep them out of the fight. They had a somewhat grander strategic mission than just skirmishing with the gooks.

Later that day, the point element of the company happened upon an NVA squad that was setting up an antiaircraft gun. Another firefight ensued, and by then the Lurps were beginning to feel a little neglected and therefore cynical. As soon as he heard someone scream "Medic!" Teddy Bear asked his teammates if anyone needed a resupply. Two or three 1/327th paratroopers were wounded, none too seriously, and since their own buddies were well supplied, they gave the Lurps their chow.

Teddy Bear was itching to plant his remaining boxes. He was beginning to lose his patience with this line company that couldn't move a few hundred meters without having to get in a fight. He was also beginning to feel like his team was a useless appendage to the company, so he volunteered to check out some of the cliffs surrounding the valley. There had been recent aerial reports of trucks, tanks, and enemy troop movements in the immediate area, and Teddy Bear thought his team could be of use. The company commander declined his offer, however, saying that the last thing he needed was to have to be rescuing a Lurp team. Being a reasonable sort, Teddy Bear could see the captain's point.

That evening they based up on a wooded hilltop that was overlooked by another, higher, wooded hilltop. Later that night, the company took a number of direct rocket hits from that larger hill—but miraculously, there were no serious casualties. Still, it was a touchy, nervous night. Early the next morning, the Lurps crossed a stream ahead of the company, then stood security as the other paratroopers crossed. Teddy Bear couldn't help looking at each man as he passed, wondering how many of them might die before the day was over. He was not in a particularly cheery mood.

At around 0830 hours, the company halted, and the company commander called Teddy Bear over for a short conference. Now was the time for the Lurps to move out and plant their remaining black boxes, and Teddy Bear could tell that the company commander was as glad to be getting rid of the Lurps as the Lurps were to be getting away from what was, by Lurp standards, a loud and unwieldy element. The company commander must have still felt some responsibility for the Lurps, however, because he offered Teddy Bear a platoon—a whole platoon!—for security. They went over the map together, and the company commander told Teddy Bear most specifically where he did *not* want him to go. Beyond a certain point, there were supposed to be tanks and NVA in prepared positions, and the company commander ordered Teddy Bear not to go beyond this point. This point, of course, was not far enough up the valley to enable the Lurps to plant their boxes where they'd been ordered to plant them.

Teddy Bear Gaskell had been a Lurp long enough to know that orders were often issued by people looking at maps back in the rear and were sometimes better considered mere guidelines when they clashed with the situation on the ground or ran counter to the good judgment of the men in the field. When he'd joined the Lurp detachment, two years before, he had been the detachment's first real cherry. Most of the other men on the teams had previous tours with Special Forces or had been incountry with the 101st since its arrival, and they had taught him well. One of the most important things they had taught him was about "orders." Back then, the Lurps had standing orders to kill *anyone* who might compromise their missions, but those standing orders were almost universally ignored. On a mission in September 1966, the team Teddy Bear was on happened to be spotted by a child, two old ladies, and an old man. The team leader, Sergeant "Fish" Carpenter, had radioed in for extraction and was told to kill the civilians and continue the mission. Instead of doing this, the TL waited for a moment, then called in that he'd taken care of the civilians but that he still needed an extraction because the VC were on to them anyway. The first part was, of course, a lie. But the second part was true. The civilians had been VC sympathizers, and they did put the local VC onto the team. Even so, nobody regretted not killing them. Professional soldiers did not obey "standing orders" to kill noncombatants, and that's all there was to it. Knowing when and how to disobey an order was something a man had to learn in the real world, not out of some training manual. It was always a judgment call, and Teddy Bear decided not to let this company commander's orders supersede his orders from the CIA types. With equal logic, he could have decided against the CIA types and in accord with the company commander's wishes. He could have even flipped a coin to decide, except that he didn't have a coin to flip.

With the infantry platoon coming along behind them, the team moved out along the road until they came to the point they were not supposed to cross. The platoon leader did not seem to know they weren't supposed to go any farther, and that was fine with Teddy Bear.

Just before the road took a quick bend to the right, the Lurp point man, Crash Clark, found an American fragmentation grenade in the middle of the road. As far as anyone knew, there'd been no Americans this far up the road, and so the grenade had apparently either been dropped or planted there by the enemy. The Lurps and the infantry platoon moved on, leaving the grenade where it was.

The road there was terraced into a hillside, with the high ground on the right and a clear ravine to the left of the road. The road was in the open. There was another hill on the other side of the ravine, and it was thickly jungled, but the hill to the right was much more open, with only high grass, scrub brush, and a few trees. Jaybird was checking out the ravine and found a small tunnel dug under the road from the side of the ravine. Teddy Bear was beginning to wonder why they were moving down the road. Maybe it was the presence of a whole infantry platoon making him careless, and maybe it was because that was how the company commander had told them to travel. Maybe, too, it was because the road and the ravine had to be checked out. Regardless, it didn't seem too smart. But now Jaybird had found a tunnel, and Teddy Bear moved forward to check it out.

As he was looking into the tunnel, firing broke out. Teddy Bear didn't know where the fire was coming from, but he knew that they were in a good place for an ambush—good for the ambushers, at least. He turned and yelled to Crash Clark and Jaybird that they had to take the high ground. Just as he was about to start for the high ground he got hit, and the impact knocked him over onto his back.

Teddy Bear had never even imagined anything could hurt this much. The pain seemed to travel from his ass to the top of his head, and for just an instant he thought his brain was going to explode. Bullets were hitting all around him, and he was sure he was about to die. He was entirely in the open, and if the fire was coming from the jungled high ground across the ravine, there seemed no way the enemy could keep on missing. Hoping that the next shot wasn't going to hurt as much as the first one, Teddy Bear managed to check his abdomen for exit wounds. Finding none, he checked his groin and genitals. He felt something warm and wet, and hoping it was urine or feces, he pulled his hand away—only to find it covered with blood. As he rolled over, he could see his blood mixing with the dirt, and for just a couple of seconds, he almost gave up.

But then the bullets stopped hitting directly around him, and he discovered that he could still move. It hurt horribly to move—but right then, moving was what really mattered. Teddy Bear initiated the destruct sequence on the black box he was carrying and tried to pull himself back onto the road.

There was firing all around. The infantry trooper right behind Thomas took a burst of machine gun fire and was slammed into the hillside. Down the line, someone was yelling for a medic. Jaybird moved back, looking over the edge of the road for his team leader. Bullets stitched in front of him, throwing dirt in his face. He yelled for Teddy Bear and heard an answer in front of, and below, him. Teddy Bear was still in the ravine, completely exposed. Jaybird yelled that he was coming to get him, but Teddy Bear yelled back that the enemy was moving on the ridge. Jaybird looked up and saw two NVA in khaki uniforms. He stitched the closest man from the crotch to the chest, and the man's AK went flying. The second NVA tried to cut to his left, and Jaybird shot him, too, then hurried to change magazines. By now, Teddy Bear had crawled back up to the road and lay panting next to Jaybird. Jaybird reached out to touch him—not to check him out so much as to assure him. His hand came away covered with blood.

Crash Clark was already up the hill, on the high ground, firing away. From the volume of fire coming his way, it was obvious that Crash was holding back at least two full squads of enemy. Figuring Teddy Bear was out of the fight, Jaybird asked him for a bandolier of ammo. Teddy Bear gave it to him. When Jaybird started up the slope to help Clark, Teddy Bear tried to go with him. No matter what he did, the pain was almost unbearable, and moving didn't make it that much worse.

When the rest of the team joined Clark, there were bushes moving above them, muzzle flashes in the bushes, and bullets flying everywhere. Teddy Bear and then Jaybird yelled for the guy who was taking Miller's place to get the artillery on the radio, but Miller's replacement had gone catatonic and didn't respond. And then, as if things weren't already going badly enough for poor Teddy Bear, his weapon jammed. Everyone else was firing at the bushes, but the enemy wasn't quitting. A couple of grenades came flying down at the Lurps, and one of them went off behind Teddy Bear. Fortunately, these were not American grenades, and instead of being ripped apart by blast and shrapnel, Teddy Bear took only a half dozen small pieces of metal in his back, his neck, and the back of his head. He was not too happy about being hit again, but at least he hadn't been killed or paralyzed.

Crash Clark was running low on ammo, and he yelled down for more. Teddy Bear reached for Clark's rucksack, which he'd dropped nearby, and fished out a bandolier, but just as he was handing it up to him, another salvo of grenades came flying down on them—and again, one of them went off close by, knocking him headfirst down the slope to the road.

That was when Teddy Bear decided to quit the army. This war just wasn't worth all this trouble.

By now, the infantry platoon was taking up some of Crash Clark's slack upslope, so Jaybird and Thomas hurried down to their team leader. Teddy Bear didn't want them cutting his tiger pants to get to the wound, but Jaybird told him he wouldn't be needing his tigers anymore. Jaybird stuffed a dressing between the cheeks of Teddy Bear's ass and told him that with an entrance and exit wound in each cheek, he now had five assholes. Teddy Bear tried to laugh, but it hurt too much. They looked up, and there was Crash Clark, firing away with an M-16 in each hand. Somehow, he must've cleared the stoppage in Teddy Bear's weapon.

Despite the fact that he'd had already quit the army and given up on this war—and despite the fact that he had taken a round through both buttock cheeks and the shrapnel from at least two grenades in his back, neck, and the back of his head, Teddy Bear somehow managed to get to his feet and walk back down the road to try to get more of the infantrymen to come up and give Clark a hand.

With the help of his teammates and the infantry platoon, Crash Clark managed to keep the enemy from advancing on them. Firing two weapons at once, he managed to drive the enemy back long enough for the Americans to begin withdrawing. When Clark finally made his way back to Teddy Bear, Thomas and Jaybird Magill went off to help tend the other wounded.

On the way back to the rest of the company, Teddy Bear couldn't help noticing that the infantry platoon was carrying dead and wounded comrades in makeshift poncho litters, and that some of the men were in a serious state of denial about their dead comrades, talking to them as if they were still alive. Seeing this, he was determined not to let himself become a burden, and so he tried to walk all the way back to the company they'd left earlier that morning. It was a brave try, but he didn't make it all the way unassisted. Dizzy from pain and loss of blood, he fell into a shallow stream and couldn't get up. Jaybird and Thomas helped him up, then helped him the rest of the way back to the infantry company—where medevac helicopters were already on their way.

The last thing Teddy Bear remembers before being evacuated was the company commander of that line infantry company kneeling down next to him, holding a map in his face and yelling at him, asking him how in the hell he could be so goddamn irresponsible, going so far up that goddamn road.

By then, the morphine was already taking effect, and Teddy Bear didn't have the energy to explain that he was just obeying his orders, just trying to get his black boxes to the area the CIA types wanted them planted. The company commander had lost men, and he had a right to be pissed. And besides, as far as Teddy Bear was concerned, with him out of it, the war was already lost and there was no use in trying to explain it, no use in making excuses for having done his best.

The whole thing had turned out to be a real pork chop.

# Chapter Eleven

By the end of June, the missions began to come down hot and heavy, but reliable helicopter support was still a problem. The 101st Airborne Division certainly had enough helicopters, but there was still no dedicated helicopter support for the Lurps. Inserting, extracting, and supporting Lurp teams was not a job that just any rotary wing aircrew could perform well. Just as the Lurps had to practice their skills at rappelling, using ladders, and McQuire rigs, so the aircrews had to practice. Most of the time when the Lurps did get a chance to practice these skills back in the rear, the aircrews were inexperienced. The training sessions were not so much about training the Lurps as training the aircrews. Occasionally there were accidents, although, fortunately, none of them was fatal. For example, during a session of McQuire rig training in April, Staff Sergeant Burnell was slammed into a bunker with such force a normal man might have been seriously injured. Burnell was not, however, a normal man, and he recovered quickly.

Everyone hoped for parachute jumps—training jumps, maybe onto the beach—but there weren't any. The Lurps were still drawing jump pay, but jumps wouldn't really have been relevant training when almost all their missions were into thickly jungled mountains where it was difficult to find a hole in the jungle canopy big enough for rappelling ropes or McQuire rigs, and next to impossible to find a parachute landing zone. Besides, any jumps would probably be chopper blasts, and compared to slack jump rappelling and getting smashed into bunkers in McQuire rigs, chopper blasts didn't seem all that exciting.

The specialized skills an aircrew needed to insert and extract Lurp teams using these methods were not the only skills that were often lacking in the aircrews sometimes assigned to the Lurps. Basic navigation from point A to point B could also be a problem. It wasn't just that the pilots sometimes put the teams in on the wrong LZ, as had happened to Rey Martinez's team. Sometimes they missed the recon zone altogether.

On a first-light insertion in late June, Sergeant Joe Gregory's team was put in so far from its assigned recon zone they were off the map sheet. Going in, Gregory and the bellyman knew something was wrong. They were following along on their maps, and they could see that they were way south of where they should have been and that the helicopters were following the wrong river. The bellyman was frantic, arguing with the pilots, and perhaps there was some argument in the Command and Control helicopter as well, but the rest of the team did not pick up on the argument, for they were looking out the open doors, lost in their own thoughts, psyching themselves up for the job at hand and trusting the powers that be to at least put them in the right recon zone, if not the right LZ.

The ship came in rather slowly over a hilltop landing zone, and then came to a hover. Before the bellyman or Gregory could stop them, two of the men had already unassed the ship, and once this had happened, the rest of the team had no choice but to follow them in. Almost immediately, everyone knew that this was the wrong LZ, but the ship was taking off, and so they headed for the woodline to lay dog and get their commo checks. For thirty minutes they stayed there in a tight security wheel, and then the word came down that they were to continue the mission despite the fact that the helicopters had been pulled by some authority higher than the company, the team was in the wrong place, and the maps were useless.

This was a major bearfuck, and the temptation was to stay tight and just lay dog near the LZ until things got straightened out. That, however, was not the way Lurps operated. As far as they knew, they hadn't been compromised. They had been ordered to continue the mission, and so they did.

A short point recon showed that there was only one way off the hilltop—and that was a high-speed trail leading downhill to the northwest. It was never good policy to move on enemy trails, but there was no alternative. The hilltop where the team had been inserted was open, but the slopes were covered with impenetrable bamboo thickets and the only way down was the trail.

Moving very cautiously, their weapons moving with their eyes, the Lurps set out. At first, the trail was easy going as it contoured gently along the hillside. Because the trail was muddy, the tail gunner had his work cut out for him obliterating the team's tracks. Everybody felt a little uneasy about moving on the trail, even though the thick bamboo pressing in on all sides and lacing overhead to keep out the sky gave them no choice.

The farther they followed the trail, the steeper it became. Finally, they came to a place where the trail headed straight down the slope, and there the team paused, for no longer was the trail just a trail. Now it was almost a staircase, with log steps set into the hillside. There was nothing to do but follow it down. Before long, the team had descended into a narrow valley where, if anything, the vegetation was even more impenetrable than upslope, for the bamboo was choked with ferns and vines.

Through the middle of this little valley, a narrow stream cut a swath through the bamboo. The trail led into the stream, then up on the other side. The team crossed carefully, and as soon as they were across the stream, they saw footprints in the mud. The prints were full of water, and there were prints on top of prints, as if a small party of men had paused there, milling around, perhaps filling their canteens and taking a break. While the rest of the team stood security at a distance around them, Magill and Gregory examined the prints and decided that they couldn't have been made by more than three or four people, for all that there seemed to be at least two infantry squads' worth of prints. Charlie had definitely done some milling around here—wherever the hell "here" was.

The trail continued up the far slope, heading almost due north, straight up the slope. Whoever had left those footprints by the stream had come down this trail, and judging by the slip marks and smears, they'd had a hard time keeping their feet. There were no fresh footprints headed north, and there had been no visible footprints going up the trail the Lurps had just come down. The only sensible explanation was that the small party of enemy had gone off downstream—or maybe upstream— probably checking on fish traps.

The bamboo was thinner on the far side and soon gave out to trees. After making sure that all their tracks were smeared, Gregory's team continued on the trail for a way and then backstepped five meters in their own tracks before cutting into woods. On the backstepping retreat, Kenn Miller lost his footing, fell on his ass in the mud, and slid, bouncing on his ass and rucksack, grabbing for vines and saplings, and looking none too dignified, down past Sergeant Gregory and Sp4 John Renear, where he finally hit some bamboo and stopped.

The team moved out through the trees, angling along the contours of the slope, zigzagging back to keep an eye on the trail, but staying off it, skirting it, alert and slow and quiet. Because they were moving cautiously and had no particular place to go, not knowing where they were, the Lurps took breaks and lay dog often. Each time they went to ground in their security wheel, Gregory tried to raise the relay team, but even with pole antennae screwed in, neither radio could raise the relay, They could hear the relay team, and the relay team could just barely hear them, but not clearly enough for it to be considered real communications. Finally, Gregory had the senior RTO, John Renear, sling a wire antenna over a tree branch, and that worked.

There was no way the relay team could tell Gregory's team where it was. The team was off the mapsheet, for one thing, and having the coordinates wasn't going to do any good. The relay told Renear to "wait one," and the Lurps waited. Finally, the relay team came back with word that someone would be flying over in three-zero minutes, and the team was to pinpoint its location. The method of pinpointing the location was left to Gregory.

When Gregory got the word, he passed it on to the rest of the team. Gregory was a big one for keeping the team informed, and so he passed the word that he was going to move the team up a little higher in the next half hour and hoped to find a break in the canopy so that he could try to use a mirror after bringing the ship into sight by clock directions off the sound.

After a determined hump, the team found a tear in the canopy big enough for them to flash a mirror and big enough to drop McQuire rigs, if extraction was in the offing. Right on schedule, one helicopter flew over, caught the flash of Gregory's mirror, and flew on. The Lurps still didn't know where they were, but it was reassuring to know that somebody on their side did know.

Toward mid-afternoon, the team moved onto a bluff that would have overlooked the trail and the fording point if the vegetation hadn't been so thick. Although they couldn't see the trail itself, they would be able to catch glimpses of anyone moving along it, and if anyone on the trail, or down at the stream, made any noise, with any luck they'd be able to hear it. Overhead, there was a double canopy of treetops, but enough sunlight broke through to make patches on the ground. The ground itself was a carpet of fallen leaves, and of course, there were leeches, but fewer of them than farther down slope. Unfortunately, there was only one way off the bluff, and that was the way they had come.

Gregory signaled a couple of the men to put out claymores, and then he got a commo check with the relay. Moving to the high ground had done wonders for their commo. Now they could raise the relay team easily on a pole antenna, and weakly with a whip antenna. The job now was to lay dog and monitor the trail.

Suddenly, there was movement in the trees under which they'd planted their claymores, and then more movement in the branches directly overhead. When a small brown face parted the leaves to look around, the six

Lurps froze and held their fire, and the face looked away without appearing to have seen them.

It was a gibbon, and he wasn't alone. Apparently unaware of the six armed men beneath them, a small band of gibbons proceeded to move in, cavorting in the branches, chattering and squealing at each other, having a high old time. For an hour, the Lurps split their attention between the trail beneath them and the gibbons in the treetops above them. Some of the long-armed little apes were dark and some of them were light brown, almost yellow, and even though he caught only brief glimpses of them, Miller, at least, was sure he could tell the females from the males, and he couldn't help reflecting that the females were cute enough to where it might not be too bad a life, being a gibbon. Gibbons were apes, not monkeys, which meant they were at least as smart as dogs, and they seemed to be having a splendid time swinging around and playing in the trees, stopping to snack whenever they felt like it. Miller wasn't sure, but he thought he remembered reading somewhere that gibbons were the hardest of all apes to approach in the wild. Of course, maybe he remembered wrong, and it was gorillas, not gibbons. But even so, he figured gibbons had to be pretty good in the woods, and it was an honor to be out with a team good enough to get this close without spooking them.

After about an hour, the gibbons finally moved on, and when they were gone, the Lurps moved on, too. They didn't go far before halting for the night. Gregory had, of course, kept the relay informed of the team's movement, and somebody was surely plotting them on a map, so if they'd had a target, they could have at least called in fire on it—gunships or fastmovers, if in fact they were out of the artillery net. During the night, they heard someone shouting off in the distance, but to their disappointment they saw no lines of heavily burdened men with dim little oil lamps moving along the trail, or any other target.

In the morning, word came over the radio that the team was to return to its insertion LZ for extraction at 1100 hours. Eleven hundred hours wasn't the best time for an extraction, and it didn't give Gregory's team much time to get to the LZ. It is a cardinal principle of patrolling that you never go back the same way you came in, and another cardinal rule that Lurp teams never travel on enemy trails. But sometimes there isn't much choice and you've got to break a few cardinal rules. If Gregory's team was going to make it to that LZ in time for extraction, they'd have to go back the way they'd come.

There was no time for slow and careful patrolling, and all the way down to the stream, then across, and then up those steps, the Lurps were expecting a fight and dreading an ambush. They made the LZ just as the extraction ship came flaring up over the LZ. The ship swung wide, then locked into a hover, and there, looming up in the cargo bay, was an awesome black giant of a man, Sergeant First Class Willie Champion, the commo platoon sergeant.

With grass and bamboo crackling from the rotor wash behind them, the Lurps ran for the extraction ship. It sounded like the whole North Vietnamese Army was opening up on them, but at first the Lurps figured it was only the bamboo. Then a quick line of pale tracers shot through the helicopter, coming low through one door and high out the other door, passing within inches of SFC Champion's right arm and, miraculously, hitting nothing.

Both door gunners opened up, the gunner on the left side sweeping wide arcs with his machine gun, the gunner on the right confining his fire so as not to hit the

Lurps. Despite the fact that he presented a large and splendid target, Champion stayed in place, and as the Lurps reached the hovering extraction ship, he reached out with one enormous hand, quickly grabbed them, one by one, by the rucksack or web gear straps, and tossed them into the helicopter.

As soon as the whole team was aboard, the ship lifted off, cranked on the speed, and began to climb, the door gunners still pouring fire onto the LZ and the slopes of the hill. Once they got their breath, the Lurps on Gregory's team began to carry on, laughing with relief, praising Sergeant Champion, and thanking him for saving their asses.

This was not what Sergeant Champion wanted to hear. He was a quiet, modest man—quiet and modest in the way that the best really big men tend to be. The veteran of at least one previous tour with Special Forces, Champion made it clear to everyone on the team that he had done nothing, that nothing dangerous had happened, that he hadn't noticed that line of tracers because that line of tracers hadn't come through the helicopter, and he wanted no one to mention this when they got back to the rear. He made it clear that he aimed to have a nice quiet tour this time, overseeing radios, coordinating signals, and sending out relay teams. He was not there to do anything dangerous. He insisted that he was a coward, and with a ferocious scowl, he let it be known that he didn't want any of these mouthy young Lurps telling any lies about this extraction. Everyone could just stop thanking him and forget the whole damn thing. If they had any illusions that he was going to put his ass in any danger this tour—particularly for the likes of them—they could keep their damn illusions to themselves and not go breathing a word of them to anyone else.

Gregory's team got the message but didn't much obey it. When they got back to the rear and had been debriefed, they lost no time in telling the other Lurps what a bearfuck of a mission they'd been on and how splendid SFC Champion had looked, filling that door with the tracers going past him, snatching Lurps into the extraction ship like they didn't weigh more than empty rucksacks. There was a lot of bitching about the pilots who had put the team in and the fact that Lurps were being sent out without dedicated helicopters standing by in case they got in trouble—but there was nothing but praise for the crew that had picked them up. Whoever it was who put them in had definitely screwed up. But it was the Kingsmen of B Company 101st Aviation who extracted them, and if the division ever got around to giving the Lurp company the dedicated helicopter support it needed, the Lurps hoped it would be the Kingsmen—and so did the Kingsmen.

# Chapter Twelve

Not everyone—not even everyone who volunteered for it and survived some of the in-unit training—was cut out to be a Lurp. It might seem glamorous and exciting to go out into the jungles and mountains, in enemy territory, miles from friendly troops, with only four to twelve men, and to sneak around with painted faces and camouflaged uniforms. But the reality of being out there so far from everyone else except a handful of teammates, and perhaps the enemy, was often more than some men could take.

In July 1968, SSG Burnell took a team out on a first-light insertion, which actually went in at first light, into a reconnaissance zone about seven kilometers northwest of Fire Base Birmingham. Though not a one of them had gone through the Ranger School where Burnell had already established a fine personal legend as a particularly hard-core and colorfully sadistic instructor, and not a one of them had been in Vietnam any longer than he had, Burnell had some good men on his team. He had Tony Tercero, Raider Laing, Barry Golden, and Glen Martinez—all of them with at least as much time in the field here in Vietnam as Burnell had. It was the sixth man who had everybody worried. He was a good enough fellow back in the rear, and he was picking up the skills in company training. But he'd already freaked out and got a little spooky on an overnight ambush patrol right outside Camp Eagle, and nobody was too happy at having him on the team. Having been one of the "Crispy Critters" back in June 1966, when A Company 2/502 was being overrun and Captain William Carpenter was forced to call napalm down on his own company position, there was a reason the man was jumpy. But a reason is not an excuse. He was clearly not cut out to be a Lurp, and he shouldn't have been given to Burnell's team for this mission by way of a second chance. He was clearly too easily spooked for the job at hand, and he shouldn't have been given a second chance at all.

The sun was behind the helicopters when the team went in, and the pilots had flown two false insertions, then come over the real LZ at treetop level and dawdled but a few seconds while the team jumped out and ran for the woodline to lay dog. Burnell's RTO, Barry Golden, got clear commo checks with the C&C ship and the relay team on Birmingham, and after a few minutes of listening around, Burnell had Goldy release the helicopters that had been lingering off station a few klicks away. The team lay dog, letting the helicopter racket fade away and the normal sounds of the jungle return, then Burnell sent Tercero and Raider Laing off on a short 180-degree recon. They came back with nothing unusual or alarming to report, so Burny moved the team a hundred meters or so farther into the jungle, and they lay dog again. There were no signal shots, no banging of sticks, no sounds of movement, no signs of the enemy just yet. Intelligence had another of their sometimes mythical enemy base camps in the area, and there were sure to be at least *some* NVA somewhere in the RZ. But the insertion seemed to have gone in smoothly and undetected, and it was reasonable to assume that they'd come in on a cold and safe landing zone. As they lay dog, every man on the team was alert. Weapon ready, every man covered his security zone, peering into the impenetrable black, green, and brown weave of vegetation and shadow that cut visibility down to just a few meters. With ears cocked, every man listened and concentrated, sorting the sounds, sniffing the fetid air . . . Nobody on the team much doubted that the enemy was out there somewhere in the recon zone, but only one man on the team saw or heard them the second time the team lay dog—and he promptly panicked and opened up, spraying the innocent vegetation on full auto. It was, of course, the man who'd freaked out before.

By the time the rest of them got him calmed down, transported back to the insertion LZ, and extracted, the jumpy would-be Lurp was on the first step of his journey to a more fitting line of work somewhere else in the division, and the remaining Lurps on Burnell's team set off to continue their mission, their good insertion now all blown to hell and probably compromised.

Trying to more or less keep to the patrol route on the map overlays they'd filed back at the TOC and presented in the premission briefback, the team moved into the jungled valley northwest of the LZ. Tony Tercero was on point, with Raider Laing walking his slack. Out there, the enemy would be moving on trails, and the Lurps were looking for trails they could parallel in the bush. Tercero was sure he'd come across at least one trail in this valley, but he didn't. There were game paths, but no trails, and the game paths showed no sign of human passage.

By late afternoon, Burnell's team was contouring along the side of a ridge, paralleling a hardpacked trail about a meter wide. Just before dusk, the team heard voices. They soon caught a glimpse of people moving on the trail ten meters away, but couldn't get a good count of them. Goldy called in a report of the sighting, but there wasn't much concrete information he could give. Burnell moved the team a little closer to the trail when it came time to finally set up for the night, and that night they counted two separate platoon-size elements walking past, weapons slung, oil lamps glowing, showing no sign that they had any idea there was an American Lurp team in the area. Maybe the team's insertion hadn't been noticed after all. And maybe these NVA moving through on the trail just hadn't been clued in. At any rate, they didn't appear overly apprehensive, and that was a good sign.

At first light, the Lurps were already on the move in the direction from which the NVA had come, heading toward the next valley, still paralleling that trail. Tony Tercero was walking point with one of the "silenced" Sten guns he'd brought to the company from FOB 1, and when he first heard voices, he was reluctant to even alert Raider. The last thing Tony wanted was to be wrong and have people thinking he was spooking out, like the guy they'd had to have extracted the morning before.

But no, this wasn't some sort of nervous hallucination. There really were voices up ahead, and soon everyone could hear them. Tony led the team to a small bluff overlooking the stream that flowed through this valley, and parting the ferns and vines and broadleaf plants that grew in this spot of sunlight, the Lurps peered out. This valley was grassier, more open, than the valley they'd been in the day before, and the Lurps saw four or five hatless NVA soldiers standing security with their backs to the stream, while at least two women chatted in singsong Vietnamese and washed clothes at the edge of the stream. There was more than enough brush near the stream to effectively hide the women, but they appeared to be washing clothes instead of bathing—which disappointed a couple of the Lurps somewhat, since they hadn't seen any naked women for a while and had never knowingly seen any naked enemy women.

It is not easy to explain, but impossible to deny, that sometimes a sixth or seventh sense alerts people when they are being watched. While Goldy was hunkered down whispering into the headset of his radio, sending in his report so quietly that even the men next to him couldn't hear him, one of the NVA soldiers raised his rifle and began to sweep the ridge with his eyes. When he paused, squinting up at the position the Lurps had taken, Tony knew they'd been spotted, so he opened up on the soldier and then hosed down his companions with the "silenced" Sten gun—which wasn't exactly all that silent, or all that accurate, either.

Suddenly there were many more NVA in that valley than the Lurps had seen before—and all of them seemed to be firing up at the ridge. The team booked out, and with an unknown but substantial force of NVA shouting and firing after them, the Lurps headed upslope, Goldy on the radio, calling in the contact.

There was no need now to cautiously pick and fold their way through the jungle, so the team broke bush. The enemy was making lots of noise, shouting and calling back and forth, reconning by fire, crashing about in the undergrowth, and silent movement was no longer of premium importance to the Lurps. What counted now was speed, and putting distance between themselves and the enemy—that, and finding an LZ from which they could be extracted. Before long, the C&C helicopter was overhead, and after getting a fix on the team, radioed down a compass azimuth to a bomb crater on the crest of the ridge a few hundred meters to the south. If it hadn't been compromised on the insertion, or the extraction of the man who'd freaked out, the original landing zone was certainly compromised now, and this bomb crater seemed to be the only possible way out.

Too hard-pressed to keep adjusting their route of march to zigzag off and back onto the compass azimuth the chopper had given them, the Lurps broke bush straight ahead. It was thick there, thick and thorny, and where the overhead canopy broke enough to let in adequate sunlight there were stands of resilient young bamboo. On point, Tercero threw himself on the vegetation, trying to bull a path for the team, but since he weighed slightly less than 150 pounds, more often than not the vegetation just bounced him back. It was tense, frustrating, exhausting work, and finally SSG Burnell, the biggest and burliest man on the team, had to take over point, for the enemy seemed to be getting closer.

At last the Lurps made it to the bomb crater, and as they did, the extraction ship came to a hover overhead and the bellyman kicked out the ladder. Worn out from his uphill battle against the thickets, Tercero held the bottom rung, steadying the ladder as his teammates climbed up and aboard the ship. It is one thing to climb a swaying ladder into a helicopter when fresh and unburdened, but Tercero was exhausted, his energy reserves depleted, his Sten gun, CAR-15, load-bearing equipment, and rucksack adding an additional eighty or ninety pounds to his weight. When it was his time to climb aboard, he got a good start, but then his boot slipped on a rung and, kicking wildly, he just barely managed to get it back on the rung. Pulling himself with his arms and pushing with his legs, he dragged himself halfway up the ladder before realizing that he was taking too long, slowing down the extraction, so he clipped himself to the ladder with his snap link and signaled the bellyman that he was secure. It was just in time, for as the ship lifted and picked up forward speed, the bottom of the ladder barely clearing the treetops, NVA soldiers came boiling out of the woodline with their weapons blazing.

Clinging to the ladder, Tony was content to let the door gunners and the gunships flying behind in escort deal with the dudes boiling up around the bomb crater. There weren't any rounds coming his way that he was aware of, and from his point of view, the gooks were just being sore losers at this point. Even with the wind in his ears and the roar and clatter of the rotors overhead, he could hear the gunships firing rockets, and secondary explosions going off down in the valley. Unless he fell off the ladder or got flown into a tree, he was on his way safely home. Now his only real worry was that his teammates had noticed how thoroughly those vines and thickets and those brakes of young bamboo had kicked his young 149-pound ass.

He needn't have worried about that. Everyone knew that Tony Tercero was cut out to be a Lurp. And besides, that bamboo had even kicked SSG Burnell's ass.

# Chapter Thirteen

Staff Sergeant Phil Byron's Team Ten was not Rey Martinez's old Team Ten. It just had the same numerical designation, and by midsummer 1968, the numerical designations—and all too often, even the personnel of the teams—were subject to change from mission to mission. On one memorable earlier mission, Byron's team had found an abandoned NVA classroom amphitheater, counted dozens of NVA soldiers passing within a meter of their position at night, charted fighting positions, crept down a river between well-traveled enemy trails as if under some sort of cloak of invisibility, discovered enemy river landings, and brought back a surprisingly complete picture of an area formerly known as "Mystery Mountain" without ever alerting the enemy to their presence.

On that mission, Byron had had at least two first-mission cherries on his team. Byron's team was now somewhat more experienced.

His ATL, Sergeant John Burford, was an experienced paratrooper who'd come back into the army for Vietnam, and Byron himself was an even more experienced paratrooper who had served with a battalion recon platoon of the 1st Cav on his first tour in Vietnam. The point man, Don "The Snake" Harris, was a soft-spoken young Lurp who'd grown up in the mountains and woods of Tennessee and felt right at home in the mountains and woods of Vietnam. PFC John Looney, a quiet, studious-looking Lurp who already had a reputation for being unflappably competent on the radio, was carrying the main radio. He was a new guy, but he wasn't exactly a cherry. Looney had been out with other teams before Byron's, and had been with Byron on the mission to Mystery Mountain. Sp4 Larry Saenz wasn't exactly a cherry either, at least not a cherry in Vietnam. He had been in-country a year already, stuck in the rear with the 501st Signal, and he'd extended for Lurps instead of going back to the States. In theory, he was supposed to have been assigned to the Lurp commo platoon, and only occasionally to fill in on short teams, but Saenz wanted more action on this tour than he'd had in the last one. He had been on one previous mission with Byron and at least three or four missions with other teams. PFC Larry Chambers, however, was definitely a cherry—a promising cherry, but a cherry even so. This was to be his first mission with Sergeant Byron, and his first long-range patrol mission.

The mission was to perform an area reconnaissance in another one of the many areas where intelligence suspected there might be an enemy regimental base camp. By this time, some of the Lurps were beginning to get the idea that intelligence had no idea whatever where the enemy was hiding his regimental base camps, for there seemed to be one suspected in almost every recon zone. If there had been a real live enemy regiment everywhere intelligence suspected there might be a base camp, there would have been about six million NVA in I Corps alone, and no need for the Lurps to go out looking for them.

As was standard procedure, the team studied the map, planned the mission, prepared map overlays, and presented a briefback in the TOC to the company commander, executive officer, Operations NCO, helicopter pilots, and any others who would be directly involved in the mission. With that taken care of, the men got their equipment ready, taping down everything that would rattle, checking again and again to make sure they had everything and had it in the right place, and then they were free to get some sleep.

As usual, nobody slept much, if at all, and by oh-dark-thirty hours they were dressed out in their cammies and ass-kicking gear, their faces and hands painted and the butterflies already beginning to churn in their stomachs. They picked up their rucksacks and weapons and headed down to the chopper pad as a team.

This turned out to be a real first-light insertion, the ship coming around from the east of the LZ with the rising sun behind it and the six Lurps in the door and on the skids, ready to jump down into the elephant grass. Within seconds, the ship was gone and the Lurps were running for the woodline. This was the critical moment, the moment that had kept them from sleeping the night before. They were committed, they were exposed, they'd come in on a big, noisy machine, and now they were vulnerable to being cut down if there was anyone waiting in the woodline.

This time, there wasn't anyone waiting in ambush just off the LZ, but as the team lay dog twenty meters into the woods, they heard a signal shot. It was just one shot off to the north, with no answering shots. It almost certainly wasn't an accidental discharge or someone doing a little hunting. Coming this soon after an insertion, it had to be a signal shot. It didn't necessarily mean that the team's presence in the area had been compromised, but it almost certainly meant that someone had seen the helicopter coming in—and from that, any halfway intelligent NVA was likely to assume that there might be a recon team in the area. A few minutes after that first shot there were four more, and the Lurps began to wonder if maybe something else was going on. Maybe the enemy actually was hunting.

A few kilometers to the east of where the team lay dog stretched a gently rolling area of elephant grass with low, scattered trees. It looked like an African savannah, but without the wildlife. To the west, the jungle grew thicker and the foothills that led into the mountains began. If there was an enemy base camp in this recon zone, it would be somewhere to the west. To the north and the south were the same sorts of terrain and vegetation as where the team lay dog—and they were already in the woods, though not deep in them.

When the team moved out, Byron had Harris take the team east, down a finger of the hill they'd come in on. They'd look for trails first, and if they found the trails, then they might have a chance of finding that base camp—if there was a base camp in this area. Just because intelligence suspected that there might be one was no guarantee that there wasn't one. If there was a base camp there, it would have trails leading to it. The plan was to move east, then, just short of the grasslands, to work around to the north, looking for trails, and maybe check out the area the shots seemed to have come from.

The team lurped along slowly and carefully, pausing often to listen all around. By late morning, they were headed north, when they came upon a high-speed trail covered with footprints. While the rest of the team lay dog, Burford, Harris, and Looney went off on a point recon. Paralleling the trail, they moved through a narrow valley where a stream crowded the trail, so they had to move along the side of a steep slope, and then they had no choice but to move on the trail—which, fortunately, was hardpacked, so they did not leave bootprints. Finally, the trail descended toward the stream, and here the Lurps found a large eddy pool. Near the pool, they found footprints with water still oozing into them. They also found cigarette butts and candy wrappers. Burford tested one of the candy wrappers with his tongue, and he could still taste the sugar. That meant the wrapper was fresh. Although there was no brass lying around, this appeared to be the place where the shooters they'd heard on insertion had been.

Moving on, the Lurps discovered that the trail led along the stream in the water. At one point, the stream was blocked by a fallen tree, and it was easy to see where the enemy had stepped out of the water to go around it. Here and there, mud was still dripping from the enemy's passage. Burford decided it was time to get back to the rest of the team.

They spent the rest of the day finding trails, paralleling them, monitoring, and calling them in. Calling them in was not easy, for the team had shaky commo. At one point, Burford had to climb a tree with an antenna. Unfortunately, the tree was covered with biting ants. Burford came down the tree much more quickly than he'd gone up it.

That night, the team set up in thick vegetation where they'd be able to hear anyone trying to approach. In the middle of the night, the Lurps heard movement, and then they saw lights bobbing about in the jungle. Everyone was tense. Staff Sergeant Byron might not have seemed tense to his teammates, and as usual, Looney did not seem particularly excited. But the other Lurps could feel each other's tension—and they prayed that the enemy would not come close enough to feel it, too.

Eventually, the enemy moved on, and in the morning, so did the Lurps. But before the team moved out, Burford and Harris pulled a quick 360-degree recon around their position to make sure the enemy had not set an ambush for them. They spent that day exploring and monitoring the trail from which the enemy had come the night before. They spent the second night far from the trails, and the only excitement came when a mongoose or weasel or small cat of some sort chased a bird through their position.

The third day was spent mapping and monitoring the trail. Although the team's mission was to find an enemy base camp, the boundaries of their assigned recon zone would not allow them to follow the main trail they'd found far enough to find any base camp that might be back there.

That night, they set up close enough to monitor the trail for foot traffic. Dusk was just about to turn into full dark night when ten to fifteen enemy soldiers came down the trail, headed east, toward the grassland and the villages beyond it. Everyone froze. At one point, an enemy soldier looked directly at Larry Chambers and John Looney, but their camouflage paint darkened their faces and hands, and in the failing light he didn't see them. When the enemy soldiers were past, Byron called in the sighting and coordinated some new artillery preplots in case they were needed in the morning. Looney leaned over and whispered something to Chambers about how he had lost his cherry. In a conventional infantry unit, it took a good firefight for a new man to lose his cherry, but in the Lurps, sometimes a man's first real test was in staying cool and avoiding a firefight. Chambers did not bother to whisper back that he'd been too scared to move.

In the morning, Byron had the team conceal itself a little better, then wait to see if the enemy came back along the trail. Sure enough, at about 0500, just as the first faint wash of daylight was filtering down through the canopy, the Lurps heard voices. Soon they could see enemy soldiers moving along the trail. There were eleven in the first group, and behind them came a group of seven. The enemy soldiers were laughing and jabbering, smoking and joking. Their equipment was rattling, they were carrying their weapons slung, and their general state of alertness and noise discipline was abysmal.

Shortly after 0700 hours, Byron called for an artillery fire mission on some of the preplotted concentrations he'd called in the night before. If the timing was right, the enemy was going to be right on the preplots when the rounds started falling.

The Lurps could not know what effect the artillery was having. They were now under orders to stay in position and continue monitoring the trail. All day, they stayed in position, hardly moving, while the heat and the leeches and the strain of inactivity preyed on them. Right on schedule, the enemy was back at dusk, headed east. This time there were eighteen of them, and none of them seemed to have any idea that they were under surveillance of an American Lurp team.

Word came over the radio that the team was to be extracted at 1600 hours, and two fresh teams inserted to pull an ambush. No one on Byron's team was too happy about this, figuring that they had done all the real work and deserved to have a little fun. But at the same time, they knew that they were tired, and they knew that there were too few of them to ambush so large an element without rigging an elaborate daisy chain of claymores along the kill zone, which was not a good idea, as close as they were to the trail. An adequate daisy chain also wasn't logistically possible, due to the limited footage of det cord they had brought along for what was supposed to be a reconnaissance mission.

Maybe it made sense to replace the team with a heavy

team, but Byron and Burford were worried that the heavy team would be coming in too late. For all the effort the Kingsmen and other special operations pilots put into making them as covert as possible, helicopter insertions were inherently noisy, and if the heavy team waited until 1600 hours to insert, the enemy was likely to be already moving east and close enough to hear them come in. A first-light insertion would be no better. A high noon insertion struck both SSG Byron and Sergeant Burford as ideal, and it would give the ambush team time to move into position. But that just wasn't in the offing.

Byron's team made it to the grasslands early enough to pull a thorough reconnaissance of the heavy team's insertion LZ and their extraction LZ. Right on schedule, the heavy team came in, and Byron's team—minus point man Don Harris, who was staying behind to guide the ambush element into position—loaded on the second helicopter and headed back to Camp Eagle.

Byron's team was just finishing up its debriefing when word came that the heavy team was in contact. The company commander and aircrews and bellymen raced down to the chopper pad. Byron's men were still in their tiger fatigues, the camouflage paint still on their faces and hands, when the choppers came back with the two teams that made up the heavy team—one under Sergeant Jeff Ignacio and one under Sergeant Joe Gregory.

One of the Lurps on SSG Byron's team was embarrassed when Sergeant Ignacio held up a yellow rubber constriction band and, after a glance at the buttonhole of his tiger fatigue jacket, where he usually wore his band in imitation of the medics, asked him if it was his. The Lurp from Byron's team glanced at his fatigue jacket and immediately made a silent oath that in the future he would carry his constriction bands stuffed into his serum albumin blood volume expander can, and not in his buttonhole. It was his constriction band, and he hadn't noticed when he lost it. Ignacio said he had taken it off one of the bodies in the kill zone of the rather too hasty ambush they'd pulled, and the Lurp from Byron's team took it back rather abashedly. The way he saw it, the constriction band had worked free and fallen away without his noticing and then been picked up by the enemy later. The enemy must have been tracking them at some point on their way to the LZ. How else would the constriction band end up in the kill zone of the heavy team's ambush? Lurps tried to never leave any sign of their passage behind them, and losing something as apparently innocuous as a constriction band could be a deadly mistake if the enemy found it and, putting two and two together, came up with the conclusion that it most certainly wasn't innocuous.

Later that night, one of the pilots came around asking if anyone had lost a strobe light along that trail. When the Lurps who had been on the ground determined that they'd brought back all their strobe lights, the pilot shrugged and said his initial judgment must've been right. He'd just come back from taking the company commander out on an overflight of the area, and the light they'd seen down there must've been flashlights or oil lanterns moving along the trail, their glow seeming to flash due to the treetops.

The next day, the Lurps were back in the area, and discovered that the enemy hadn't found all the bodies, but had policed up all of the brass. It was a fairly satisfying mission for Byron's team, though not as satisfying as the mission to Mystery Mountain. The heavy team under Sergeant Gregory and Sergeant Ignacio had the satisfaction of pulling a fruitful ambush, but couldn't help wishing they'd had a chance to set up beforehand and rack up a more respectable body count. It wasn't a perfect mission, but at least this time the Lurps had the satisfaction of knowing that some action had been taken as a result of their efforts. Of course, it was the Lurps themselves who had to exploit a situation the Lurps had discovered, but that made sense to everyone who gave it a moment's thought.

It was a lesson that F Company, 58th Infantry (LRP) would have good cause to remember under more unhappy circumstances in the future: If you want something done right, sometimes you've just got to do it yourself.

# Chapter Fourteen

From June 10 onward, hardly a day passed without at least two Lurp teams out on missions, and some of the missions were very productive. There were plenty of enemy troops out along the Laotian border, north and south of the Ashau, and in the dread valley itself. As might be expected, there were plenty of enemy to be found, and very few of the recon zones proved to be "dry holes." There were also plenty of NVA in the vicinity of Nui Khe and the place the Lurps called "Leech Island." It didn't really seem to matter where a team was sent—the Lurps were finding enemy soldiers, or signs of recent enemy passage, almost everywhere, and only rarely was the enemy finding the Lurps. Although not every mission turned into a contact mission, almost every mission brought back valuable information. And when there was contact, the Lurps were always on the winning side of it.

Fortunately, none of these contacts turned into pitched battles. There wasn't much sense in a six-man recon team—or even a twelve-man "heavy team"—initiating a fight with a much larger enemy element, and almost all of the contacts were at the initiation of the Lurps, not the NVA.

Sometimes, however, the enemy could surprise the Lurps in ways they had not anticipated. Toward the end of June, SFC Brubaker took a team out along the Vietnamese-Laotian border and Sp4 Whitmore and PFC Linderer had the experience of putting at least ten rounds, at close range, into an enemy soldier who wouldn't go down. This soldier was tall, big-boned, amazingly resilient, and dressed somewhat differently from the other NVA the team had seen in the area. When the team returned to Camp Eagle from the mission, and described him during the debriefing, a major from intelligence spoke up and said that he was probably one of the Chinese advisers reported to be in the area. Vietnamese or Chinese, he was a very tough dude, and some of the men who had seen Sp4 Whitmore and PFC Linderer fire him up took to calling him "Super Gook" and hoping the man would end up surviving his wounds and somehow be evacuated back wherever the hell he'd come from. After taking all the rounds he'd taken without going down, it would be a shame for him to die—and tough as he was, it would be an even bigger shame for him to recover and stick around to get even.

The pace of operations continued well into the summer. For once the company had adequate helicopters for operations and training. It wasn't always the Kingsmen, or the Black Widows, or the better crews from the 17th Cav—which meant they weren't always crews the Lurps could trust if a team had to rappel in, or be extracted under fire from a hasty, unsecured LZ by McQuire rigs or a dangling, swaying ladder. There were no insertions by rappelling in July, no parachute insertions—just as there would be no parachute insertions for the 101st Lurps during the course of the war—and there were only two teams that came out by McQuires in the whole month of July.

It was in July that F Company, 58th Infantry (Long

Range Patrol) first appeared as a comer on the 101st Airborne Division's company-by-company body count tallies. Although each of the line infantry battalions had at least one company with a higher body count, each of those companies had also suffered casualties. The last real combat casualty F/58 LRP had suffered since moving up to I Corps was Teddy Bear Gaskell, and Teddy Bear just got shot in the ass, not killed or horribly mangled and disabled. The Lurps were either very lucky or very good.

Of course, F/58 was still something of a bastard unit. As a general thing, they worked for G-2, but they didn't belong to G-2. On paper, they were still administratively linked to the 326th Engineers, but the Lurps weren't allowed near the engineers, and the engineers stayed away from the Lurps. The 101st's 2nd Squadron, 17th Cavalry—a weird mix of rotary wing aviation and infantry—was lobbying for command of the Lurps but didn't exactly have it yet. Having no officers of its own higher than a captain, the company was not getting much in the way of official credit for most of its accomplishments, but word was getting out that it deserved some.

By then, of course, the Lurps did not have an entirely savory reputation back in the Camp Eagle rear, nor down at the *rear* rear area at Bien Hoa. There was nothing unusual about this, for Lurps and such people almost always manage to maintain a somewhat unruly and unsavory reputation among rear echelon types, and their dash and independent air of go-to-hell eliteness does tend to lead the envious to huffing about "freebooters" or waxing spiteful and jealous about overprivileged profile artists and phony tin heroes. Word was that Captain Fitts had to deal with some of this talk up at the officers club one night, and the way the Lurps heard the story, they heartily approved of Captain Fitts's response. Word was that he'd decked either a major or a lieutenant colonel who was badmouthing Green Berets and then got around to badmouthing the Lurps.

Adding all of this up with the actual high jinks of the Lurps back at Camp Eagle between missions, and the things they were suspected of doing—both in the field and back at Camp Eagle—but didn't really do, the long-range patrol company quite naturally became the object of some attention.

On one occasion, a whole galaxy of Vietnamese and American brass descended on the company on short notice, expecting a show. Enough men were found with proper haircuts and proper uniforms to supply one. There were no parachute jumps, and no demonstrations of the Fulton Skyhook. There were, however, demonstrations of rappelling, which was still a new concept at that time to every unit in the division except the Lurps and Pathfinders. There were mock extractions by McQuire rig and ladder, and a ladder insertion, too. One of the teams ran through some immediate action drills down on the chopper pad, without actually firing, and another team appeared and stood at an almost respectful position of attention in front of the assembled brass in tiger fatigues and full field gear, with full paint on their faces and the backs of their hands. There was a field expedient static display laid out on a brand-new poncho liner the supply sergeant broke out especially for the occasion, and Captain Fitts was probably relieved that his hoodlums kept the modified, unauthorized, classified, stolen, silenced, and otherwise illegal weapons safely out of sight.

In July, the company sent out three augmented heavy

teams of eighteen men each, putting almost every operational Lurp in the company in the field at the same time.
The general consensus was that eighteen men was too
many men for the missions at hand, and no one was
too disappointed that the missions had been into "dry
holes." The company planted black boxes on dedicated
black box missions that rarely lasted all day, and also
planted black boxes as a secondary mission on recon
patrols that lasted as long as eight days. At one point,
rumor leaking out of the TOC was that the company was
about to be given a couple of missions across the Laotian
border—but these were cancelled by Control, or "Higher," or somebody, before the mission planning could
really begin.

Also in July, the company worked with the 1st ARVN
Division's famous Black Panther Reconnaissance Company—which was famous primarily for having staged a
gallant assault on the final Communist strongholds during
the retaking of the Citadel of Hue. Without much warning
to the Lurps, a platoon of Black Panther recon troops was
moved into the company area, and two Vietnamese soldiers were assigned to each team. The Black Panther platoon came complete with a salty old Aussie adviser who
had seen it all during the course of about a half dozen
wars, large and small. The Lurps took to the adviser, who
had previous experience with the Aussie SAS, a lot more
readily than they took to the Black Panthers.

There was the language problem. A few of the Lurps—
very few of them—could get by after a fashion in Vietnamese, and about half the Black Panther ARVNs knew
at least a few useful phrases of GI English, but that
wasn't enough, and the Aussie couldn't do all the inter-
preting for everyone. Then there were the cultural problems. The Black Panthers didn't quite strike the Lurps as

manly enough to be recon troopers—mainly because the
Black Panthers were polite after a Vietnamese fashion
and didn't see anything faggoty in holding hands with
each other to show brotherhood, and also because they
were physically small and delicate-looking. Even the
American Lurps who were small did not look delicate,
and this was a big point against the Black Panthers.

The fact that the Black Panthers did not seem any
more enthusiastic about going out, just two of them, with
six Americans they didn't know and couldn't really communicate with, any more than the Americans fancied
taking a couple of excess ARVNs out on their teams, did
not bode well for this particular experiment, and the few
mixed teams that went out did not particularly distin-
guish themselves. Still, the experiment was not entirely a
waste. Individual American Lurps and individual Vietnamese Black Panther recon troopers did take the first
steps in getting to know each other, and in the future
when the two units worked from the same location, they
ran separate teams and got along rather well, considering
the language gap, the culture gap, and all the other gaps
between them.

It was toward the end of July that word came down
that Captain Fitts would be leaving the company, headed
back to Special Forces. The executive officer, Lieutenant
Gay, took temporary command of F/58 on the departure
of Captain Fitts. Lieutenant Gay was a well-liked and
well-respected officer, the only officer in the company
who had taken a team out under his own command. If he
had remained in command of the Lurp company, none of
the Lurps would have complained too much about it,
though most of them probably would have preferred an
NCO—say, SFC Willie Champion—as commander.

Of course, the United States Army and the 101st

Airborne Division weren't about to put an NCO in command of an elite long-range patrol company. Even a first lieutenant wasn't enough. A captain had to be found, and almost before the dust from Captain Fitts's jeep had even settled down on the company sign, a captain had been found.

It was Captain Shepherd, who as Lieutenant Shepherd had been hanging around the company down at Bien Hoa months before, alienating everyone. Word was that Captain Fitts had run him off back then, but in Captain Fitts's absence, he was back—this time as a captain and company commander.

The word among the troops was that before being commissioned an officer and a gentleman, Captain Shepherd had served as an enlisted man in the 82nd Airborne and as a junior NCO in SF. You certainly wouldn't know it by the way he assumed command of the Lurp company. He announced that there would be three mandatory formations every day. His first company formation was widely interpreted as a declaration of war. Captain Shepherd soon made it clear that he was going to straighten out this company. He wasted no time letting the Lurps know that he considered them undisciplined, slovenly, unmanly, shirkers, and phonies. This was actually fairly mild compared to what the Lurps considered him.

There would be no more use of vehicles for any purpose without the company commander's specific authorization. All men on work details, including filling sandbags and burning shit, were to be fully dressed in proper uniforms at all times. Captain Shepherd was a real stickler when it came to proper uniforms. No one was to take off his shirt or remove his headgear. The proper headgear in the company area was to be black baseball caps with the Recondo arrowhead, and nothing else.

There were to be no Lurp hats worn except in the field. Headbands and drive-on rags were unauthorized under all conditions. There were to be no berets of any sort worn under any conditions—not even the camouflage beret that Brooks wore to the field or the black Ranger instructor's beret SSG Burnell occasionally wore back in the rear. Everyone entering the orderly room or Tactical Operations Center for any reason was to be dressed in complete uniform, with all the authorized badges and tags and patches, but no unauthorized items, such as the red-and-black "1/Long Range Recon/101" 1st Brigade Lurp tab, or even the black-and-gold "101/Long Range Patrol/Div" Lurp scroll that had preceded the current locally authorized F/58 Lurp scroll. Captain Shepherd forbade the nonoperational wear of tiger stripes—and even the new "flower power" leaf-pattern camouflage suits—and within a day of his arrival, he was already rumored to be considering the confiscation of all non-TOE weapons and radios, all indigenous patrol rations, indigenous ponchos, individual fighting knives, tiger fatigues, Ho Chi Minh sandals, black pajamas, enemy web gear, belt buckles, and carrying pouches.

On his first or second evening as company commander, Captain Shepherd had apparently been going over some mission files, for he made a nasty comment about Terrible Team Ten's being extracted on the word of a mere E-5 to the Operations NCO, who was no friend of Rey Martinez but tried to defend him by explaining that the team really had been seriously compromised and the mission had been a good one anyway. Captain Shepherd made it clear that he wouldn't tolerate dissension from a mere SFC. He called in Sergeant Joe Gregory, and when Gregory reported to him, Captain Shepherd immediately lit into him, berating him for getting his team lost, bragging that he'd had buck sergeants hauled in front of court-martials for less.

The only time Sergeant Gregory could remember his team ever really being lost was the time they were put in out of his recon zone and off the mapsheet, but Joe Gregory was a well-disciplined soldier, and having run into some real dickhead officers in both the army and the Marine Corps, he took Captain Shepherd's ass-chewing in stride, and had enough military courtesy not to argue back.

The next day, Captain Shepherd interrupted the post-mission debriefing of SSG Bob McKinnon's team to argue that McKinnon's extraction LZ was fifty meters from where McKinnon had reported it, and there were repressed smiles all around when the major in charge of the debriefing told Captain Shepherd to shut up.

Just about everyone in F/58 LRP suffered some sort of threat or insult from the new company commander. At least two of the senior NCOs were threatened with court-martials just for doing their jobs the best way they saw fit, and it didn't take a mind reader to tell that even the first sergeant, Operations NCO, platoon sergeants, and company lieutenants were not all that happy with Captain Shepherd's leadership of the long-range patrol company.

Before he had been in the company three days, Captain Shepherd had already managed to alienate, insult, offend, or terrify almost every man in the company. Article 15 company punishments and busts of one or two pay grades for negligible offenses and imagined ones were coming down so fast the company payroll must've dropped 10 percent.

The new company commander might have been a fine soldier in his day, but once some of his operational and Command and Control ideas leaked out, it became clear to almost everyone that he was now an unbalanced martinet just waiting to manifest himself in some disastrous fashion.

The only bright spot in Captain Shepherd's brief reign over the Lurp company was the day a lieutenant colonel came to the newly instituted noon formation and announced that a line company had recently captured documents announcing a large cash award for the capture of an American Lurp. The assembled Lurps stood proud in the enemy's esteem, and some wit in the back of the formation wondered aloud how much they'd give for Captain Shepherd.

The next day, Captain Shepherd announced at formation that animals other than scout dogs and tracker dogs assigned to the proper units were unauthorized in the United States Army. The mascot Dixie Dog would have to go. This did not sit well with the Lurps. And since most of them considered Dixie more a part of the company than they did Captain Shepherd, everyone, even the first sergeant, joined in the conspiracy to hide Dixie until Captain Shepherd got another, different hair up his ass and forgot about cleansing the Lurp company of animals. Hell, if you got rid of all the animals, you wouldn't just be getting rid of Dixie—you'd be getting rid of all the Lurps!

No one knows who did it—or at least no one who knows will ever tell—but Captain Shepherd was quite effectively removed from the command of the long-range patrol company after only a week or so of command.

As company commander, Captain Shepherd had to stay aloof from even the other officers and senior NCOs, so he had a small, well-sandbagged tent of his own near the TOC. At 0330 hours in the morning of July 30, 1968, Captain Shepherd stopped in the TOC to check on the two teams in the field. The man on radio watch said that they'd been sending in negative sit-reps, calling in on schedule, and Shepherd nodded, then said he'd be heading back to his quarters and expected to be informed of any changes in the situation reports. Twenty seconds after Captain Shepherd left the TOC, there was an explosion about as loud as the impact of a small mortar, followed by a scream of pain. Captain Shepherd had stepped on a "toe-popper" mine that someone had planted at the entrance to his tent. The mine had severely mangled his right foot. Doc Proctor gave him first aid and a shot of morphine, and then oversaw his removal to the division dispensary. The next day, a squad of Criminal Investigation Division (CID) snoops descended on the company. Every man was questioned, and every man was asked pretty much the same basic questions. "Did you do it?" Everyone said "No." "Do you know who did it?" Everyone smirked at the thought that Lurps would snitch on Lurps and answered "No." "Do you know anyone capable of doing such a thing?" To this, the answer was a proud and resounding "Yes!" When asked if he himself was capable of such a thing, the general answer given the CID was something along the lines of, "Sure, but I don't have the patience to stand in line."

The next morning, there was a formation. With a hint of a smile on his face, First Sergeant Walker announced that the CID's comments about the company were very interesting. According to the CID, 40 percent of the men in the company were psychotic. Forty percent suffered from delusions of grandeur. The remainder were merely criminally insane.

There was another formation that evening. A tall, strac (army for "neurotically neat"), black major introduced himself as the new, temporary, company commander. He said that he and several other officers had drawn straws for the job and he had lost. He did not seem like a bad guy, but he was obviously not tremendously happy to be given temporary command of the company, and did not spend a great deal of time in the company area.

Three days later, a new company commander arrived, and the major lost no time in getting away. The new CO was Captain Ken Eklund, and at his first formation he told the company that he was well aware of what had happened to Captain Shepherd, then he smiled and said that he hoped the company had got that sort of thing out of its system. Captain Eklund made it clear that he had volunteered for the company when all the other available officers were lying low and hoping it would be disbanded. He said that the division staff was all for disbanding the unit, but the new commanding general, Major General Melvin Zais, was willing to give it another chance. Captain Eklund said that he was grateful that General Zais was giving the company another chance and giving him the chance to command it. He said that he had come over as a platoon leader with the 1st Brigade in 1965 and was very proud of the fact that during an entire year of heavy combat, his platoon had not lost one man killed in action. He said that he hoped to repeat that accomplishment with the Lurps. This cheered the Lurps considerably, but Captain Eklund's next announcement put the damper on the good cheer. For the time being, the company was on administrative stand-down and would be pulling no missions. Before turning the formation over to First Sergeant Walker for dismissal, Captain Eklund assured the men that he would do everything in his power to see that the company got the missions, support, and respect that it deserved.

Within a few days, F/58 Lurp teams were back in the Ashau Valley.

# Chapter Fifteen

The Lurp company was still under a cloud. No matter how Captain Eklund begged, cajoled, and lobbied, the division was still down on the Lurps for what had happened to Captain Shepherd. Even so, the Lurps did have a mission to perform. On August 10, two teams were inserted, one just north of the Ashau Valley, with the mission of looking for an NVA radar-guided .51-caliber antiaircraft gun, and the other team six kilometers to the southeast, with the mission of performing a general area reconnaissance. As things worked out, it was this team that found a .51-caliber machine gun. Sp4 Glen Martinez hosed down the gun crew, killing two NVA and sending two more running, and though it slowed them down considerably, with the enemy beating the bush for them, the Lurps managed to get away with the gun itself. The other team—the one tasked with the mission of finding a .51— didn't find such a gun but did call artillery fire from a newly opened firebase down on a complex of enemy positions, raising a secondary explosion, then booked out of the area before the enemy could find them. Both teams were extracted safely, and both teams had conducted successful missions. But rumor had it that the Lurp company was still in danger of being disbanded.

In the next few days, three more teams went out on

long-range patrols—two of which made contact. One of these teams was under newly promoted Sergeant Al Contreros as team leader. Contreros was an extremely enthusiastic Lurp who wore a Special Forces "De Opresso Liber" crest on his Lurp hat to remind himself that the Cuban people were still oppressed under Castro. He made a somewhat better impression on the company cadre than he did with the men on the teams. His team was moving along a ridgeline, parallel to a high-speed trail, when they caught a glimpse of a single enemy soldier bopping along that trail with his weapon—an SKS rifle—slung on his back over a small rucksack. Moving quickly, but carefully, through the jungle, the team passed the enemy soldier, and though they weren't moving quite as silently as they might have wished, the enemy didn't hear them. A live prisoner is far more valuable than a dead enemy, but this area was too far from even a good McQuire rig extraction point, and Contreros was apparently in no mood for snatching a prisoner, then herding him all the way to a pickup point. Setting up a hasty ambush along the trail, they killed the enemy soldier and discovered that his rucksack was full of documents. It was time to move, to get out of the area, but Contreros was in no big hurry. He customarily camouflaged his face flat black, without any green, and now, dipping his finger in the dead soldier's blood, he dabbed it on his face like war paint. Then, handing his field camera to a rather disgusted teammate, he posed for a picture with the dead soldier. His entire team was in a hurry to get away, but Contreros had to have his face paint, had to have his picture. Only then did the team move on.

In addition to these missions, the Lurps pulled local security ambushes and patrols within a few kilometers of the Camp Eagle perimeter. These were usually considered training missions, a chance for commo platoon Lurps to get out in the field with the patrol teams, a chance to break men in on new team positions. But these could still be dangerous patrols. On at least one occasion, a team had to abandon its ambush position when the perimeter came under a probing attack and .50-caliber machine-gun rounds—American rounds—began ricocheting into the area. Spotter helicopters and gunships took to the air, and the team had to lie *very* low, for fear of being spotted by the choppers and fired on by mistake. When they moved back into position, the enemy, returning from the perimeter, came through their kill zone, but the team was advised not to ambush them, for fear that the choppers would open up on them in the confusion. In the morning, this team detained a party of none-too-innocent-looking civilians and discovered grenades and C-4 plastic explosive. A two-and-one-half-ton truck manned by military police was sent out to pick up the detainees, but the Lurps had to walk back and make their way through a perimeter manned by still jumpy troops. They doubted they'd get any credit for the detainees. Any credit would probably go to the MPs.

On August 15, three more teams went out. Two of the teams discovered enemy caches, and the other team monitored the passage of a large party of NVA soldiers, but being severely outnumbered and lacking good commo at the moment, the team was not about to bring the NVA under fire with their own organic weapons and was unable to call artillery or gunships down on them. Though no one was compromised, and the missions were shaping up nicely, all three teams were extracted the next day—three days earlier than scheduled. Sergeant Ray Zoschak's team had a good extraction LZ, but one of the teams had to come out by ladder into a hovering helicopter, and another had to come out by McQuire rigs. Neither team was under fire at the time, and there were no Lurp casualties, but when they got back to the company area, there was a lot of wondering why the missions had been so abruptly terminated.

The next day, word came that the company was to stand down for at least the next two weeks. It was, everyone assumed, some sort of reaction to the Shepherd incident, and there was a great deal of worry that the division had decided to disband the company.

The second day of the stand-down, the weather turned bad—very bad. Even if the company had not been on stand-down, the extremely low cloud ceiling and unceasing rains would have made it very difficult—perhaps impossible, even with Kingsmen pilots and Lurps on radio relay—for teams to be inserted and extracted, or to maintain communications in the field.

As the unseasonable monsoon continued, so did the Lurp company's stand-down from operations. Captain Eklund was still knocking himself out, trying to get missions, and occasionally division headquarters forgot about the stand-down and gave him a few. Unfortunately, these missions all ended up being aborted due to the weather, often after a team or two of Lurps had spent the day before plotting and planning and coordinating, and half the scheduled insertion day waiting in the rain by the Acid Pad, all dressed up and with someplace to go but no way of getting there. Cancelled missions were about the only break in the general run of inactivity, and they were having a bad effect on morale.

One Lurp who probably found the mission cancellations particularly frustrating was Sp4 John Gambino. Gambino was a quiet, soft-spoken, unshakable fellow from commo platoon who had already done a lot of radio relay and was just beginning to go out with the recon teams. He didn't talk about it much, but back in the States, he'd apparently had to spend a long time waiting for security clearance due to his last name, and the fact that he was closely related to the powerful *cosa nostra* don Carlo Gambino. His time in the army had already been consumed with too much delay, and the bad weather must have seemed like some sort of cosmic conspiracy against him.

On August 26, the company mascot, Dixie, was joined by a new dog, who was immediately dubbed Tiger due to the resemblance of his coat to a dirty set of tiger fatigues. Tiger was scruffy, lazy, opportunistic, sneaky, and horny, and he fit into the Lurp company so well that many years later, a novel about Lurps was named after him.

The miserable weather continued through the rest of August and into the beginning of September. The Lurps themselves were not too delicate to operate in inclement weather, but if the weather conditions were such that helicopters could not fly, the Lurps had no way to get to work. The Lurps were Airborne qualified, but weather that was too bad for helicopters was also too bad for parachutes. A couple of the team leaders volunteered to walk their teams out to whatever recon zones "Higher" might want checked out, but this was not considered practical, and—with the possible exception of Al Contreros—even the team leaders who made this proposal were relieved when it was turned down.

On August 30, word came that the company was going to be relocated to a position adjacent to the 2/17th Cavalry—and more important, that the company was going to be coming under the operational control of the 17th Cav.

On the surface, putting the Lurps under the 17th Cav

made sense. The Cav had helicopters galore, plus a platoon of airmobile infantry that could act as a reaction force for the Lurps. Attaching the Lurps to the 17th Cav made more sense than attaching them to the 326th Engineers, but some of the old hands were not too happy about it—worrying, among other things, that this would mean that only Cav pilots would be flying for them in the future. Nobody wanted to see the splendid working relationship between the Kingsmen and the Lurps come to an end.

The good news was that the company was going to be living in plywood barracks. The bad news was the weather. Typhoons whipped the Hue–Phu Bai area while the new company area was being prepared, and between the typhoons, the rain and low cloud ceilings, and resulting lack of missions, continued.

When the bad weather temporarily broke, the mission alerts started coming down like yesterday's rain, and morale picked up. If the enlisted Lurps knew what the Cav had in mind for them, morale might have plummeted lower than ever. Lurps were Rangers, and Rangers were supposed to be commandos, not cavalry scouts. In centuries past, American Rangers had been cav troopers, and Ranger Mosby's 6th Virginia Partisan Cavalry was still honored on the Ranger School crest. But this was the 1960s, and twentieth-century Rangers had elevated themselves into the infantry, the Airborne infantry. They might take some inspiration from Ranger Mosby, but unlike the modern cavalry, they didn't hark back on a lineage that included George Armstrong Custer.

One evening, Captain Eklund returned from a meeting with the Cav's squadron commander in an absolute fury. According to Keith Hammond, who had driven him to the meeting, the Cav commander had come up with the absolutely insane idea of inserting Lurp teams with cavalry charge bugle calls coming off loudspeakers mounted on the insertion ship and colored smoke streaming from the skids. According to Hammond, who had been waiting right outside, Eklund really lit into the Cav commander, a lieutenant colonel, calling him at least six kinds of asshole and a dozen kinds of fool, then stomped out of the meeting and settled into the jeep, telling Hammond that he had just thrown his career away and was probably about to face a court-martial. When word of this got out, Captain Eklund's status in the company shot up, but Lurp spirits crashed to an all-time low.

Fortunately, the Cav commander more or less came to his senses—probably either because his pilots and air-rifle platoon leaders talked some courteous good sense to him or else because General Zais heard about his madness. There was no more talk of cavalry charge Lurp insertions.

Still, the relationship between the 2/17th Cavalry and the Lurps was to be an occasionally rocky one to the end of the war.

It was at about this time that the company almost lost some of its more experienced men. Jaybird Magill had already gone home at the end of his extension, leaving only two of the men who'd come from the 1st Brigade still in the company. These two might have started looking for another home if SSG Derby Jones hadn't had the habit of stopping by every now and then to make sure they weren't being abused or expended in too obviously stupid a fashion. Derby was now working as bodyguard and RTO for Colonel John Deitrich, one of the few senior officers left in the 101st still adhering to the 1st Brigade tradition established by the likes of Hank Emerson and David Hackworth. Colonel Deitrich was a soldier's soldier, Airborne to the bone, and though his heart was with the enlisted men and company officers, he was not without influence at division headquarters. When Derby said there was no real need to start looking for a new home just yet, the last two 1st Brigade Lurps figured they could stick around.

Sergeant Ray Zoschak wasn't so sure. "Zo" was not the sort to go telling everyone what was on his mind. He'd already decided to extend his tour an additional six months, but he was spending a lot of time hanging around MAVC-SOG Command and Control North's FOB 1 at Phu Bai, and some of his fellow Lurps were a little worried that he'd be going to SOG.

At this time, the 101st Airborne Division had one battalion, 3/506, operating independently of the division down in II Corps. In the 101st Airborne, the battalion recon platoons had always been elite units. Three or four of them had tremendous reputations and records, but they had a different mission from Lurps and did not generally operate in six-man teams, or operate very far from the other companies of their battalions. The good thing about battalion recon platoons was that they gave a man an opportunity to see more combat than a Lurp had any business seeing. That had been enough to lure Ernie Winston to the Tiger Force and Superspade Hite to the Hawk Recon Platoon. The bad thing was that the battalion recon platoons were too often just used as bait, and this could be a downright deadly role—Ernie Winston was killed with the Tiger Force, and Superspade got wounded with the Hawks. It was more the fashion for guys in the recon platoons to transfer or extend for the Lurps than it was for Lurps to go to a battalion recon platoon. But what the 3/506 was doing was different. The recon platoon had become a provisional Lurp detachment, operating in the same mode and to about the same standards as F/58—and they were pulling a lot more missions at the moment.

John Sours, Frank Souza, Jim Schwartz, and Gary Linderer decided to put in for a transfer to the 3/506 recon platoon. Captain Eklund called them in to the orderly room and gave them a little talk, counseling patience and promising them that as soon as the weather broke to the satisfaction of the aviation assets—and there he paused to make it clear he didn't blame the pilots themselves, for they were willing to fly into anything short of a mountain for the Lurps; it was their commanders and division headquarters being so cautious—as soon as the weather broke, they'd be getting missions worth sticking around for.

Captain Eklund had some plans of his own, and he figured he was in a position to put them in front of the division. The company was going back into the Ashau and the Rung Roung. Captain Eklund was reluctant to make any outright promises, and he had to show some respect for security, but he figured his Lurps were supposed to all be carrying at least provisional Secret clearances, and this was obviously a case of "need to know," so he mentioned the likelihood of missions up around Khe Sanh and hinted at the possibility of a few missions over the fence—without, of course, openly acknowledging that any American recon teams had ever made a covert crossing of any established international borders. The Lurps all knew what SOG was doing—and what Lurps, SEALs, Force Recon, and non-SOG Special Forces units were at least rumored to sometimes be doing—and they knew that their pilots sometimes joked about working for "Kingsmen International Airlines," but they were properly tactful about mentioning such officially deniable doings out in the open, even among themselves.

That's why Captain Eklund only hinted at missions

across the fence, but he needn't have bothered. His concern in calling them in for some straight talk was enough to keep Sours, Souza, Schwartz, and Linderer from transfering out of the company.

Everyone was watching the weather, hoping for a break. The break came in the second week of September. Two teams went in, one from each patrol platoon.

The team from the First Platoon, McKinnon's team, made contact right off the LZ. The enemy had moved in behind them, between them and the LZ, but the rear security had seen them before they saw him, and he opened up first. The team went into an immediate action drill that pretty much consisted of letting the rear security fire off a magazine and drop a grenade while everyone booked out at high speed. Then they slowed down and stepped high, moving alertly, cautiously, and tensely. They could hear the enemy moving on three sides of them, and they moved into the thickest jungle they could find.

A Lurp heading for the thick jungle was like a navy frogman heading for the water. The jungle offered concealment, and the Lurps were clothed and painted to look like the jungle. Sound did not travel well where the jungle was thick, and the Lurps were very quiet anyway. The jungle slowed down everyone, but it was Lurp wisdom that real jungle slowed down Charlie more than it slowed down a Lurp. Charlie was a creature of trails, but the Lurps were creatures of rough ground and bush. It was only natural for them to head for the deepest jungle and steepest terrain they could find.

There was, however, one disadvantage to rough terrain and thick vegetation—and that was the lack of helicopter landing zones.

With the enemy chasing them, and plenty of thick jungle around, Sergeant McKinnon did not want to expose his team out in the open on an LZ, although there were more than a couple of potential LZs in his recon zone. McKinnon and his men were Lurps, and they didn't need any stinkin' LZs. McKinnon had already called for a McQuire rig extraction, and his big problem was to get as far away from the enemy as he could, in as unlikely a place to escape by helicopter as it was possible for the enemy to imagine. If the enemy hadn't been briefed on McQuire rigs, this extraction was likely to be a piece of cake—except, of course, for the part about being pulled up through branches and leaves, which was likely to be the case out there.

Finally, the team found a place where there was a small hole in the canopy, and the ships came in. The first ship, which lifted out the first three Lurps, didn't drag anyone through the branches or draw any enemy fire, but the enemy caught on quickly, and when the second ship came in to pick up the three remaining Lurps, the NVA opened up with small arms fire on the chopper, the Lurps dangling 120 feet beneath it, and the Command and Control ship circling about a hundred meters above and a hundred meters to the rear of the extraction ships. It was just small arms fire, and with the racket the choppers were kicking up, no one was all that aware of it until the second extraction ship climbed high enough to lift its load of three dangling Lurps above the canopy, and a round clipped the rope holding Sergeant Quick.

To the horror of everyone watching—probably even the enemy—Sergeant Quick plummeted down and disappeared into the maw of the jungle. Both door gunners on the extraction ship caught glimpses of enemy soldiers and opened up with their machine guns, but Quick had already hit the ground—landing so close to the enemy his impact scared them—and landing so hard the shock knocked him unconscious.

A Lurp was down there, unconscious, surrounded by the enemy, and Warrant Officer Dave Poley immediately figured out what he could do to rectify the situation. The first thing was to get the other two Lurps into the ship, which meant burning for the closest patch of open ground and hoping everyone moved fast—which they did. The Command and Control ship and gunship escorts stayed on station, and within three or four minutes Poley's ship was back over Quick's position. Poley brought the ship down low enough for the rotor wash to blow back the tree limbs and give his crew and the Lurps aboard a visual fix on where Sergeant Quick was lying, and then he continued to bring the ship down—his rotors chopping away tree limbs, enlarging the narrow rend in the canopy. For a full minute or two, the enemy was too shocked and confused to react. But then they opened up. Poley ignored the incoming fire and continued to bring his ship down until he was low enough for McKinnon and his point man to jump out, run for Quick, and drag him back to the chopper just as he was regaining consciousness. Then, his rotors still chopping the vegetation, Poley brought the ship back up out of the hole he'd cut in the jungle and took his Lurps home.

For this action, WO David Poley was awarded the Distinguished Flying Cross—and threatened with a court-martial if he ever did anything that foolhardy and destructive of rotor blades again. Such threats, of course, meant little to Poley. This was not the first time, nor would it be the last time, he was to sacrifice a few feet of rotor blade to get Lurps out of a tight spot. His crew members and the Lurps on his ship didn't get any new medals, but Poley made sure they knew he had accepted the damn medal on their behalf, so they wouldn't have to get spruced up and spit-shined and have to deal with an awards presentation of their own. By this point, Mr. Poley and the other Kingsmen pilots and gunners were at least as cynical about medals as the Lurps were, and just as Ray Zoschak was about to become the most cynical about medals of the Lurps, Mr. Poley was probably already the most cynical of the Kingsmen. Nobody who did this sort of thing for a living did it for medals. They did it for their buddies.

Quick was bruised and scraped, but otherwise unhurt. He had just a few weeks left on his tour, and despite his protests that his close call had only proven how good his luck was running, Captain Eklund decided to put him to work in the company area, maybe let him fly bellyman, but not send him out on another mission unless it became absolutely necessary.

For the rest of September, the rains returned, the cloud ceiling rarely got off the ground, and due to the abysmal flying conditions most of the scheduled missions were aborted before they could be launched. One of the teams that managed to get inserted was an ad hoc team made up of various Lurps who were temporarily without a team. This team was put under Sergeant Chester Smith— known as "Black Smitty" to differentiate him from the two other "Smittys" in the company, both of whom were white—and as his ATL, Smitty was taking "Crazy Adams." Even by Lurp standards, Adams was crazy. He was on his third tour in Vietnam—the first having been with the 1st Cavalry Division in 1965, the second with Special Forces—and he was probably the most kill-crazed Lurp in the company. Adams was also probably the most politically cynical Lurp since Crash Clark went back to the States. Back in the rear, Crazy Adams got a big kick out of listening to Country Joe McDonald and his band, "the Fish," mock the war effort and savage LBJ. Sp4 Adams had once been an E-6, and he often argued with Sergeant Smith back in the rear, trying to convince him that since nobody in "Higher" could be trusted to do the right thing about any enemy they might find on a recon mission, it was up to the Lurp team itself to deal with them—at least anything less than a battalion or a dug-in company that already knew there were Lurps in the neighborhood. Back in the rear, it was great sport to gather around Smitty and Crazy Adams, listening to Country Joe and the Fish, hearing Adams's crazy talk and watching Smitty shake his head at such foolishness. Crazy Adams was crazy enough back in the rear to be a fairly popular fellow with some of his brother Lurps. But more than a few of those brother Lurps had some real doubts about going out into the field with him, since he didn't seem quite cautious and rational enough, and didn't seem to have much interest in ever leaving the war alive as long as he could take a lot of people—including probably his own teammates—with him.

Those who had actually been to the field with Adams valued the experience, for seeing Adams really come alive like some sort of ravenous and cunning wolf in the field was strangely inspiring to even the most sensible Lurp. They enjoyed going to the field with Crazy Adams. But nobody wanted to go out with Crazy Adams as team leader.

Fortunately, Smitty was going to be TL, the other men on the team were somewhat more sane than Crazy Adams, and the mission wasn't into the Ashau Valley, the Rung Roung, or anyplace that looked too extreme on the map or sounded too promising at the briefing. Smitty's team would be checking out an "Area of

Interest" for one of the infantry battalions, probably because the infantry battalion in question wasn't quite daring enough in the employment of its own recon platoon. This did not look to be anything more than a routine mission, and possibly a very cold recon zone.

Then again, all Lurps knew there was no such thing as a routine mission, no such sure thing as a cold RZ. Hadn't Doc Norton gotten gored by a goddamn water buffalo on a bullshit sweep through the ville right outside the perimeter? Life was dangerous for a Lurp, no matter where he went.

Smitty's team went in on a first-light insertion and spent the first two days monitoring and paralleling trails—of which there was an abundance in their recon zone. None of the trails showed signs of recent use, however, and on the second day the team moved west, skirting alongside the broadest of the trails they'd found. The vegetation was not particularly thick, but the weather out there was much better than the weather back at Camp Eagle, and sunlight streamed through the single canopy, falling in mottled patches on the carpet of dead leaves on the ground. Leeches were strangely absent, but there was a profusion of birds in the trees, and Adams, who was walking point with Smitty as his slack, kept finding little slugs of feces, which he declared to be anteater shit. This area had all the signs of a cold RZ—but none of the Lurps really believed that any recon zone was a cold one until they were safely out of it.

There were intermittent sounds of movement throughout the second night, but listening carefully, the Lurps were pretty sure that these were not the sounds of human movement. They were probably anteaters, or some such creature. Whatever they were, they did not sound like predators or particularly challenging prey.

On the morning of the third day, the team moved into the bushes overlooking a deep ravine through which ran a small river with numerous little pools. There was a trail down to the water on the opposing slope, across the ravine. For an hour, the team stayed in the concealing brush, watching the river and the pools and that trail, and suffering from the leeches, which were now terrible. Smitty called in and tried to register the spot they were overlooking as an artillery concentration, but the relay team came back over the horn with the news that the team was a little bit beyond the reach of the guns of Fire Support Base Birmingham and "Higher" wanted them to pull back. Since it was passed down to Captain Eklund, and passed on by Captain Eklund through the Lurp relay team on Firebase Birmingham, it came through as a suggestion rather than an order, but it was clear what "Higher" wanted.

This lack of artillery seemed strange, since the whole RZ was supposed to be well within reach of Birmingham. Of course, operating outside the artillery net was nothing unusual, but finding such holes in the net was a little unusual. Smitty's team was at the edge of its recon zone, and after monitoring the river and ravine for a few more minutes, Smitty had Adams lead the team back to a little knoll covered with saplings and ferns a couple of hundred meters to the southeast. Sp4 Miller switched frequency on the artillery radio, ran a wire antenna up into the saplings, and called in a commo check on the command net. With the wire up, the second radio didn't need to go through the relay and could communicate directly with the rear at Camp Eagle. The rear wanted to know if Smitty had any new artillery preplots, but Smitty showed Miller the plots he already had and shook his head. He could direct off them, if the arty at Birmingham had its

shit in order. Miller sent the message back, then switched
back to the artillery push for a commo check and confir-
mation that they could hit the preplots.

While the other men lay on their bellies in the ferns,
weapons out to make a security wheel with overlapping
fields of fire all around, Crazy Adams huddled with
Smitty, whispering in his ear. Smitty listened, shook his
head, whispered something back, then shook his head
again and shrugged. Whispering, he passed the word that
Adams was sure he'd heard voices as they were moving
and wanted to pull a little "point recon" back to the place
where they'd overlooked the river. PFC John Meszaros
rolled his eyes and gave Miller a wry little smile when he
got the word. Everyone in the company knew that Crazy
Adams had a tendency to go a little farther, and stay a
little longer, on his point recons than most of the Lurps
thought wise. But he couldn't go too far without crossing
that ravine and river, and he had Smitty with him, and
Smitty had good sense. Adams shrugged out of his rucksack, but Smitty was carrying his own command net
radio, and he kept his rucksack on his back.

The team leader and assistant team leader had been
gone only thirty minutes or so when the rest of the team
heard two grenade explosions, then a long burst of automatic weapons fire, another grenade explosion, then
another burst of fire. All of the fire sounded like M-16
and CAR-15 fire, and the grenades had sounded like
American M-26 frags, but it was hard to be certain—and
at any rate, the four Lurps on the knoll were rather
alarmed, for Smitty was carrying a radio, and yet there
had been no transmission.

Suddenly, Smitty and Adams came running back, right
along the route they said they'd be returning. Adams was
laughing gleefully, and Smitty looked pissed off. Adams

grabbed his rucksack, and Smitty gestured for Miller to haul ass and leave the wire antenna hanging. Before long, they heard mortars crumping behind them, two hundred meters or so off to the northwest. Adams threw his head back, laughing. The mortars were way off, and he seemed to find that tremendously funny. When the whole team could hear voices shouting behind them—somewhat too close behind them for comfort—Crazy Adams laughed again. But Crazy Adams wasn't crazy enough to want to stick around and develop the situation. It was time to haul ass and get to an LZ. Fortunately, there were plenty of LZs in the area, and the team was out safely within the hour. Though he admitted it had been fun, after the debriefing, Smitty lit into Adams for opening up on the small party of four NVA they'd found filling canteens down by the river. This was supposed to have been a five-day area reconnaissance mission, and Adams had blown it on the third day in order to add to his personal body count.

As it turned out, they were lucky to get out when they did. Louie Ondrus's team and Ralph Timmons's team had to spend an extra day socked in, out in their recon zones, when the weather turned nasty again.

A few days later, Ray Zoschak's team went in—and as was usual with Zo, he soon found the enemy. Unfortunately, the enemy soon knew that they'd been found, and when it came time to be extracted, Zo's team had to come out by McQuire rigs under fire. It was Kingsmen pilot W. T. Grant's first opportunity to extract a team by McQuires, and he did a perfect job of it. But as soon as he and the other extraction ship let their Lurps off at the closest firebase, they had to pull in the ropes and head back out to extract a team under SFC Brubaker. This was another touchy extraction, for Brubaker's team had been chased off its first pickup LZ and had to make its way to another with the NVA in pursuit. Grant and his crew managed to extract Bru's team and get the Lurps safely back to Camp Eagle.

As platoon sergeant, Brubaker really wasn't supposed to be taking teams out, but he'd come over with the understanding that he would, and he took every opportunity to do so. The opportunities weren't many, and since Brubaker had never been very happy in F/58, he was already looking to either go back to Special Forces or go to the advisory detachment assigned to the Vietnamese Airborne. Shortly after returning from this mission, he got word that a slot was open at the Vietnamese Airborne, and he made his move.

Missions continued to come down throughout the rest of September, and teams continued to troop down to the Acid Pad in the predawn darkness to wait with the helicopter crews, only to have the insertions aborted or postponed due to the weather. The Lurps, however, did not stay inactive. There were classes in the company area, security patrols and ambushes outside the Camp Eagle perimeter, sessions on the rappelling tower down at FOB 1 or the ARVN firing range, and there was the urgent task of getting a club for the company—for the Lurps were not very welcome in the other makeshift clubs around Camp Eagle and needed a place to relax together.

Captain Eklund must have heard about Tony Tercero's previous mission to Da Nang, and he called on Tony to do his magic again—only this time, to *buy* what he needed, not to "reappropriate" it. Once again, Tony came through, both with building material and with an abundance of beer and soda, and everyone pitched in to help. Before long, the Lurp Lounge was in operation. It was an exclusive club for the Lurps and aircrews and only a few occasional, rigorously selected, outside guests. Of course, having their own club did not stop the Lurps from making occasional forays to the other clubs at Camp Eagle, and the fact that the arrogant, hell-raising Lurps were not really welcome anywhere except their own club made these forays all the more interesting.

On September 23, the bad weather broke, and Lurp spirits soared. That same evening, word came that the 501st Signal battalion was showing stag films at their club, and a good number of Lurps decided to attend. But there was an unexpected cover charge, beer prices had been doubled, the club was packed with REMFs, and after an hour and a half of drinking overpriced beer, the porno films were still not forthcoming. Everyone started to get a little testy. When an E-7 from the 501st Signal came around to kick the Lurps out for not buying enough overpriced beer, one of the Lurps nailed him with a short, straight, right hand, and the brawl was on. The club was very crowded, and as usual the Lurps were outnumbered. Hostiles pressed in close on all sides—so close the bigger Lurps didn't have quite enough room to punch and kick and throw people around, and just let the smaller guys do most of the effective fighting. With their larger buddies giving what help they could, these smaller Lurps had a field day cracking REMF ribs, kneeing REMF groins, and stomping on REMF insteps. As usual the Lurps counted the brawl a good time and a victory, and as usual, the Lurps got blamed for everything.

It was time to get these animals back out in the field.

# Chapter Sixteen

September 1968 ended in a sad fashion. On the night of the twenty-ninth, Sergeant John Quick was celebrating his upcoming return to the States by drinking with the Kingsmen pilots who had saved him when he'd been shot out of his McQuire rig a few weeks before. Sergeant Quick had once been a survival instructor, and although he wasn't quite as extreme as Sergeant Burnell, who occasionally dined on lightbulbs and razor blades, there wasn't much in the way of raw meat he wasn't willing to try. When someone came in with a big toad from the paddy down by the chopper pad, Sergeant Quick chowed right down on it. It was a fatal mistake. Toxins in the toad's skin reacted with the alcohol in Sergeant Quick's system, and by morning he was dead.

Throughout October, there was an abundance of rain, an abundance of bad flying weather, and an abundance of aborted and cancelled missions—but also an abundance of missions that went in. A man might come back from a mission with one team only to find himself getting ready to go out with another team the next day. Team integrity was pretty much a thing of the past. Although the strongest team leaders managed to maintain a stable cadre of three or four regulars, hardly a team in the company went out twice in a row with the same five or six

men, and at least two men—the last of the Lurps who had
joined the company from the 1/101 LRRP, and a Lurp
who'd come over from Fort Campbell with the company—were not even sure which platoon they formally
belonged to anymore, much less which teams, because
they were going out with everyone. The bad side of this
was obvious, for a Lurp team was supposed to be a *team*.
But there was a good side, too. Going out with different
teams, filling different slots on those teams, was certainly
good training, if not exactly the safest, smartest way to
do this sort of job, and in October 1968, many of the men
who would become team leaders in 1969 learned to
handle all the jobs on a Lurp team by performing in a
variety of slots, on a variety of teams, and on a variety of
missions.

In October, the company pulled a handful of black box
missions, planting sensors out along enemy infiltration
routes. On one of these missions, toward the end of the
month, the enemy called the team up on the radio and, in
very good English, told them exactly where they were
and offered them a compass azimuth from their present
position to a suitable extraction LZ. The team was
promised safe conduct out if it complied, and was
informed that the alternative was to be annihilated. After
switching to the alternate Command and Control frequency—which was probably also compromised—and
consulting with Captain Eklund in the air overhead, the
Lurps decided that this was a case of discretion being the
better part of valor. With the C&C ship scouting against
ambushes ahead of them, the team made its way to the LZ
the enemy had designated and got out of there safely. It
was a spooky, galling, and humiliating experience, but a
day or two later, after the frequencies, call signs, and
codebooks had been changed, and all the other teams had

been extracted as compromised, that same team and two more were back in the same general area and planted their devices without any trouble until the extraction, when one of the ships went down—fortunately, without injury to Lurps or aircrew. There were also a couple of aircraft-recovery missions in October. In neither case were there any survivors of the downed aircraft, nor any contact with the enemy near the crash sites.

At least two raids on suspected enemy communications sites were planned, but they were cancelled when someone in "Higher Higher" decided that the targets weren't really there. And of course, there were recon patrols—almost all of them with the secondary mission of snatching a prisoner if the opportunity presented itself, which it didn't. Sergeant Zoschak's team, consisting of Zo, Jim Schwartz, Gary Linderer, Barry Golden, Ken Munoz, and Mike Reiff, went on a three-day trail-monitoring mission that was extended to six days. There were too many enemy, and the enemy were too alert for the Lurps to snatch a prisoner. Sergeant Al Contreros's team, consisting of Contreros and his regulars, Jim Venable, Jim Bacon, and Riley Cox, and supplemented by Terry Thayer and Kenn Miller, almost snatched a lone NVA soldier on a trail along the side of a thickly jungled mountain just east of the Rung Roung, but ended up having to kill their target rather than capture him when he took off running and hollering, unslinging his weapon in a most unfriendly fashion as he ran. Intelligence wanted prisoners, and so did the Lurps, but prisoner snatches were highly dependent on the element of luck, as well as the element of surprise, and luck was not running well for the snatch teams.

On October 27, Captain Eklund ordered the company to prepare to field six teams of ten men each for saturation patrolling in an area along the Laotian border and slightly north of the company's usual areas of operation. Saturation patrolling was a relatively new concept in the employment of Lurp teams. The idea was to put as many teams as possible into as concentrated an area as they could safely operate in without bumping into each other, and thereby assure that whatever was out there would be discovered. Intelligence already had a pretty good idea that there were four thousand enemy soldiers concentrated in this particular area, and as the likelihood of compromise and contact was considered great, the thinking was that six teams of ten men would be more effective than ten teams of six men. This belief was not shared by all of the Lurps, many of whom felt that the extra firepower of a ten-man team would hardly compensate for the superior stealth and mobility of six-man teams. Ten men would also necessitate an extra helicopter for each insertion and extraction. Fielding sixty Lurps at one time was going to put a severe strain on the company's manpower, and the ten-man teams would have to be augmented with men from the commo platoon—all of whom trained with the company but many of whom had never been on a mission. The recon zones for this operation were to be only a grid square in size, and adjoining each other, and although no one objected much to smaller recon zones, there were more than a few men who worried that having teams operating so close to each other only increased the likelihood of one team being driven into another team's area, which contributed to the possibility of confusion and potential fratricide. Lurps were accustomed to working in areas where there were no friendly troops—and, in this part of I Corps, no civilians.

In announcing the pending operation, Captain Eklund

did not seem too happy about it, and neither were some of the men on the teams. This operation was cancelled before the company could make up the ten-man teams, and there was only some minor grumbling and disappointment. The reason for the cancellation seems to have been that intelligence decided that there were ten thousand enemy soldiers in the area, not just four thousand, and it wasn't thought prudent to send sixty Lurps against ten thousand NVA. Four thousand was apparently a reasonable number for sixty Lurps to deal with, but ten thousand was stretching things a little.

The day after the cancellation of the saturation patrols, Burford's team and Gregory's team were put in on missions, made contact very soon after insertion, and were extracted in the afternoon, leaving a number of dead NVA behind them.

Then the weather turned bad again, and October ended with a whole series of missions that were aborted before they could be launched due to impossible flying conditions.

November began with two missions on the first. Al Contreros's team and John Burford's team went in on first-light insertions, were compromised right off the insertion LZs, and after brief exchanges of gunfire, were safely extracted. On landing at the Acid Pad, the rear security man on Burford's team was delighted to discover that his old buddy from AIT and jump school, Barry Schreiber, had been command pilot on the extraction ship. Prior to this, the only times he'd flown with Schreiber, Schreiber was flying co-pilot, not aircraft commander. But the Lurp didn't get a chance to congratulate Schreiber, because as soon as Burford's team unloaded the helicopter, the ships had to go extract Contreros's team, which had not broken contact and was headed for its extraction LZ. Besides, Schreiber would soon be flying as a co-pilot again—as W. T. Grant's co-pilot, in fact—since that slot guaranteed that he'd be flying Lurps and FOB missions more regularly than he would as an aircraft commander.

Contreros's and Burford's missions were failures in that the teams had not been able to perform much in the way of area reconnaissance, but they were successes in that they left behind them a respectable number of dead NVA. That helped to lift the company out of its doldrums.

On the night of November 2, the cities of Hue and Phu Bai were rocketed, and so was Camp Eagle. The next day, two teams were alerted for missions—Ray Zoschak's team, to Nui Khe mountain, and Snuffy Smith's team, to the south of Nui Khe, near Leech Island. They were both to be first light insertions, but the only team with much hope of actually getting on the ground anywhere near first light was Zo's since it was scheduled to be inserted first. As soon as Zo's team was inserted, the ships would return to Eagle to pick up Snuffy Smith's team and fly it out to its recon zone.

Too often, the Lurps didn't have much idea exactly how their missions were supposed to fit into the "big picture." But this time it was very clear. Intelligence had the rockets that hit Hue and Camp Eagle coming from Nui Khe, and the rockets that hit Phu Bai coming from the vicinity of Leech Island. The Lurps' mission was to find the rocket teams and destroy them. They would have artillery, gunships, and Tac Air on call to do the actual destruction, but if they found targets, and for some reason had no option but to take them out with their own organic weapons, they'd do it that way.

Zo told his team that with all that support on call, about the only reason he could see that they'd have to fire their own weapons would be if someone fucked up. As usual, Zo made it very clear that nobody was going to fuck up on his team. If, on the other hand, the enemy fucked up, and the team caught him really half-stepping ... well, maybe then they'd do the killing themselves. But with any luck, they'd be spotting targets and calling in supporting fire, and come back without expending any of their own ammunition. Snuffy Smith probably told his team pretty much the same thing. It was just basic good sense, but it was also the sort of thing team leaders had to stress just so the Lurps going out with them wouldn't figure they weren't fully developing the concept of the mission. It was always necessary to have a basic concept of the mission before you got down to planning it out and preparing the map overlays.

If the Lurps were going to find their targets, they'd need to be inserted without compromise. Inserting Snuffy's team wasn't going to present any unusual difficulties beyond whatever the enemy might come up with. But getting Zo's team on Nui Khe presented certain problems. Almost all the possible LZs were in the valley, and these lowland LZs were just too visible from the high ground. Nobody wanted to put a team in with Charlie looking down on the insertion and maybe even shooting down on it as well. Besides, Zo wanted to go in with the tactical advantage of high ground. His concept of the mission, and his plans for it, as reflected on his map overlays and briefback presentation, consisted in good part of target spotting, and if at all possible he intended to do it from a safe enough distance that he could watch the show and direct fire. There had to be more than one rocket team down there, and although a very good—and very lucky—Lurp team might be able to find one of them and destroy it, getting rid of one rocket team wasn't going to do much to stop the rockets. Captain Eklund had said that "Higher" wanted teams in both recon zones until the rocket attacks stopped. If Zo's team could put a stop to the rockets coming from the foot and slopes of Nui Khe—or if Snuffy's team could stop the rockets hitting Phu Bai—then the other teams wouldn't have to go in, and keep on going into these same RZs over and over again until somebody's luck ran out completely. The sooner the Lurps put an end to the rockets, the sooner the Lurp company could get on with more important business farther west, in some of the recon zones no allied teams had penetrated since Project Delta went back to Nha Trang and on to further adventures in other places.

Zo didn't take any particular delight in coldblooded calculation, but he didn't shirk when it was necessary. He figured that the only way his team was going to put a stop to the rocket attacks on Hue and Camp Eagle was to catch the bastards in the act and bring smoke down on all the launch sites at once. For that, he was going to need to stick to the high ground.

It was Captain William "Wild Bill" Meachum's idea to go over the top and put Zo's team in right on the abandoned firebase at the peak of Nui Khe. Meachum reasoned that an insertion lower than the summit would be too easily observed, but although an insertion at the highest point, right at first light, might get a lot of enemy necks craning, it wasn't going to be easy to actually see—unless the enemy was right there on the abandoned firebase. And if the enemy was there, then the Lurps and helicopters would at least have the advantage of not having anyone shooting *down* on them. Meachum said that army helicopters flew over that abandoned firebase on a regular basis, and often dawdled over it, looking for signs of enemy occupation. If it turned out to actually be occupied by the enemy when the team went in, then the Lurps and Kingsmen were going to be in deep trouble. But Meachum was hooked in to pilot scuttlebutt, and he said it had been a while since anyone took any serious ground fire from the peak of Nui Khe, despite the fact that some of the helicopters that often dawdled over the summit really dawdled, offering a fat and tempting target. Though he could have left it unsaid, Meachum pointed out that a Kingsmen helicopter landing Lurps would hardly be seen to dawdle.

Captain Eklund and Sergeant Zoschak agreed. It was either the top of the mountain or insertion five or six kilometers behind the Rocket Belt and a slow hump into the recon zone—and there wasn't time for that.

The pilots liked the LZ. Zo liked the tactical advantage of starting out on the high ground. And Captain Eklund liked the thought that he'd be getting a team in quickly. If he had a Lurp team in there to catch the rocket teams in the act next time they launched, Division was going to finally have to put that Captain Shepherd incident behind it and start treating his Lurps the way they ought to be treated—with dedicated support and good missions. The men deserved promotions, awards and decorations, and R&R allocations—most of which were being effectively withheld at the moment. And for moral reasons, as well as reasons of morale, Captain Eklund probably figured it was important to stop those damn rockets. Hitting Camp Eagle was honest warfare, and while Captain Eklund might curse the NVA for doing it, he couldn't really blame them or hold it against them. But hitting Hue and Phu Bai? That was pure terrorism, and the bastards had to be stopped.

To the extent they thought about anything beyond the mission at hand, the Lurps on Zo's and Snuffy's teams would have probably agreed with that judgment. But they weren't thinking much of the big picture. They were too consumed with preparing for their insertion at first light on the morning of November 4. About as much into the "big picture" as anyone talked about was the night of the third, when one of the men on Snuffy's team looked up from taping his equipment and said something about the prospect that these two missions might set the tone for the whole month of November, at the end of which he was going home.

Someone else mentioned that Zo was going home on extension leave even before the end of November, and somebody else said that Mr. Poley was going with him. Another Lurp regretted aloud the fact that Mr. Poley wasn't flying this mission, since he was off flying for CCN Phu Bai, or Force Recon, or some other, lesser, unit of the 101st. At this, Snuffy Smith laughed and pointed out that they had Grant's crew putting them in, Meachum and his crew putting in Zoschak, and with these crews it was downright stingy to begrudge CCN, Force Recon, or some other unit in the 101st the use of Mr. Poley's talents and those of his crew and helicopter—at least on a temporary basis. Even if Zo's team did have a special sort of relationship with Poley's crew, you didn't hear them bitching about the aircrews, did you? Not with Grant's crew, and Meachum and his crew, you didn't. With them flying for you, you might still have a lot to think about, but you didn't have to worry about your pilots and gunners running out of balls.

# Chapter Seventeen

By almost any standards, Sergeant Zoschak had a good team for this mission. Zo himself was, by general agreement, probably the best team leader left in the company, and the fact that he'd soon be going home on extension leave didn't make much difference in his spirit, for Zo was immune to such common weaknesses as "short-timer's syndrome." As point man and ATL he had Gary Linderer. Terry Clifton was walking Linderer's slack. Zo would come right behind them in order of march, and behind him would be his senior RTO, Billy Walkabout, carrying the command radio. Behind Walkabout would be Dave Biedron, carrying the support radio. Walking drag to provide rear security and sanitize their trail would be Jim Schwartz, who had been on Zo's team longer than anyone. Every man on the team had at least ten missions behind him, except for Clifton, and Clifton had a year of combat service in an Airborne infantry company behind him before extending for Lurps.

Shortly after first light, the team flew directly from Camp Eagle to Nui Khe. Captain Meachum brought the ship in fast and low over the abandoned firebase atop the mountain. The original plan had been to put the team down on the perforated steel plate chopper pad in the center of the firebase, but at the last instant, Meachum veered off and put the Lurps in atop the old command bunker. Some sixth sense had told him to veer off, and when Meachum was gone and the team was on the ground, Zo checked out the chopper pad and discovered a two-hundred-pound air force bomb buried nose up and rigged with a pressure detonator, right under the PSP at the edge of the pad. Any weight on the metal grating would have vaporized the team and blown the chopper to pieces.

Zo called in the discovery, and word came back that it would be destroyed by artillery after the mission was completed, but for now to give it a wide berth. Linderer couldn't help thinking that if Captain Shepherd was still company commander, he probably would have had them blow it in place before continuing the mission—or worse, blow themselves in place trying to disarm it.

Almost as soon as they'd called in the bomb, the Lurps saw the enemy. While the other men monitored three figures running down the sides of Nui Khe, Zo and Clifton very carefully searched the abandoned firebase. As expected, the enemy had been all over the place, scrounging through the gear left behind—of which there was still a shameful abundance—but there were no more booby traps.

Back when the firebase was active, fields of fire had been cleared for a few hundred meters around it, and the only cover or concealment up there were boulders and fallen trees. Around 0900 hours, the team began to patrol down the eastern finger of the mountain, heading toward the tree line at the end of the finger. The Lurps felt uncomfortably exposed, and it was hard to shake the feeling that they were being watched. Just short of the tree line, Zo halted the team in a cluster of boulders and sent Linderer and Clifton off on a point recon to check out the woodline. Flitting from boulder to boulder, fallen tree to fallen tree, the two Lurps moved cautiously forward, expecting to be ambushed at any second. But when they got to the woodline, they found it clear and without signs of recent enemy occupation.

Stepping back into the open, they motioned the rest of the team forward. But as soon as the other four Lurps started to move, they all heard the sound of mortars leaving a tube in the valley to the north of them. They quickly sought cover in the boulders and hugged the ground as three mortar rounds impacted halfway up the slope. Zo called Linderer and Clifton back, and they raced to join the rest of the team, making it back to their position just as a second salvo hit the opposite side of the ridge. Now they were bracketed, and though the ridge offered the enemy mortar men a narrow target, they knew they were in trouble. Zo and Biedron moved a few meters off the side of the ridge to where they could overlook the enemy mortar position, and got the artillery on the horn. Within a minute or so, artillery from Firebase Brick was dropping rounds into the valley, and Zo was having a high old time adjusting and correcting fire, walking those rounds up and down the valley. When two secondary explosions erupted beneath them, sending up billows of thick smoke, Zo looked back at the rest of the team with a big grin on his face. The team had been on the ground only a couple of hours and was already compromised, but it was sure hurting the enemy.

The mortars had stopped, but Linderer spotted movement on the south finger. Several enemy soldiers were rushing uphill, trying to beat the Lurps back to the peak. Now there was no need to maintain complete sound discipline, for the enemy knew where they were. Linderer hollered to Zo, telling him what he'd seen, and Zo hollered back for him to get the rest of the team back to the top. When Linderer glanced over his shoulder on the run, he could see Zo and Biedron squatted down among the rocks, calling in another fire mission.

Linderer, Schwartz, Walkabout, and Clifton ran for the abandoned firebase, half expecting to find the enemy firing down at them from behind the concertina wire that still surrounded it. They won the race to the top and took up the best defensive positions they could, while they waited nervously for their team leader and artillery RTO to join them. After a few minutes, Zo and Biedron appeared, panting hard from their run but looking remarkably calm, considering the circumstances.

When Linderer had spotted the enemy soldiers, they were closer to the top than the Lurps were, and now he wondered where they had gone. He looked around at the other Lurps. There they were, six men, trying to cover a perimeter designed for at least a company. They had the high ground, but if the enemy made a concerted push on them, their position did not seem tenable.

Zo began calling in fire missions from two different firebases, bringing rounds in on the valleys, both flanks of the eastern ridge, and along the woodline of the south finger. There were almost certainly enemy troops between them and the artillery, but at the moment, the enemy seemed to be keeping his head down. Suddenly the Lurps heard a helicopter overhead and a little distance to the east, away from the artillery's gun-target lines. It was Captain Eklund in the C&C ship. He radioed that he had four Cobra gunships on station, and as soon as Zo called off the arty he would have them work out on the slopes. Zo immediately had Biedron call in a cease-fire, then went up on the command net and told Eklund he was clear to bring in the snakes. While debris from the last artillery rounds was still falling, the C&C ship made one quick pass, low over the south ridge, and Captain Eklund tossed out a yellow smoke grenade. As soon as the C&C ship was out of the way, the Cobras came swooping in with rocket fire. As the third Cobra made its rocket run, Gary Linderer saw three NVA soldiers make a break just ahead of the exploding rockets and run up the finger below him. When they got to the crest of the ridge, they hesitated, then turned and ran back for the woodline. They were about a hundred meters away from Linderer's position. He put his selector switch on semi, took careful aim, hit two of the men, then emptied his magazine into the foliage where the third man had disappeared.

After what seemed only a short time, the Cobras had expended their ordnance, and had to break off and return to Camp Eagle to rearm. The C&C ship stayed overhead, and Captain Eklund came up on the horn, telling Zo that he had a pair of F-4s coming in hot. The Lurps were in for a show.

The first F-4 came screaming in from over the Perfume River and let fly a two-hundred-pound bomb. He was lower than the Lurps when he made his bomb run, and as he climbed up and away from the explosion, the Lurps were able to look down into the cockpit at the pilot and his backseater. On the third bomb run, the F-4s got a massive secondary explosion, and Linderer suddenly understood why the enemy had tried to mortar them on the high ground rather than wait to ambush them farther down in the jungle. This was the third big secondary explosion of the morning, and that meant the enemy had something down there he definitely didn't want to risk having a Lurp team discover.

By the time the F-4s were finished, the Cobras were rearmed, back on station, and ready to go back to work.

The men at the rearming point must have made record time today. That was fast work, and much appreciated.

It's amazing how slowly time can crawl sometimes— and just as amazing how quickly it can pass when you're living life on the edge. The first time Linderer looked at his watch, it was almost 1630 hours. Since the team obviously wasn't going to be able to continue its originally planned mission, Captain Eklund decided to extract it. Zo called back, reminding Captain Eklund to warn the pilots *not* to put down on the PSP chopper pad. Captain Eklund soon came back with the word that the team would have to hold tight for another hour because Snuffy's team, down by Leech Island, had made contact and was already being extracted. When he got the news, Zo just shrugged and passed it on to his teammates.

Half an hour passed, and then Clifton spotted movement in the trees below his position. Zo got on the horn and passed the word that the enemy seemed to be preparing to come pay a personal visit, and he'd appreciate it if the Cobras covering Snuffy's extraction might come around in time to get in on the fun. After a slight delay, word came back that a single slick would be coming out to extract the team. Linderer moved over to Clifton's position to see what was going on. It was hard to believe that the enemy would try coming up this slope, steep as it was, and he figured that maybe it was a diversion, with the real attack coming from elsewhere. Then again, Mr. Charles was known to be braver than he was smart, and there was little doubt that he had a definite case of the ass at the Lurps for all the trouble they'd caused. Linderer and Clifton tossed some grenades down the slope, and the movement stopped.

By the time Linderer got back to his own position, a lone slick had appeared high overhead. The pilot radioed for a sit-rep, and Walkabout reminded him about the bomb under the chopper pad, but didn't say anything else too discouraging. The pilot asked for smoke, identified the purple Zo tossed into the center of the abandoned firebase, then spiraled down for the top of the old command bunker, where the Lurps leaped aboard, hardly daring to relax until the ship was well clear of Nui Khe and on its final approach for the Lurp compound Acid Pad back at Camp Eagle.

It was almost dusk when Zo's team off-loaded the ship on the Acid Pad, and the whole company, including Snuffy's team, fell out to welcome them back. The welcome was, however, short-lived. The Command and Control ship landed right behind the slick that had extracted Zo's team, and when Captain Eklund got off, the grim look on his face was enough to put the chill on all the celebration. "Higher" wanted the team reinserted, down into the valley this time—and "Higher" wanted it done *that very night*!

This was complete madness, and Captain Eklund didn't pretend it was anything else. He let Zo know that if he refused the mission, he would be proud to testify on his behalf at the court-martial—providing, of course, that he himself wasn't also being court-martialed. Zo brushed away this offer and instead asked Captain Eklund if he could at least have a man to replace Schwartz, who was suffering from heat prostration and needed to see a medic. Although it was suicidal folly to go into that valley, at night, on an unscouted LZ, after all that had gone on that day to prove that the enemy was there in great strength, and all that had happened to rile the enemy up, there was no shortage of volunteers to take Schwartz's place. Reluctantly, Zo took his pick.

He chose Larry Saenz, who had just come back from

Leech Island with Snuffy Smith's team. Saenz was a good Lurp, and he was still ready for the field, but everyone—even Saenz—suspected that Zo hadn't chosen him because he was a good Lurp or because he was still dressed and geared up for the field. Of all the men who volunteered, Saenz was the one whom Zo knew least, and since this looked like a suicide mission, he couldn't bear to choose one of his closer friends. It seemed a good choice to Linderer and Clifton, who knew Saenz a little better than Zo did, for Saenz was a good man and an experienced RTO. Even if he wouldn't be carrying a radio this time, it was always good to have an extra commo man along when a team seemed certain to take casualties, and there was no telling who might end up taking over the radio.

It was 1930 hours when the insertion flight took off from the Acid Pad and headed for Nui Khe. This time, they did not fly directly to Nui Khe. Instead, the ships flew out toward Firebase Birmingham, then dropped low and headed back east, then south for Nui Khe. The pilots were hoping it would look like an aerial reconnaissance rather than an insertion, and the men on the team were probably hoping that this was just a bad dream. The C&C ship was in the lead, and as it flew over the valley, the belly light kicked on briefly and swept back and forth, the beam hesitating briefly on a large, anvil-shaped boulder before continuing to sweep as the ship flew up the valley. Behind, and without lights, came the insertion ship. When it came to the anvil-shaped boulder, Meachum put the ship into a hover, and the Lurps and bellyman were about to kick out the ladder when the left skid grazed the edge of the boulder and they realized they were low enough to jump out.

The six Lurps landed on the boulder, and as the ship

continued on its way, they jumped about eight feet from the boulder down to the ground. The ground was soft, as if recently plowed, and the Lurps realized that it had probably been churned up by that day's artillery or air strikes. With the choppers gone, the silence was heavy, close, and ominous. No one believed for a moment that the insertion had gone unnoticed.

There was no sense in moving off into the jungle to lay dog. If the Lurps even made it to the jungle, they would just be putting themselves in a position where they'd have to fight their way back to an LZ. The thing to do now was to lay dog with their backs to the boulder, listening. It would be rash to move right then, before they had some sense of where the enemy was and how he was moving. Zo called in a sit-rep, reporting negative contact—negative for the moment, at least—and the choppers headed back to Camp Eagle, leaving the Lurps feeling very alone out there in the darkness, in the midst of a very pissed-off and vindictive enemy. The next move was going to have to be the enemy's, and the Lurps were going to have to react to it. Get some sense of what the enemy was up to first, *then* move.

The Lurps did not have long to wait. The first voices seemed to be coming from the opposite slope, a couple of hundred meters away—maybe closer—maybe *much* closer. Someone shouted out a shrill command, and the voices stopped. Minutes crept past, the Lurps listening intently, peering into the darkness, hoping for some sense of what the enemy was up to so they would have some idea which way to move. Suddenly the silence was broken by the sound of sticks tapping together—then more sticks, and more—a whole line of them, a few hundred meters across. It was a large force of enemy coming on line, using the tapping sticks to stay abreast in the darkness.

Now the Lurps heard the sound of more sticks tapping behind them, and then more sticks above them on the slopes of Nui Khe. Soon the sound of tapping sticks could be heard in all directions, and the Lurps realized that there was no direction in which they could move without having to fight their way out. The enemy had them completely surrounded. They were trapped. There would be no slipping through this encirclement. If they couldn't get an extraction ship in—and get it in soon— they would have to try to break out fighting and then make an escape-and-evasion attempt. The chances of pulling it off seemed slim to the point of impossibility.

Suddenly the sound of a bugle rang out up the valley. It was like something out of a Korean War movie, just before the Red Chinese hordes launched a human wave attack against an American position, and it even chilled Zoschak to hear it.

Zo ordered his teammates to set up four claymores facing upslope behind the team. He whispered for his teammates to wait until the enemy was right on them before blowing the claymores. If they could blow a hole in the enemy's line, they'd have a chance to charge through that way and E&E upslope to the abandoned firebase on the peak of Nui Khe.

Gary Linderer couldn't help remembering how steep that slope had been when he and Clifton had been rolling grenades down it earlier that day. Even if they broke out, there just didn't seem any way they were going to make it up Nui Khe without having to fight all the way. And even if they somehow managed to break out and make it to the top of Nui Khe, what were the chances that the firebase was going to be abandoned and unwatched?

Almost none. Realistically speaking, that was the chance they'd have if they didn't get extracted very soon—none.

None of the Lurps was going to let himself or any of his comrades be taken alive. It was better to die fighting, better to save that last grenade and take some of them along, than to trust the NVA to show professional courtesy and Geneva Convention solicitude to captured Lurps after a day like this.

Captain Eklund came back on the net, whispering. He said that ships were on the way and the extraction was going to be a replay of the insertion. If possible, the team was to get back atop that anvil-shaped boulder, and when the C&C ship came over, Zo was to hit his strobe light. It was going to have to be a ladder extraction, he said, for the insertion ship had clipped trees with its rotor after putting them in.

Zo rogered the transmission, then whispered urgently for his teammates to take the charging handles of their claymores with them and climb back up on the boulder. The banging of the sticks was getting closer, and as the Lurps climbed back onto the flat rock they'd come in on, whistles began shrilling in all directions.

Now the Lurps heard that most welcome of sounds—the *thump-thump* of helicopters coming their way. They weren't out yet, but they might have a chance.

As they turned for their final approach to the valley, Captain "Wild Bill" Meachum, in the extraction ship, glanced at his instruments and cursed wildly for a second, then called W. T. Grant and Ken Roach, in the chase ship.

"One-Eight, this is Two-Five. My altitude indicator just went tits-up. I'm pulling up; it's your extraction."

Of all the times for a goddamned equipment failure,

this just had to be the worst. Grant and Roach had begged to insert Zo's team the second time, but Meachum wouldn't hear of it. Now he was having to turn the extraction over to Grant, and suddenly he was more scared than he'd been when it was still his extraction. He hadn't been all that scared for himself and his crew, but now that it was Grant's, he was scared for them—and for the Lurps. Some things were easier to do than to watch.

For his part, W. T. Grant was now perhaps a little less scared than he'd been when he was worrying about Meachum. This was his extraction now, and there was no time for fear or worry. He was only sixty seconds out. He called Captain Eklund in the C&C ship.

"Guard Six, this is One-Eight. I'm going as low as I can, and I won't be able to see the strobe until I'm on it. Vector me in if I need it."

When Captain Eklund rogered the transmission, Grant switched to his internal and told his co-pilot, Ken "The Teenybopper" Roach, to hit the position lights so they could see how close they were to the trees. His altitude indicator was working fine, but he didn't know how tall the trees were. Roach hit the lights and then started guiding Grant in—up a little now, down a little now— keeping the skids a few feet above the treetops. As soon as Grant could see the strobe light, he went up on the command net, telling Zo to kill it. It was normal Lurp procedure when signaling a chopper overhead to put the strobe light in the barrel of an M-79 grenade launcher so it wouldn't wash over the team, but that wouldn't work with the chopper coming so low, and holding that strobe up like the torch on the Statue of Liberty, for just those few seconds, Zo had made himself into the flashiest human target in the whole world. As soon as he got the word, the light was out and the lines of pale tracers were so much easier to see. They were high and wide, as if the strobe light had ruined the enemy's night vision and thrown the tracers off target.

As Grant was entering his short final approach, Wild Bill Meachum came over the horn, telling him that the whole valley was lighting up with muzzle flashes. Grant told Meachum that was just what he wanted to hear right then, and called him an asshole. Meachum chuckled softly in reply. Grant was a cool one, and a little last-second banter was just what he needed to make him even cooler.

Right over the boulder, Grant brought the ship to a sudden hover, trying to keep one skid on the rock for stability. He ordered his door gunners to open up, but "Loser," on the right—who was usually not a loser at all when the feces hit the fan—told him he was facing a solid rock wall on that side and didn't relish shooting himself with his own machine gun, so "Sugar Bear," on the left, opened up alone.

By this time, Grant could hear M-16 fire from the team and AK fire all around, even over the noise of his rotors. The bellyman kicked out the ladder, and looking down, Grant could see one Lurp grab it and start scrambling up, then the others. The helicopter was shaking as the Lurps climbed aboard, but Linderer and Zoschak were still down there, shooting. Although he knew he couldn't be heard over the racket of his ship and all the firing, Grant hollered down for them to get a move on, they didn't have to kill all the gooks themselves. Linderer grabbed the ladder and pulled himself up, and Zo blew the claymores, damn near scaring Linderer off the ladder. Finally, Zoschak grabbed the ladder, clipped himself to a rung with the snap link on his web gear suspender, and gave the thumbs-up.

With Zo hanging onto the ladder, the extraction ship took off, racing up and out of the enemy fire with torque at the max. When they were at last safely up and away, and out of range of enemy fire, Grant released the controls to Roach and with shaking hands lit a cigarette, then tossed the pack back to the Lurps—all of them except Zoschak, of course, for Zo was riding home still clipped to the ladder below.

For four days, around the clock, the area around Nui Khe was hit with everything from 105s and aerial rockets to a B-52 Arc Light mission, as Uncle Sam poured in the ordnance and put the taxpayers' money to work. The rocket attacks on Hue and Camp Eagle stopped—for those four days. But then, on the evening of the eighth, the NVA managed to fire off four rockets at Camp Eagle. The rockets seemed to be aimed at the Lurp compound and the nearby 17th Cav, but they did little damage, and no rockets were launched against the civilian populations of Hue and Phu Bai.

Sure enough, the rockets came from the north side of Nui Khe, proving once again that for guts and tenacity, you had to give the enemy some real credit in this war.

A few decorations finally came down for the Lurps, and the Kingsmen involved got a few medals, too, though the pilots didn't really need more medals, and as usual the gunners didn't get what they fully deserved for riding along with the crazy bastards, keeping the ships flying, and keeping the enemy's head down when the going got rough.

As if they'd been a personal sort of message to the Lurps, those four rockets on the evening of the eighth were the last for a spell, and "Higher" dropped its plan to keep rotating teams in on just those two recon zones.

\* \* \*

Almost everyone, including Zoschak himself, had assumed that Nui Khe would probably be his last mission before going home on extension leave—if not his last mission on this mortal coil. But he was wrong. Just a few days after that little doubleheader out by Nui Khe, Zo was out again, with Saenz as a full-time team member, on what was supposed to be a four-day area reconnaissance mission.

On the first day, Zo's team managed to come across an enemy unit of somewhere between platoon and company size, and followed it, unseen, until it broke up into smaller elements, after which they spent the next three days following what seemed to be the largest of the elements and was therefore probably the command element. More than once during this time they lost the enemy unit, but never for long, and by the time "Higher" began demanding some sort of resolution—preferably gunships and extraction of the team—Zo had already gotten the enemy squad's schedule down right nicely and taken note of a few of its more obvious weaknesses. When the time came to bring the mission to an end, Zo had his team wait until the enemy stacked arms for chow, and then he and his team hit them—but didn't kill all of them right off. At one point, Zo was forced to call for gunship support and extraction, for the survivors of the large squad he'd hit showed some balls, and another squad or two must've come to their assistance more quickly than Zo had expected. But just as the Kingsmen slicks and 17th Cav gunships were cranking up to come help them, Zo called back telling them to disregard that last transmission and relax—but stay close to their ships. When asked what had happened to the NVA they were fighting, Zo's reply was characteristically laconic. He said that they had died.

Ray Zoschak was a modest fellow, and enough of a genuine hero to allow himself a good laugh at heroics, and particularly inflated heroics. It would have amused him no end to know that, somehow, his team and its supporting fires were reported to have killed at least 151 NVA on that mission, wiping out a whole company. But he would have been the first to scoff and say it was nothing but an overstrength squad, and they probably hadn't killed or seriously wounded more than eight or nine people, and that the rest had probably got away.

Shortly after this mission, Zoschak himself finally got away on his extension leave, wearing the first of his Silver Stars. He took Mr. Poley with him, and it seems only sensible to assume they cut quite a bold swath through the civilian population back home.

When they got back from their leaves and learned all that had happened in the month they were gone, Zo and Poley would curse themselves mercilessly for not having been there.

# Chapter Eighteen

On November 14, 1968, four F/58 Lurp teams went into recon zones on a north-south axis just east of the Ashau Valley. Because the cloud ceiling didn't lift until mid-morning, it was late morning before the last team went in, and that was not a good time to insert Americans by helicopter anywhere near the Ashau Valley. "Higher" apparently considered these missions so pressing that the few more hours it would have taken to wait for last-light insertions could not be wasted. Under less pressing circumstances—a brigade commander wanting some general information about a potential Area of Operations, or the division wanting to check out the far edge of its assigned Area of Interest—the decision to postpone the insertions until last light, or to try again the next day, might have been left to Captain Eklund and the pilots. But there was a sense of urgency about these missions, and in their long, uncertain wait by the chopper pad for the fog to lift enough out in the mountains for the helicopters, the Lurps on the teams picked up on the urgency. Although it contributed somewhat to their already enormous self-esteem to think that their missions were too urgent to put off until last light or the next morning, the thought of inserting by helicopter so late in the morning, and so far out, was a little disconcerting to almost all the Lurps and air-crews.

The Lurps on the four teams pulling the missions hadn't been briefed on the big picture, the strategic implications of these missions. But they weren't entirely stupid, and to the extent that they concerned themselves with the doings of very senior officers and civilian field marshals, they understood that "Higher" probably didn't stop with the division commander this time. These missions might not take the Lurps across any deniable inter-national borders, or even into the Ashau Valley itself. But as the morning dragged on and the Lurps who cared about such things speculated and gossiped with the heli-copter crews, the conviction grew that these were mis-sions that would have gone to MACV-SOG if the Green Berets and their indigenous teammates over at FOB 1 hadn't been so hard-pressed, understrength, and other-wise engaged at the time.

Of course, the Green Berets at FOB 1 never talked about their missions, and the Lurps knew better than to ask. But because F/58 LRP, Command and Control North's FOB 1, and the Force Recon Marines (when they were lucky) shared helicopter crews, enlisted door gun-ners were a great conduit of information. The Lurps always had a pretty good idea what the local Green Berets and Recon Marines were up to.

Despite the fact that he was too elite to personally shoot the shit with mere door gunners, Sergeant Al Con-treros always had his own ideas about strategic implica-tions, and as the teams waited by the chopper pad, he waxed portentous about how these missions were so important they were probably being directed from the secret War Room in the White House basement. The Communists were gearing up for a new Tet offensive, he was sure, but this time they were going to be stopped before they got ten kilometers east of the Ashau. According to Contreros, the Lurps were getting the missions instead of FOB 1 because MACV-SOG recon teams were overwhelmingly manned by indigenous personnel, some of whom were surely Communist agents. Contreros was of the opinion that Force Recon Marines were as trustworthy as 101st Airborne Lurps, but not nearly so adaptable, being hampered by the notorious "Marine Corps mentality," and that's why *they* weren't getting the missions. Contreros told Kenn Miller, who had just returned from R&R and wished he was going on one of the other teams, that he expected to be running missions into North Vietnam by spring—that's how stoked up he was on his own strategic role.

Finally, word came to board the ships, and the pilots cranked up. When all four insertions went well, everyone—even Miller—breathed a little easier.

That first afternoon, all four teams found heavily traveled high-speed trails. Commo was generally good, and so were the opportunities to observe enemy troop movement. For three days and three nights, the NVA kept the four Lurp teams very alert and observant, and the four teams kept the radio relay teams on the firebases and the TOC back at Camp Eagle busy taking their sitreps and SALUTE reports. SALUTE was an acronym for Size-Activity-Location-Uniform (or Unit)-Time (and Terrain)-Equipment observed, a mnemonic device to aid the memory when reporting an enemy sighting. And although not a one of the twenty-four Lurps in the field was even minimally qualified to so much as venture a guess about the *units* of the North Vietnamese soldiers they were seeing—and though they couldn't always get an accurate count, or see all the equipment—they were seeing beaucoup bad guys, and these bad guys were plenty well equipped.

The missions were originally scheduled for four days and nights, but on the seventeenth, one of the teams got spotted, and after a brief exchange of automatic fire that probably didn't do more than give both sides a scare and an adrenaline rush, the Lurps and the NVA both broke contact—the NVA no doubt to regroup and call in help from their buddies, the Lurps wisely heading for the closest preplotted LZ, calling for extraction along the way. There had to be at least a couple of regiments' worth of NVA within an hour's hump on those high-speed trails that seemed to be everywhere, and now that their presence was compromised, it was time for the Lurps to go home, and go home quickly.

While he was out extracting this compromised team with his favorite 2/17th Cav and Kingsmen chopper crews, Captain Eklund decided to go ahead and also extract the next closest team. This was done after taking the first team home and refueling. While it was carrying the second team home, the little armada of three slicks and two gunships took some ineffective but sobering .51-caliber antiaircraft fire, the fat glowing tracers arching short beneath the C&C ship and almost mesmerizing Captain Eklund with their beauty.

The remaining two teams came out without incident on the morning of the eighteenth, and on the afternoon of that very same day, a mission order came down for F/58 to furnish two twelve-man heavy teams for insertion at last light the next day into the Rung Roung.

Due to rotations and extension leaves, the company was very short of personnel, which meant that the Lurps who'd just come back from east of the Ashau were going to be going back out without even enough turnaround time to care for their equipment, wash the camouflage paint out of the creases of their faces, or adequately prepare for the new missions. There was a little sour joking along the lines of "Out of the Ashau, into the Rung Roung," and a lot of hurried effort to get ready.

The team leaders of the two heavy teams were to be Sergeant Contreros and SSG Burnell, and since the two recon zones were not far apart, they took the overflight together. It was a quick, high-level overflight, but it was apparent, even from a quick pass high above, that there was only one possible LZ in all of Contreros's recon zone. When the two team leaders got back to Camp Eagle, there was a lot of work waiting for them. For one thing, the available personnel had to be apportioned between the two teams. One of the men slated to go out with Contreros, Kenn Miller, requested that he be allowed to go out on Burnell's team instead because Burnell was the only team leader in the company he hadn't been out with before, and he'd had his fill of Contreros. Besides, Lieutenant Williams was going out as Burnell's ATL, and it was a novelty to go out on a mission with an officer. When Arthur Herringhausen volunteered to change places and go out on Contreros's team, the switch was made. Terry Clifton, who was originally scheduled to go out on Burnell's team, then decided to change places with Jim Schwartz so that he could go to the field with his best friend, Gary Linderer. Linderer told him he was crazy, for Burnell's team had all the LZs, but Clifton laughed it off. Both teams were going into the Rung Roung, and Linderer was sorely mistaken if he thought Burnell's team had an abundance of LZs.

The Rung Roung was right up there with the Ashau when it came to hairy places to pull a mission, and everyone packed a heavy load of grenades, claymores, and ammunition. The chances of making contact were excellent—and built into the missions. Burnell's team was to observe enemy troop movement, with a secondary mission of locating and destroying a COSVN radio site that intelligence claimed to have pinpointed for the team. It had been decided to send a Lurp heavy team after the radio site, rather than an air strike, because it was hoped that the Lurps would be able to capture equipment, codes, commo logs, and maybe a prisoner or two. Contreros's team had the mission of ambushing whatever small parties of enemy soldiers they might find traveling on the abundant trails in their area, and it was hoped that they might even be able to capture or kill the commander of the 5th NVA Regiment or some of his staff officers. Always one to let slip his special knowledge of the big picture, Contreros told his team that they were also going to be acting as a blocking force for an infantry battalion being inserted on the other side of where the 5th NVA regiment had its base camp. This was not comforting news, particularly to those who knew Contreros well, for Contreros seemed to take a little too much pleasure in the thought of a whole battalion chasing a whole regiment his way. Even Gary Linderer, who had never been out with Contreros before, knew that Al was just a little bit too gung-ho—and a damn sight too medal-hungry—for his own good and the good of the men on his team.

It gets dark early in Vietnam in November, and Burnell's team left Camp Eagle aboard two slicks at 1615 hours. It wouldn't be a true last-light insertion, for they'd have a couple of hours of light once they got on the ground—but they'd need it. Burnell's team was going in on a bare mountaintop that had once, briefly, served as a firebase. In their wake, aboard a separate flight of helicopters, would come a Lurp radio relay team, a handful of Pathfinders, and a security detachment of air-rifle troops from the 17th Cav. Burnell's heavy team would need the remaining hours of daylight to get off the mountain and down into their recon zone.

There were four insertion ships available for this mission, and when Burnell's team took off, Contreros's team waited aboard their helicopters. Before long, the pilots cranked the engines, and the insertion ships lifted off the chopper pad. They'd be rendezvousing with the Command and Control ship and the gunships out over the mountains after Burnell's team went in.

As they flew west, the Lurps on Contreros's team looked out the helicopter doors and down at the darkly ominous shadows and hills. When the insertion ships were on station, the C&C ship and gunships that had accompanied Burnell's team were already waiting for them in high orbit.

There were no good places to make false insertions, no route for a low approach, and the ships had to spiral down to get close to the LZ. The LZ was just a small, grassy clearing off a long, winding ridge, and no sane infantry company—no sane conventional pilots—would even consider it a landing zone, except under emergency conditions. But to the Lurps and the Kingsmen, it looked more than adequate from the air.

Dusk was already coming on as Wild Bill Meachum's ship, carrying Contreros and the first chalk of his heavy team, hovered over the LZ. To the men aboard Mr. Grant's ship, the first helicopter seemed to hover there a long time, the main rotor clipping tree branches, and the rotor wash causing a storm in the tall elephant grass. But then Lurps began dropping from the skids, and Meachum's ship lifted up and out. Back in Grant's ship, John Sours was monitoring his radio and yelled out over the helicopter noise, saying that Captain Eklund had ordered an abort, but one of the men was already out, so the rest had gone with him. Now, it was time for the second chalk, in Grant's ship, to go in.

As the second group of Lurps got out on the skids, Grant's rotors were already chopping wood and scattering leaves. The ship was as low as it could get, and the waving elephant grass was still a good eight or ten feet below the skids. The six Lurps squatted down, then hung from their arms on the skids before dropping off. From a hanging position under the skids, it was only four feet down to the elephant grass. But from the top to the bottom of the elephant grass, it had to be a twelve-foot drop—twelve feet under eighty or a hundred pounds of pack and equipment onto hard, broken ground, and hidden teak logs.

The drop jarred everyone, but it really injured John Sours. His best friend since Jump School and Pathfinder School, Frank Souza, wanted to call the choppers back and get him medevacked out, but Sours wouldn't hear of it. He said that all he had was a mere two twisted ankles, and he didn't intend to let his ankles slow him down. With Sours limping painfully, the second chalk moved off the LZ to join the first chalk in the woodline. All the men who'd gone in with Contreros had a few bruises and bumps from the insertion, but none of them was hurt as badly as Sours.

After laying dog and releasing the ships, the heavy team moved into double-canopy jungle with fairly light undergrowth. It wasn't dark yet, and the Lurps had decent fields of vision, but the jungle was a gloom of twilight, and it was a little like looking through thick, greenish water. Ten meters from where they'd laid dog off the LZ, they found a well-maintained high-speed trail running east to west along the base of the ridge. The branches overhead had been laced together to conceal the trail from the air, and it bore so much sign of recent passage the bootprints had pretty much obliterated each other. Maybe a graduate of the British tracking school in Malaysia could have made sense of the prints, but even Contreros couldn't claim that level of expertise, so he sent a two-man point recon to the west and another to the east.

Herringhausen and Reiff went to the west, Linderer and Souza to the east. Contreros wanted information about the trail, and he wanted it before it got too dark, so both point recon elements were encouraged to move as far as they could and to move as fast as they could.

If anything, the trail seemed to get wider, harder packed, the farther east Linderer and Souza paralleled it. They hadn't gone more than fifty meters when they spotted a little trail watcher's bunker, which fortunately turned out to be unoccupied at the moment. The farther east they moved, the higher the trail climbed on the ridge, and before long Linderer and Souza could no longer parallel it, so they made a knowingly rash decision to move up onto it, and follow it a little farther. Light was beginning to fail. When they were already a hundred and fifty meters from Contreros and the others, Linderer and Souza heard a signal shot about three hundred meters farther east. Souza was on point, and when he heard the shot, he stepped backward as if in slow motion and motioned to Linderer. It was time to get back.

Reiff and Herringhausen had already returned and briefed Contreros. They'd seen more than enough enemy sign to convince them that this area was definitely hot. When Linderer and Souza reported the bunker, Contreros only nodded. When they reported the warning shot, he said he'd heard it, too, and had assumed, at first, that it was them, except that it sounded too far away. When they reported a little knoll they had found along the trail, Contreros finally showed some real enthusiasm. When Linderer and Souza agreed that it might make a good ambush site, Contreros gave the sign for everyone to saddle up and get back in the rucksack straps, for they were moving out.

The move was not easy on Sours. His ankles were more than merely twisted. They were broken and already badly swollen. Linderer and Souza moved with him, both of them worried, both of them fretting silently about the possibility that Sours would have to move fast in a contact or try to escape and evade on those ankles. It was already past nautical twilight when the Lurps moved into position on that knoll and began to run out their claymores. It was too dark to reliably daisy-chain them together, so placement was critical. The idea was to make an L-shaped ambush, hitting the trail from the side with the claymores and small arms fire and sweeping down it with overlapping claymores. When the claymores were set up and camouflaged as well as possible in the darkness, the Lurps who'd planted them returned to their positions and hooked up the charging handles. Some of the men were only ten meters from their claymores, within danger range of the backblast, and some of them were almost as close to the even more deadly outer sweep of one of the downtrail claymores. If they had to blow this ambush, they'd have to get just as low to the ground as they could. Fortunately, there was a slight rise, almost a small berm, between them and the kill zone. Still, five of the Lurps—Jim Venable, Steve Czepurny, Billy Walkabout, Gary Linderer, and Art Herringhausen—were within five meters of the trail.

Weapons, grenades, spare magazines, and claymore charging handles close at hand, the men on Contreros's heavy team settled into position for the night. Alert and silent, they listened intently to the sounds of the jungle, almost certain that before the night was through, they would have enemy traffic on their trail.

An hour or so before midnight, a light drizzle fell, and when it was over the Lurps spotted the dim glow of oil lanterns coming down the trail toward them from the east.

More often than not, when Lurps saw the enemy passing on a trail they were monitoring, the enemy was moving as if secure in the knowledge that this was *their* rear area, talking, smoking, carrying their weapons slung. That was not the case that night. The first enemy patrol really did seem to be a patrol. They were moving with weapons in hand and on the alert. The Lurps slipped the safeties off their claymore charging handles, eased their rifles off safe, and lay there quietly, hardly breathing, as the enemy passed. It certainly seemed that the enemy was aware that there were Lurps in the area. They were moving in a patrol formation, with a small fire team or squad-size point element followed by a much larger body of troops. The Lurps had the distinct impression that the point element was being offered as bait to spring any ambushes so that the larger element—which seemed to be at least platoon-size—could then move in and clean up. Even Contreros was not rash enough to take this bait.

All night, the heavy team stayed in position, and at intervals throughout the night, groups of enemy passed them without ever knowing they were there. Once or twice it was only a couple of soldiers. But usually it was the same pattern as earlier—a squad or fire team followed by a platoon or more. The Lurps sat tight and let the enemy pass.

By dawn, Sours's ankles were so swollen he couldn't lace his boots and so painful they couldn't bear his weight. It was obvious that he'd have to be extracted. Contreros directed Terry Clifton, Riley "The Bulldozer" Cox, and Frank Souza to take Sours back to the LZ while he called for a medevac ship equipped with a cable and litter. With his brother Lurps supporting him and providing security, Sours limped painfully off into the jungle, avoiding the trail. At about 0730 hours, the Lurps still in position next to the trail could hear the medevac ship, and Contreros whispered into his radio headset, reminding the crew that they'd be looking for a flash panel, not a smoke grenade. Within five minutes of first hearing its approach, the Lurps by the trail heard the helicopter lift away from the LZ and move down the valley. Shortly afterward they were rejoined by Clifton, Cox, and Souza.

Almost immediately, two signal shots rang out, sounding as if they came from two or three hundred meters to the east. This seemed to be a good sign. There was no way to be certain, but the Lurps figured that the enemy had mistaken the medevac of Sours for an extraction of the whole team and was giving the "all clear."

If this had been purely a reconnaissance mission, the team would have moved out as soon as Sours was medevacked. But this was not a pure area recon. It was a surveillance mission, and an ambush mission, and because the ambush site was almost perfect, the heavy team stayed in position. Daylight showed that the claymores were well placed, the mines themselves and their wires well concealed. There was no sign of American bootprints on the trail, and the Lurps were well camouflaged and behind cover, slight as it was. If a manageable group of enemy came bopping down that trail thinking the Lurps had been extracted, they were going to be in for a sudden, fatal surprise.

Shortly before 0900, someone did come bopping down that trail. The Lurps heard the enemy soldiers before they saw them. There were three of them, in green uniforms, and they were jabbering away, just as carefree as could be. It was impossible to be sure, but from the sound and the way they moved, they did not seem to have anyone behind them. The Lurps waited, frozen, their hands on the charging handles of their claymores, their fingers inside the trigger guards of their rifles if they had no claymores. Everyone was waiting tensely for Contreros to initiate the ambush, but Contreros decided to let these three NVA pass and wait for a more promising target.

Half an hour later, the Lurps heard voices again. Contreros rose up on his knees and craned forward to peer down the trail. His face was camouflaged black, without a trace of green, and he was in deep shadow. As long as he didn't move quickly, or smile, or let his eyes get too wide with excitement, he was almost invisible. Gary Linderer looked at Contreros, then looked down the trail just as the first NVA soldier appeared in his kill zone. The man was wearing olive drab fatigues, a boonie hat, a towel around his neck, and a rucksack on his back. For just an instant, Linderer thought he might be a South Vietnamese soldier, but before he could even reason this out to the conclusion that there weren't supposed to be any South Vietnamese soldiers out here, Contreros snapped his fingers, signaling the ambush. Linderer squeezed the charging handle, and his claymore went off simultaneously with the other five. There was a deafening roar. Sticks and leaves and debris from the backblast washed over the ambushers, and the Lurps opened up with their M-16s and CAR-15s, hosing down the kill zone on full automatic.

When the firing stopped, there was a long, horrible moaning out on the trail. Linderer rose cautiously, and as he did he caught some movement from the corner of his eye. It was the enemy point man. Somehow, he had survived the ambush and he was sprinting back down the trail in the direction of that trailwatcher's bunker. Linderer opened up on full automatic, draining a whole magazine, hitting limbs all around the man but not seeming to hit him. Souza leaped up and took off after the enemy point man, firing as he ran. The point man's towel went flying as he took a hit that should have stopped him, but he just hunched over and kept on going, then cut off the trail into the jungle and headed back the way he had come. There was blood on his towel, and blood where he'd cut off the trail, but the wound hadn't stopped him, or apparently even slowed him down much. This was good luck for the NVA point man but bad luck for the Lurps.

Out in the kill zone, the security team was going to work. Linderer and Souza joined them. One of the enemy soldiers was still clinging to life, still moaning. It was briefly hoped that the soldier might be dragged away and medevacked as a prisoner. Counting his chickens after the eggs were already broken, Contreros called in that he had a prisoner. But the moaning soldier's wounds were too grievous, and when the moaning stopped, everyone knew he was dead.

Except it wasn't a he—it was a she. To their shock, Linderer and Souza discovered that two of the three dead in front of Linderer's claymore position were female. Even mangled as he was, the male appeared to be some sort of staff officer. His hands were soft, and there were broken, gore-splattered eyeglasses a few feet from his body. Both of the females were mangled, too, but one of them had survived long enough to moan and get the team leader's hopes up. If she had to be out there at all, Linderer wished she'd gone instantly, like the others.

There was another female among the dead. When they had stripped the bodies of weapons and equipment, the Lurps understood the presence of females a little better. They had ambushed a medical unit, and the three dead women were apparently nurses. This momentarily shook Gary Linderer, for his fiancée back home was a nurse. When he discovered that at least one of the nurses had been armed, he felt a little better. His fiancée didn't run around with any soldiers but him, and she didn't go about armed.

The dead NVA had not been heavily armed. Only one of the men had been carrying an AK. Two of the men had holstered 1911-style .45 pistols on their hips. One of the nurses had been carrying a third .45 in the bottom of her rucksack. All three nurses had been humping rucksacks, and all three rucksacks were full of medical supplies. One of the men had been carrying a rucksack full of documents, but no one was carrying much in the way of canteens and field gear. By NVA standards, these people had been REMFs. Their lack of much field gear, food, or water indicated that they had not planned on moving very far. Their lack of security indicated that they'd considered themselves fairly safe. These were not the sort of people the NVA sent down the trail when they feared there might be Lurps lurking about. Those two signal shots earlier must have been an "all clear" message. The enemy must have assumed the whole team had been extracted with Sours.

Now, of course, was the time to book out of there. The last thing any sane person does is stick around the site of a successful ambush—but that is just what Al Contreros decided to do. He'd reported the ambush and the "prisoner," and then he'd reported the rucksack full of documents. Captain Eklund had called back that a reaction force was on the way to "develop the situation" and that the team was going to be extracted, given fresh ammo and claymores on the helicopter, then be reinserted on the other side of the ridge, closer to Burnell's recon zone.

Captain Eklund didn't say anything about getting the team away from the ambush site, because that was standard operational procedure and just good common sense, and he assumed Contreros knew it. His job was to support the teams and help them when they needed help—not to micromanage their movement or insult experienced team leaders by reminding them of the most elementary basics. Every Lurp knew that ambushes had to be hit-and-run affairs and that the only thing to do after springing one was to book out as soon as you'd searched and stripped, and maybe booby-trapped, the bodies.

Contreros knew that it was time to get moving, but he seemed in no hurry. The sticky-sweet stench of death was heavy in the air, and now every NVA for a kilometer or two in every direction surely knew that the Lurps had not all been extracted. Still, Contreros did not move his team. When they saw that they'd be staying, Cox and Walkabout calmly broke open their Lurp ration bags and had a little breakfast, their rifles in their laps, at the ready. Most of the other Lurps were nervous and fuming. Venable pleaded with Contreros in whispers, but Contreros shook his head and would not be moved. Linderer eased over and tried to reason with him, but Contreros let him know that he knew exactly what he was doing, and he wasn't moving the team before the reaction force came in. The fact that beaucoup NVA were surely on their way at that very moment, and wouldn't be too kindly disposed toward American Lurps when they saw what the Lurps had done, didn't seem to faze Contreros at all. He seemed to be planning to ambush the ambush, and he seemed right smug about his cleverness in coming up with the totally unconventional idea of doing so. The fact that it was unconventional because it was suicidally stupid didn't seem to impress Al much.

Burnell came on the horn, whispering softly to Contreros, gloating a little about the fact that Contreros had reported a prisoner a little too prematurely, and Contreros whispered something back that made Burnell smile.

Burnell's team had already found the long-abandoned COSVN radio site, some Chinese characters recently carved into a tree near the commo site, and the broken rice bowl and the skeleton of an NVA trailwatcher that Schwartz identified as one Zoschack had killed on a previous mission months before. But their recon zone seemed strangely cold, as if it had been abandoned. For a while, Burnell had been frowning with jealousy at the thought of Contreros's getting a prisoner, when he'd hoped to get one first. He'd even whispered "Die, bitch, die" over the radio when he heard the prisoner was female. Now that he knew the prisoner was dead, it was almost his duty to rag Contreros a little, and by the smile Contreros brought to Burnell's face with his reply, Contreros was taking her loss with good humor.

Being only a few klicks away, but far enough so that no one on his team had heard the claymores or the firing of Contreros's ambush, Burnell had no idea that Contreros was keeping his team right where they'd sprung the ambush. Like Captain Eklund, Burnell had more confidence in Contreros than anyone on Contreros's team had anymore.

Contreros was staying put until the reaction force came in. And if the enemy came back to police up the bodies before the reaction force got there, he was going to develop the situation himself—him and his team.

Forty-five minutes after radioing the team that a reaction force would be coming in, and the team coming out, Captain Eklund had to call back with the bad news that there would be no reaction force and there would be no extraction. All the helicopters assigned to the entire 101st Airborne Division were already committed elsewhere— all except for one "loach," a Light Observation Helicopter (LOH). Eklund told Contreros that he would be out in that LOH, trying to cover the team until it could get some real support. He told Contreros to move the team to a defensible location closer to the landing zone.

By that time, Contreros must've been thinking way ahead of everyone—not just the enemy and his own team-mates, but ahead of Captain Eklund, too. Instead of taking the team down toward the LZ, he decided to move the team higher on the ridge to the west, then have Captain Eklund, in the LOH, direct the team to a new pickup point.

Still, Contreros dawdled. The team was rucked up, but had just begun to move when the Lurps heard Captain Eklund's LOH circling overhead. The jungle canopy was somewhat thinner farther up the ridge, and Contreros sent his ATL, Jim Venable, forward to try to signal Captain Eklund with a mirror.

Venable moved ten or fifteen meters up the ridge, then paused under a break in the canopy where he could flash the LOH with his mirror. Just as he raised his arm with the mirror, several AK-47s simultaneously opened up on him, hitting him in the neck, arm, and chest. Venable went down. Cox and Souza rushed forward and dragged him back to a hasty perimeter that the rest of the team immediately formed.

Now the NVA began to pour fire down on the Lurps. The Lurps were on the ground, and most of the fire was high, showering them with twigs and leaves and sticks. Contreros got on the radio to Eklund, reporting contact and one man wounded. He needed a medevac for Venable, and he needed it quickly.

Unfortunately, Contreros must not have been too forthcoming about his location in earlier transmissions, for Captain Eklund and the LOH pilot still did not have a fix on the team's position. As Contreros asked again about a medevac, Captain Eklund broke in and informed him that two Cobra gunships had been released to come to their aid and would be on station in ten minutes. A medevac would be on the way as soon as humanly possible. In the meantime, the team was to hold tight.

An NVA platoon came charging uphill from down in the direction of the LZ. They were only forty meters or so away, running from tree to tree, firing as they came. Now the Lurps had enemy above them and below them. Clifton, Souza, and Linderer were the closest to the attackers, and responded immediately with a heavy volume of fire—"Bulldozer" Cox joining in with the shotgun he'd brought along as a supplement to his CAR-15. The Lurps could see some of the enemy go down, but they were too busy to count. The charge faltered, and as the enemy faded back into the jungle the Lurps tossed grenades down after them.

The medevac ship was only minutes out and closing fast, but Captain Eklund still hadn't been able to pinpoint the team's location. Venable's teammates had bandaged him the best they could, trying to stop the bleeding, seal the chest wound, and keep him from going into shock. Venable's spirit was strong. But it was clear that if he didn't get evacuated to a hospital soon, he was going to die.

Now the Cobras came on station. But without knowing where the team was, there was almost nothing they could do. Hoping to pinpoint the team's location for the helicopters, Walkabout tossed a smoke grenade onto the trail, but the smoke drifted down the trail, then dissipated in the trees. Captain Eklund came over the horn, saying he was going to have the LOH fly crisscross patterns, and telling Contreros to let him know when he passed overhead.

The enemy chose this moment to attack again—this time coming from the west and the south in a coordinated attack, firing as they came. The Lurps managed to stop them, but they knew it was only temporary—and they knew they couldn't keep this up forever. For all that they'd come out loaded for bear, if the fighting kept up much longer they were going to run out of ammunition and grenades.

Finally, Captain Eklund got a fix on the team's position and was able to make use of the Cobras. He had the LOH pilot come in low, skimming the treetops to the team's west, and he dropped the Cobras in, first blasting the ridgeline with rockets, then making gun runs to the south of the team.

Within seconds, the medevac was overhead, lowering a jungle penetrator through the canopy. On the first attempt, the penetrator's cable snagged in vegetation, but the second attempt brought it right down into the beleaguered team's little perimeter. Venable was quickly strapped onto the penetrator, lifted through the trees, and pulled aboard the helicopter. As the medevac ship pulled up and then away, the enemy attacked again, from the southwest, and for a moment it seemed that Venable had a better chance of surviving than any of his teammates.

But the Lurps' fire and grenades were devastating. Never one to worry about a heavy load, Riley Cox had brought close to a thousand rounds of M-16 ammo and a few hundred shotgun shells along with him, and he was out on the left flank, working away with his twelve-gauge. As the NVA began to pull back, Contreros yelled for everyone to get down, and a Cobra came swooping over them, blazing away with its miniguns. Hot brass rained down on the Lurps, and the jungle around them began to smoke.

Under the Cobras' onslaught, the NVA seemed to have abandoned its frontal assault tactics, at least for the moment. But they had not abandoned the fight. There was just enough incoming fire to force the Lurps to keep their heads down, and for the most part the Lurps now held their fire. They still had claymores, but no way to put them out. Cox signaled the others that he still had plenty of shotgun shells and hadn't yet seriously dipped into his supply of M-16 ammo, but for the others, things were getting a little tight. Most of the men were down to ten magazines or less, and two or three grenades.

When it came to ammunition, however, the Cobras were in even worse shape. They had expended their loads and would have to return to Camp Eagle to rearm and refuel. When Captain Eklund informed Contreros of this, and Contreros passed the word on to his team, morale took a definite drop. And to make matters worse, the LOH was also running on empty and would have to go back with the Cobras. Captain Eklund radioed that another pair of Cobras was on the way and would be turned over to the team when they arrived, and he promised to be back as soon as possible with whatever help he could get. But in the meantime, the Lurps were once again going to be on their own.

With the helicopters gone, silence descended ominously over the team. It wasn't really silence, for there were sounds of movement in the trees and some faint moaning downslope, but it felt like silence without the helicopters.

It was a miracle that only Venable had been wounded so far, and something of a miracle that Venable was now on his way to the hospital. But miracles don't generally come in long serial strings, and everyone, probably even including Contreros, was now worried and scared. Except for the enemy, the Lurps were alone.

But they were not without friends. As soon as the helicopters were safely away, Contreros called for an artillery fire mission, and the guns on Firebase Spear and Firebase Brick went into action. Artillery rounds began to impact all around the team—all around, but still too far out. At first, Contreros seemed reluctant to adjust fire closer than a hundred meters from the team's position, and there were plenty of enemy soldiers closer than that. With artillery rounds falling behind them, and only a few Lurps in front of them, the enemy had only one way to move, and that was right into—and over—the team. Of all the times for Contreros to turn cautious, this was not the time.

Finally, he caught on, and he began to walk the rounds to within fifty meters of the team's position. Shrapnel ripped through the treetops overhead, occasional hot jagged pieces falling within the perimeter. The Lurps hugged the ground—and fortunately, so did the NVA.

For forty-five minutes, the cannon cockers on Brick and Spear kept the rounds coming in, and the rounds kept the enemy at bay. Then, at 1330 hours, Captain Eklund came back over the horn. He was in a Huey slick, and he had four Cobras with him, ready to come in as soon as Contreros called off the artillery. By this time, the team had been in contact for four hours.

Contreros had the artillery cease firing, and the Cobras swooped in with supporting fire. Contreros was up on one knee next to his RTO, Jim Bacon, the headset pressed to his ear, looking surprisingly calm. Suddenly, Heringhausen hollered out that the enemy was moving up on the other side of the trail. Walkabout and Linderer tossed off their last grenades in the direction of the movement, then Contreros started screaming, "Pull back! Pull back! Tighten the perimeter! I'm going to bring the gunships in closer!"

The other Lurps were up now, in a crouch, firing and moving back to tighten the perimeter around the team leader, but Gary Linderer stayed down, crawling up the hill, pushing and pulling his rucksack with him. Linderer was just about to give up his crawling and make a crouched dash for Contreros's position when there was a deafening explosion and something slapped his leg.

A large cloud of black smoke billowed down the ridge, rolling over the knoll where the Lurps had been tightening their perimeter. His ears still ringing, debris still showering down on him, Linderer looked up through the smoke and couldn't believe what he was seeing. Seconds before, nine men had been crouched and fighting on their feet, but now they were gone. Everyone was down, and Linderer was sure that he was the only one alive.

Then he saw Walkabout sit up. Walkabout's hands and forearms were red, his face etched with pain. He looked at Linderer, and then both of them looked across what had been their perimeter at Riley Cox. Cox was trying to sit up, but having some difficulty doing so. He had been hit all over, but the Bulldozer was strong, and he looked wonderful to Walkabout and Linderer. The only way to put the Bulldozer out of action was to kill him, and he wasn't dead yet.

Reiff was dead, pinned to a shattered tree. Jim Bacon was alive, but horribly wounded and obviously in great pain. Contreros lay draped over Bacon's legs, apparently dead. Souza was folded over his rucksack, unmoving. Linderer looked over at Terry Clifton, his best friend, who should have been on Burnell's team. His throat was gone, his blood fanning up in a spray, then falling back on the debris-strewn jungle floor. Clifton struggled to roll over and couldn't quite manage it. He looked over at Linderer, pain, shock, and fear in his eyes, and Linderer had to look away. There was nothing he could do for his friend—nothing. It was all over for Clifton. It was all over for all of them.

Linderer must have passed out, for the next thing he knew, Walkabout was down next to him, yelling in his face, telling him that everyone else was down and asking if he could walk. Damn Walkabout! The last thing Linderer wanted just then was someone yelling in his face, asking him questions he couldn't answer. Linderer had always liked Walkabout. Everyone had always liked the stocky little Cherokee wrestler from Oklahoma. But goddamn him, didn't he know better than to come yelling in a man's face at a time like this?

"Linderer! Snap out of it!" Walkabout shouted. "Can you walk?"

Linderer shook his head, and then he snapped out of it and tried to get up. His right leg wouldn't hold him, and he collapsed back, trying to remember if he'd been hit. He was feeling no pain, but his leg wouldn't work, so he had to be hit. Everyone else was hit, and some of them were dead. It was all very confusing, all very strange, but Linderer managed to tell Walkabout to get on the radio and contact Captain Eklund. The CO had to know what was going on down there. They were all finished, and Captain Eklund had to know about it.

Walkabout ran back to Bacon's position. Bacon was already in touch with Captain Eklund, reporting the team's condition, but his own condition was not so good, and he seemed on the verge of shock. Linderer crawled over and helped Walkabout pull the team leader's body off Bacon's legs. There was a big chunk of flesh missing above Bacon's knee, and even though he was determined to stay on the radio, Linderer and Walkabout could see that he was starting to go into shock, so they gave him what help they could, slapping a dressing on his wound and trying to elevate his legs a little. They they went off to see to the others, Walkabout moving at a crouch, Linderer crawling, dragging his wounded leg.

Cox waved them off. He was sitting up in a slight depression on the west side of what had been the Lurp perimeter. He was covered with wounds, his guts half spilled into his lap, but he looked calm as he jacked another round into the chamber of his shotgun. Linderer stared at him, puzzled as to why the Bulldozer was using only his left hand. And then Linderer saw why. The Bulldozer's right wrist was flopped back over his forearm. Cox looked over at Linderer and Walkabout, both of whom were staring at him, then he grinned.

Walkabout was Cherokee, and the Bulldozer was what—half Sioux? For just an instant, Linderer marveled at the tenacity and courage of his Indian countrymen, then he crawled over to Mike Reiff. As he'd suspected, Reiff was dead, pinned to a large, scarred tree by a piece of shrapnel.

Linderer crawled over to Art Herringhausen, who, like Clifton, should have been out on Burnell's team. Linderer felt for a pulse, but there was none.

Steve Czepurny had been hit in the feet and was in considerable pain, but he signaled that he was okay, then turned back to the trail with his M-16. For some reason, the NVA was holding back and not following up the attack, so Linderer crawled back to Contreros.

The team leader had a small hole above his right ear and a large exit wound on the top of his head. He was still carrying a pulse, but it was very weak. Walkabout and Linderer moved back to Terry Clifton.

Clifton was dead. Walkabout got Linderer away from Clifton before the full emotional impact could hit him, and they moved over to Frank Souza. Souza was on his back, breathing in shallow gasps, a small penetration wound on the right side of his chest and a smaller wound on his neck. Walkabout raced back to his rucksack, and with his painful, mangled hands, he dug out the extra radio battery he'd been carrying and ran back to Linderer with it. Linderer ripped off the plastic cover and put it on Souza's chest, hoping to seal his sucking chest wound. This was the procedure he'd learned in training, but it wasn't working. He placed a field dressing over the plastic and ran the ties around Souza's chest. His hands came away bloody, so he rolled Souza over. There was a hole at least eight inches wide and eight inches deep in his back. Linderer and Walkabout looked into the wound and saw that Souza's right lung and some of his ribs were gone. Linderer and Walkabout exchanged a hopeless look. Lurps didn't carry dressings that big.

They did what they could for Souza, then Walkabout went back to the radio. Bacon was still struggling to keep functioning, but he was drifting in and out of consciousness. Walkabout took the headset from him and, wincing from the pain of squeezing the transmit button with his

wounded hands, he called Captain Eklund to ask about
the medevac. It was ten minutes out.

Linderer crawled back to his rucksack and took up the
best firing position he could, cursing himself for not
having thought to collect ammunition from the wounded
and dead. He just knew that the enemy was going to be
coming any minute to clean up the last of them, and he
was determined to take as many as he could when they
came. Looking around, he could see that he wouldn't
have much help. Walkabout's hands were barely able to
hold the radio headset. Contreros might still have a pulse,
but if he did, a pulse was all the life he had left in him.
Bacon was struggling just to stay conscious. Cox was
using his mouth and good hand to bind up his shattered
forearm. He had already stuffed a green sweat towel into
his stomach wound to keep his guts inside. He had his
shotgun across his legs, his CAR-15 on the ground next to
him, and his ammunition already laid out for easy access.

Linderer added it up quickly. Five good hands and one
pair of good legs was all they had left, and he knew it
wouldn't be enough. There was no way anyone was
going to survive the final onslaught that was sure to come
any second.

The NVA were a brave and tough bunch, but they
weren't all that smart sometimes, and fortunately, this
was one of those times. They'd hit the Lurps with some
kind of command-detonated horizontal weapon—probably one of those forty-pound claymores the Chinese supplied them—and if they'd had any sense at all, they
would have come in to finish off any survivors while the
debris was still falling. Whatever it was they'd used, it
had been devastating. The underbrush was gone, swept
away, and the overhead canopy was also gone. It was a
miracle there were any survivors at all.

Time crept past slowly. Linderer was almost impatient for the enemy to come, but the enemy did not make his assault. Rounds cracked through the trees, and there were sounds of movement all around, but the NVA just couldn't get its act together. The enemy obviously knew that there were live Lurps around that knoll, but they apparently didn't know how few of them were capable of putting up any resistance.

The medevac ship could now be heard beating its way toward the team's position. It was soon overhead, and Walkabout yelled out to Linderer that he needed his help. Linderer nodded, then looked around, fully expecting to see whole hordes of vengeful NVA swarming in on him. But except for a few quick flurries of movement off where there was still some underbrush, he saw no enemy soldiers. They were surely getting organized at last, and Linderer briefly forgot about Walkabout and the medevac and began laying out his magazines. He must've miscounted his grenades, or taken some from someone else, for he had two frags and a white phosphorous next to his rucksack. Not that it really mattered anymore, but he hoped he'd last long enough to use them.

Again, Walkabout yelled for help with the medevac. The medevac helicopter was right overhead, and Linderer looked right up at the big red cross on its belly and then at the jungle penetrator coming down on a cable. He looked over at Cox, and the Bulldozer grinned at him and waved his CAR-15. Linderer idly wondered what he'd done with his shotgun.

The medevac ship started taking heavy ground fire, and drifted, taking the penetrator away from the Lurps. Walkabout was going crazy, running around in circles, waving up at the helicopter, but the penetrator kept drifting, drifting off toward the enemy. Enemy fire was picking up.

Cobra gunships ripped overhead, trying to suppress the fire, showering the Lurps with hot expending brass, tearing into the NVA with much hotter lead and steel.

Things were getting out of control, and PFC Billy Bob Walkabout was determined to put a stop to it. He began running downslope, through NVA gunfire, right up to NVA positions, chasing that dangling, swaying, elusive jungle penetrator. Less than twenty feet in front of a line of enemy muzzle flashes, he finally caught the penetrator. Wrapping his arms around the shaft, he ran back uphill for the perimeter. Linderer and Cox opened up to give him covering fire. Cox drained a magazine, then fumbled a one-handed reload, grabbed his shotgun, and began booming away, pumping furiously with his good arm after each shot.

Walkabout staggered back to the perimeter with the jungle penetrator and manhandled it over to Linderer. Linderer held the penetrator while Walkabout worked his arms under Contreros and dragged him over. Linderer folded the struts down, making seats, then he and Walkabout wrestled Contreros into position and strapped him on. Walkabout then stepped back, and looking up through the now denuded treetops, he signaled the crew chief to tighten the slack on the cable. The cable tightened, and Walkabout looked up again, frustration verging on panic on his face. The helicopter had drifted again, and the penetrator was thirty meters from the center of the ship's belly. If Contreros went up this way, he'd be dashed against the trees—maybe even catch and pull down the helicopter if the crew chief couldn't cut the cable in time. Walkabout wrapped his arms around Contreros, lifted him and the penetrator off the ground, then, carrying the whole load, he ran, under fire, until he was directly beneath the medevac ship. The slack went out of the cable, Contreros was winched up and pulled into the ship, then the medevac helicopter banked away to the northwest and headed for the hospital at Phu Bai.

Another medevac helicopter immediately took its place, and again the enemy opened up on it. This ship, too, began to drift, and the descending penetrator angled away from Walkabout and Linderer. Walkabout shook his head, then took off downslope after it. This time, the enemy was ready for him. Bullets snapped and cracked all around him as he caught the penetrator, secured it, and hauled it back uphill. Exhausted, Walkabout collapsed on the ground next to Linderer, still hugging the penetrator. "Let's get Cox out!" he said, panting, struggling to his feet. They both looked at Cox, but Cox shook his head and yelled that he was okay, and for them to get someone else out.

Leaving Linderer holding the penetrator, Walkabout ran over to Souza, grabbed him under the armpits, and dragged him back to Linderer. Souza was pale and didn't seem to be breathing, but he still had a pulse—a very faint pulse. Walkabout and Linderer strapped him to the penetrator, and the medevac pilot brought the ship overhead again. In a few seconds, Souza was aboard the helicopter and on his way to the hospital. Linderer doubted he'd survive the flight.

Walkabout told Cox he was going next. Cox pumped his shotgun and shouted back that he wasn't hurt badly and wasn't going out until he ran out of ammo.

With all the helicopters flying around and the enemy still throwing rounds at the knoll, the only way to be heard was to shout. Linderer shouted at Cox, telling him he was going out next, but Cox only grinned back at him. He wasn't going out, and that's all there was to it.

The radio crackled. Captain Eklund said the next medevac was thirty to forty minutes out and told the Lurps they'd have to hold tight. Eklund said he was

doing everything he could to get help. It was the truth—
he was doing all he could, but he knew it wasn't enough.

Overhead, the Cobras circled and swooped down on
gun runs and rocket runs, but the situation looked
increasingly grim to the Lurps on the ground. Walkabout
and Linderer decided that they'd stay until all of the other
wounded and all of the dead were out before they'd go.
There was really nothing else they could do. They were
all in a bad way, and there didn't seem much chance any
of them were going to survive. Bacon was still losing
blood, still struggling to stay conscious. Walkabout tried
to help him with the radio, but he had real trouble
holding the headset, and the two of them seemed to be
switching back and forth, neither one of them having an
easy time of it, so Linderer crawled over to help out.
Czepurny was in pain but still covering his zone of security. Cox had just finished a short but furious battle with
some NVA trying to move up on him, putting down five
or six and driving the rest back, but even he was beginning to weaken, and he wasn't grinning anymore. Sooner
or later, Walkabout was going to run out of whatever it
was that was keeping him going. The numbness in Linderer's leg was spreading. They were all in very bad
shape.

Walkabout began to move from position to position,
gathering up ammunition and grenades and distributing
them to the other four. When Linderer told him that they
couldn't let anyone be taken alive, he nodded grimly, as
if he'd been thinking the same thing.

When Captain Eklund came over the horn, saying
something about a reaction force, Linderer told him that
if it didn't arrive in the next ten minutes, not to bother.

"Just hold on," said Captain Eklund. "We're going to
get you out."

# Chapter Nineteen

Burnell's team was only five kilometers away from Contreros's team, but it might as well have been five hundred miles away. Years afterward, some of the men on Burnell's team would vividly remember having heard the sounds of desperate battle in the other team's recon zone, but at the time, the only firing they heard clearly on their entire mission was a "mad minute" during which the air-rifle detachment securing the radio relay on the abandoned firebase on which they'd inserted scared the shit out of them by opening up to "test fire" their weapons just before sunset on the nineteenth—that, and the firing they heard in the background when they were anxiously monitoring the radios the next day. Five kilometers of mountainous jungle . . . The two teams were so close, and yet so far away from each other they seemed to be in different climates. About the only thing Contreros's team had going for it was good weather. Burnell's team had fog and cold drizzle alternating with driving rain.

Burnell's recon zone was spooky, and one of the spookiest things about it was that the enemy seemed to have abandoned it. There were plenty of trails, plenty of slightly overgrown sleeping positions, and by all the signs the Lurps could read—which didn't include the

Chinese characters carved in that tree on the finger leading out to it, but did include antennae scars on the trees directly over it—there actually had been a fairly major radio site out there not too long ago. But the radio site was abandoned now, and the remains of the trail-watcher Zo had killed a month or two before were still strewn near the trail—which was a pretty reliable sign that, good as it was, the trail hadn't seen much use lately. Something about that just didn't seem right.

Whenever one team made contact, it was standard operating procedure for all the other teams in the field to go to ground in good concealment and will themselves into invisibility. This wasn't always possible, of course, but when Contreros sprang his ambush, this is what Burnell's team tried to do.

At first the news was good. But then it began to turn bad, and then worse. His camouflaged face a mask of impotent rage and worried grief, Burnell tightened the perimeter. The Lurps around him were somber, shocked. A whole team down—a whole heavy team! In the Lurp catalog of horrors, this was second only to a whole team's disappearing without a trace or even so much as a last situation report. This time it wasn't happening to some SOG team over the fence, or some other Lurp unit. This was happening to friends, and it tortured the spirit to just helplessly lay dog, so close but so far away. . . . They were a hard-bitten lot of killers out there on Burnell's team. Those who hadn't yet actually killed anyone were still pretty hard dudes, but on November 20, 1968, the rain hid more than a few tears.

The rain let up and started again. Burnell's team shivered from the cold and emotion. Whispered updates spread out from the radios. Bacon was alive, but Walkabout and then Linderer were taking his place on the radio, so he couldn't be doing too well. Another two men were wounded but still functioning, but no one on Burnell's team knew the individual line numbers of the men on the other team, so they had no idea who these men were or the nature of their wounds. Burnell was visibly shaken to hear that Contreros was unconscious with a serious head wound. Every man on the team thought of each of the men on the other team, worrying about them, wondering who was already dead. There were Catholics, Protestants, Jews, and at least two atheists on Burnell's team, and even the atheists broke down and offered up a silent plea for their friends and brother Lurps.

A mere five klicks away from the action, the Lurps with Burnell strained to hear the artillery and the helicopters, but the rain and jungled mountains and the distance muffled the sound so that it was easier to imagine than to really hear. Whenever Walkabout or Linderer came up on the radio, there was gunfire in the background, and though they tried to stick to proper commo procedure and stay brief and professional, whenever they came over the radio they both sounded increasingly tired, scared, and impatient. And more often than not, the men with the radios on Burnell's team couldn't hear the other team's transmissions. They could hear Captain Eklund, but not the survivors on the ground. Captain Eklund was trying to sound calm and reassuring, but there was a lot of impatience in his voice, too.

Out on Burnell's team, the impatience had long since turned into angry frustration. The supposedly "Airmobile" 101st Airborne Division couldn't find the helicopters to extract its Lurp teams. And where the hell was that goddamn reaction force anyway?

Burnell offered to take his team overland to rescue the other team, but Captain Eklund told him to sit tight. Then

word came for Burnell to move the team back up to its
insertion point on the abandoned firebase. Though every
man was scared, the whole team was hot to go. They
were going to the LZ for extraction and reinsertion as a
reaction force for the other team. Hell, this should have
happened hours before—and probably would have if not
for the bad pocket of local weather and the fact that the
goddamn division had pulled the Kingsmen while damn
near the whole operational Lurp company was out in the
Rung Roung.

Burnell put the company's most respected point man,
Don "The Shadow" Harris, on point. Harris could set a
fast pace without sacrificing too much in the way of
stealth and caution, but he didn't get much chance to do
his stuff. He hadn't taken the team more than forty
meters or so when word came for it to go to ground again
and lay dog. A reaction force from the 17th Cav was
already in the air and on the way out to the other team's
rescue. Burnell's team was to stay put and stay off the
radio. The 17th Cav reaction force was on the job, at last.

And then there was a "word change." The reaction
force wasn't in the air; it wasn't on the way. Burnell's
men were to get moving again, back to their hilltop insertion LZ, to link up with the air-rifles, Pathfinders, and
Lurp radio relay. There was no word about being picked
up and reinserted, but it was best to be next to an LZ in
case that became necessary.

It was a hard, slippery climb back up the mountain
they'd come down the evening before, and when Burnell's team finally made the linkup, every man was
exhausted, emotionally and physically. The mountaintop
was socked in solid with clouds, and it was obvious
there'd be no helicopters coming in—Burnell's team
would not be going out to the aid of their comrades.

The air-rifles were tense and nervous, and rightfully so. Even with the Lurp radio relay team, and the short handful of Pathfinders, there was less than a platoon to secure the whole hilltop, and Burnell's heavy team wasn't much in the mood to give them any relief.

Burnell's personal motto at the time was "You gotta be hard," but he and Contreros were close, and even Burnell wasn't hard enough to shrug this off. Being an officer and a gentleman by the president's commission, and a good Lurp in anyone's book, Lieutenant Owen D. Williams took over long enough to order Sergeant Burford and Sergeant Smith to get the men out on the perimeter—where they'd already set up out of habit and good sense anyway—and he stayed with Burnell and the radio relay, monitoring the radios and letting Burnell grieve over Contreros and the others.

There was plenty of grief, plenty of worry, plenty of misery, and plenty of anger at the division for pulling support from teams in the field and not getting it back when they needed it. The RTOs for Lieutenant Williams and SSG Burnell, Kenn Miller and John Looney, had their radios, and there was a radio for Burford and one for Smith, too. But the Lurps were spread a little thinner than before up there, and so one of the Pathfinders, Sergeant Ron Reynolds's buddy, Richie Burns, took radios to the Lurps who needed them. Nobody wanted to hear all the bad news, but nobody wanted to be left in the dark.

Captain Wild Bill Meachum, his co-pilot Jim Cline, and their two door gunners, and WO W. T. Grant and his co-pilot Barry Schreiber, and their two door gunners started November 20 with a real case of the ass at whoever it was that had pulled them off Lurp duty. Of course, the division had its priorities and wasn't about to let a mere captain and three warrant officers straighten those priorities out. So Meachum and Grant and their crews had no choice but to follow orders like good soldiers—at least up to a point. It seemed like damn near the whole division was on the move, and they had been assigned to ferry line infantry units on conventional combat assaults with the rest of the Kingsmen. This could be very dangerous work, but the two Kingsmen crews weren't thinking much about the danger they might be going into. They were thinking about the danger those two heavy teams were in, out there in the Rung Roung without helicopter support.

The night before, when his commanding officer gave him the news that the two crews were being pulled from Lurps to spend the day moving troops around, Captain Meachum had almost gone ballistic. Of course, he couldn't very well mutiny, but he did manage to push a bargain with his commanding officer. His crew and Grant's crew belonged to different platoons. When on detached duty flying Lurps—or any of the other special operations they flew—this didn't make any difference. But flying combat assaults, Kingsmen helicopters from the Second Platoon and First Platoon did not normally fly in the same formations. This time they would. And this time, Grant's ship and Meachum's ship would fly together at the rear of the formation, where they could break off and go to the aid of the Lurps if word came down for them to do so.

Meachum and Cline, Grant and Schreiber, were monitoring the Lurp command net after Contreros sprang his ambush. When they heard Captain Eklund tell Contreros that a reaction force would be coming in and the team extracted, then reinserted closer to Burnell, Grant and

Schreiber exchanged grins, figuring they'd be released to do the job they ought to be doing. It didn't happen—not then. When the Kingsmen heard Eklund inform Contreros that there would be no reaction force, no extraction and reinsertion, because all the division's helicopters were already committed, Meachum and Cline, Grant and Schreiber, couldn't believe it.

Finally Meachum had had enough. He radioed his commanding officer, Kingsmen Six, telling him there was a Lurp team in trouble and requesting that Kingsmen 1-8 and Kingsmen 2-5 be released to do what they were supposed to be doing—which was supporting the Lurps.

Both ships were running low on fuel, and had already headed for the refueling point at Camp Eagle when Kingsmen Six came over the horn, releasing them back to Lurp duty. Refueling seemed to take an eternity, but then the two Kingsmen helicopters were on their way to Contreros's AO.

For what seemed like another, even longer, eternity, the two Kingsmen ships circled, standing by to extract the team when the word finally came—but the word didn't come. Things kept getting worse on the ground; first Venable got hit, then that massive explosion cut down the whole team. Neither Meachum nor Grant could get McQuire rigs down to the team, and for all they knew, there was no one down there capable of dealing with the rigs anyway. Grant had to relay the call for a medevac, reporting high-priority head wounds and sucking chest wounds, without any idea what the situation really was.

Dragon Six, the commanding officer of the division's aerial rocket artillery helicopters, came over the horn announcing that he was taking over the operation. Captain Eklund, who already had 17th Cav Cobras and didn't need some ignorant colonel butting in, told him to go to hell and get off the net.

The reaction force was coming—then it wasn't coming. This was the final straw for the two Kingsmen crews. They offered to go back to the Acid Pad and grab a reaction force from the Lurp company, and Eklund told them to go to it.

By this time, both Kingsmen ships were again low on fuel, but they didn't have time to refuel—and it was a good thing they didn't take on the extra weight, for when they got to the Lurp Acid Pad, the call for help had preceded them. The company was already short of personnel, and almost all the currently operational Lurps had been committed to the two heavy teams. Most of the Lurps back at Camp Eagle were short-timers waiting to go home, men coming from or going to R&R or Recondo School or extension leave, men on medical profiles, men whose jobs in the company did not normally take them to the field. Now they swarmed down the hill to the chopper pad. Some of them were in olive drab jungle fatigues, some in "flower power" leaf-pattern camouflage suits, some in tigers, some in civilian shirts and uniform pants, uniform jackets and jeans or bermuda shorts—but all of them were ready to go to the aid of their brother Lurps.

Tony Tercero was scheduled to go back to the rear at Bien Hoa for DEROS the next day, and he'd already turned in his weapon. When word came that the Kingsmen were inbound to pick up volunteers, he raced to Supply, only to find Mueller, Kirby, and Holland getting ready to head down to the chopper pad. Tercero grabbed a weapon, some magazines, and a bandolier of M-16 ammo still in the boxes, and raced down to the pad, hastily loading magazines. In his haste, he'd forgotten to dress. He was wearing a brown army T-shirt, green army boxer shorts, and rubber shower shoes, but he had a weapon and he had a bandolier of ammo. If the VC sometimes fought like this, so could he—he was a Lurp!

First Sergeant Darol Walker had gone back to the rear at Bien Hoa the day before, his tour over. Lieutenant Jim Jackson was in charge of the TOC, and he had to keep a contingent on duty manning the radios. He didn't need Tim Long, the mail clerk—and it was a good thing, because Long was already fighting his way aboard one of the choppers. He didn't need supply—and Mueller, Kirby, and Holland were already down at the pad. The men on the radios had to stay put, but there was no stopping the rest of the company.

Every available man from both patrol platoons, every available man from commo, all the supply section, and all the headquarters personnel Lieutenant Jackson didn't already have down in the TOC—everyone swarmed down to the Acid Pad and onto the helicopters. This was clearly not going to work. The ships were too overloaded to do anything but crash right there on the Acid Pad if they tried to take off. After all the stories they'd heard of panicked ARVN troops overwhelming helicopters trying to get *away* from battle, the Kingsmen crews were now having to fight off Lurps overwhelming their ships trying to get out *to* the battle. Eighteen, twenty, twenty-four men on one ship? No one could get a clear count, but there were way too many men, and the door gunners began to kick and shove and argue with their Lurp buddies.

Spotting Tercero in his underwear and shower shoes, Captain Meachum jerked his thumb and ordered him off. "No, sir," said Tercero, locking and loading his weapon. "I'm going with you!"

Mr. Grant got the same reaction when he spotted a

Lurp with a bandage or a partial cast on his leg and ordered him off. The man wouldn't budge.

These people were crazy—but that didn't make them any lighter. The four Kingsmen pilots and four Kingsmen door gunners loved the Lurps more than ever now, but they couldn't take off until they had the load down to something they had some hope of lifting and carrying all the way out to the Rung Roung. The Acid Pad was just above sea level, but the mountains between there and the LZ were a couple of thousand feet higher. Grant finally got his Lurp load down to twelve, Meachum down to eleven, and they both had to torque almost to the limit just taking their ships off from the Acid Pad. Once under way, Meachum and Grant conferred briefly over the radio. They decided to handle this like a standard heavy team insertion, except that this time each ship was carrying a heavy team of its own. It was not going to be easy.

The pilots monitored the radios. Medevac was taking heavy fire from the ground. All of the circling ships were taking at least some fire, and down on the ground the surviving Lurps were still fighting for their lives. It was now 1530 hours, and they'd been in contact since 0930.

When Captain Eklund radioed the team that a reaction force was really on the way at last, Grant and Meachum heard Gary Linderer roger the transmission, then advise their company commander that if the reaction force couldn't be there in ten minutes there was no reason to bother, for they'd be too late.

The LZ had been altered considerably by all the firepower called in on behalf of the beleaguered Lurps. The vegetation had been blown thin, the ground was easier to see, and though the LZ was still on a slope, still strewn with old logs, stumps, and newly broken tree branches—

and though the LZ was now completely compromised—the insertion went well. By the time the second ship came in, the first chalk was already moving out to secure the immediate edges of the LZ.

In the field, Lurps have never been big on formal rank. It wasn't unknown for an E-4 team leader to have an E-5 on point, an E-6 for his ATL, and the likes of Lieutenant Williams walking his rear security or carrying the second radio on a mission. Now, when the mantle of leadership fell on Tony Tercero, none of the Lurps on the reaction force questioned it. There was gunfire all around, and all the Lurps were serious, all knew instinctively what to do—even the supply clerks. Without thinking of him as anything but another Lurp, Tony put Kirby in charge of the four guys next to him, two of whom were clerks and two of whom were experienced field Lurps who out-ranked both Tony and Kirby. Tony knew where security was needed, and that's where he sent it.

There was no time to waste. The LZ had to be secured, and somebody had to get up to the team. With Tony in the lead in his boxer shorts and shower shoes, a strange weapon in hand, Tim Coleman, Joe Bielesch, John Renear, Dave Bennett, and three or four other Lurps charged up the ridge toward the sound of the gunfire. There were NVA all over the slope. A couple of them had to be killed on the run, but a dozen or so more fled right past the Lurps without anyone shooting—just a bunch of scared and worried youngsters passing each other on the hill, as Tony remembered it later.

But not all of the NVA on that slope were still alive. By that time, the dead probably outnumbered the living, and the Lurps slipped in the blood, almost tripped over bodies and parts of bodies.

"Lurps!" yelled Tony. "We're Lurps!"

Very briefly, the enemy fire increased, and up on the bloody knoll, Gary Linderer felt something slap him on the thigh and didn't realize that it was a bullet. Someone was hollering down by the LZ, and that fool Walkabout was hollering back.

"Walkabout! You idiot! Shut up!" Linderer wasn't sure if he said it or just thought it, but then the realization hit him that *he* was the fool, not Walkabout. After all this fighting, the enemy already knew exactly where they were. And those were Lurps down there by the LZ— Lurps!—a reaction force of Lurps!

Walkabout began to shout again, and so did Linderer. Lurps! Lurps! When no one else could be bothered, their brother Lurps had come to their rescue and were there at last!

There was fighting down around the LZ. A reaction force of air-rifle "Blues" from the 17th Cav had been inserted shortly after the Lurps, and though the Cav troopers themselves were brave enough and game enough, their leadership was so bad that Tony had to go back down to the LZ and pretend to be an officer to get their machine guns properly positioned, and the other Lurps had similar difficulty getting them squared away.

Occasional bursts of fire coming their way, Tony and the other reaction force Lurps on the ridge oversaw the extraction of their wounded and dead buddies, while the Lurps and Cav "Blues" fought off the enemy down by the LZ. Fortunately, the NVA seemed disorganized. This had not been a good day for them, either.

It was dark before the reaction force was finally extracted, and since no one had thought to bring a strobe light, the reaction force had to use Zippo lighters to guide in the helicopters. Among the men on the F/58 LRP reaction force, Dave Bennett, Joe Bielesch, and Tim Coleman had been wounded, and so had Mueller, Kirby, and Holland from Supply. None of them was seriously wounded, and they all shrugged off their wounds, but Mueller, Kirby, and Holland's stock among the other Lurps shot up.

Contreros carried his pulse all the way to the hospital ship, where he lost it and died. It was only his heart that had lasted out the whole battle. The rest of him had been dead from the moment that blast rolled over the knoll and cut the team down.

Reiff, Clifton, and Herringhausen had been dead for hours when extracted. Of the three, Clifton had had the worst part of it, for Reiff and Herringhausen had died instantly. Their suffering was over, but their brother Lurps and their people back home would suffer and grieve in their absence.

Czepurny's and Linderer's wounds were serious, but no longer quite so life-threatening once they got to the hospital.

Venable was in extremely critical condition, but by the time the reaction force finally went in, he was already in surgery. He had made it over the hump, surviving until he could be medevacked, and he was going to survive. Bacon was also critical but would probably survive if he could fight off infection. Miraculously, Frank Souza was still alive, according to the last reports the company got of his condition before he was evacuated to the hospital in Japan, but he wasn't really expected to survive.

Of course, the people setting those expectations were medical experts, but they weren't experts about Lurps, and Frank Souza was a Lurp. He defied their expectations and survived the hospital, and went back to his wife, and thrived so completely in civilian life that only those who know him well—or read about him in books like this one and a couple of others—have any idea how miraculous his survival truly was.

The Bulldozer, Riley Cox, had been wounded far worse than he'd let himself notice during the fighting. He'd refused extraction until there were enough Lurps on that knoll to force him to get on the jungle penetrator and keep the NVA at bay, but during the medevac helicopter ride to the hospital, it was so cold and the cold was so tempting, he almost went into shock. But that wasn't the Bulldozer. He'd paid attention in training, and he knew that shock was a killer. He wasn't going into shock—it was just *cold* in that damn medevac ship, and he wasn't going to let a little cold kill him. Word was that the doctors who got hold of Cox at the hospital at Phu Bai doubted he'd survive—but they didn't know the Bulldozer. Even the guys who knew him best—his brother Lurps—hadn't yet taken the Bulldozer's full measure. He'd get out of the hospital and make his way back to the 101st Lurps months after almost all the men who'd known him in 1968 had gone home. On the first anniversary of November 20, 1968, he was out on a mission with Frank Anderson, the only man still in L Company, 75th Rangers who'd been on that reaction force a year before, and about the only indication Anderson had that Bulldozer was marking the anniversary was that in addition to his usual heavy load of weapons and ammo, Cox was also carrying a .357 magnum revolver and a bigger knife than usual.

The post–Shepherd Incident block on promotions was still apparently in place, but a shower of medals rained down on the members of Lurp Team Two-Three and those who had come to its aid. The medevac crews probably didn't get anything new in the way of medals, and no doubt didn't care, since they had all the medals they'd any use for, and anyway were doing it out of big balls and brave morals, not for common motivations like wealth or glory or privileged access to women. The same could be said of the artillery crews who fired in support of the team—it was just another good job of work for them, too, and the only time the artillery got any medals for their efforts was when the NVA tried to overrun their firebases. On November 20, they were doing their job out of duty, courage, and morals brave enough to go all out for their fellow Americans.

The same could also be said of Captain Eklund and his pilots, the Kingsmen crews, and the 17th Cav Cobra pilots—but unlike the artillery, they were a regular part of the team and knew the people on the ground. They had played so vital a part that they all got some medals—all except the door gunners, as usual.

Walkabout was in for a Medal of Honor, and would eventually end up with a Distinguished Service Cross. He received an impact award of the Silver Star in the hospital. Gary Linderer also got an impact award of the Silver Star in the hospital, as did Cox and Bacon. To this day, both Linderer and Bacon are a little embarrassed about sharing the same level of award with Bulldozer, figuring that Cox should have been put in for a Distinguished Service Cross if what they'd done was worth a Silver Star.

Al Contreros did get a DSC, which would have meant a lot to him if he'd lived to gloat over it.

Czepurny and Souza don't talk much about medals, and whatever Clifton, Herringhausen, and Reiff got was posthumous, and far too cheap for the sacrifice. None of the medals were worth the sacrifice—medals never are.

Of course, every man on Team Two-Three got a Purple Heart, as did the wounded men from the reaction force. The Cav "Blues" did rather well by medals, since the 17th Cav was in administrative control of the Lurps, as well as their own people, and had some say about who got what. The Cav NCO in charge of the reaction force—the same man Tercero and Coleman had to threaten to shoot in order to get him functioning—got a Silver Star almost immediately, but it took more than a year for Tony Tercero to receive a mere Bronze Star with "V" device for taking command on the LZ, leading the charge uphill through the enemy to the shattered team, and taking control of the medevac of the wounded and the extraction of the company reaction force—and doing it all with an unzeroed rifle and one half-loaded bandolier of magazines, while wearing green boxer shorts and floppy rubber shower shoes. One buck sergeant from the 17th Cav "Blues" was so embarrassed by the Bronze Star with "V" awarded him for his part in the rescue he tried to find Tony Tercero to apologize and give him the medal, but Tony had already rotated back to the States.

At the postmission debriefing on the night of the twentieth, Dragon Six offered up his theory of the action, saying that the 17th Cav Cobras must have hit the team with a rocket. Major General Melvin Zais was present at the debriefing, and just let the man prattle on, making a fool of himself, but almost everyone else present—those who had actually been involved in the day's activities—wanted to throttle him to death right there in the Lurp TOC—and very well might have if General Zais hadn't been there. Dragon Six was still fuming, still casting aspersions against the professional competence of the Cav pilots, when the Lurp company's senior medic, "Doc" Bruce Proctor, walked in with a nasty handful of bolts and broken glass that had been taken out of Souza's wounds. When Proctor asked Dragon Six if this was the sort of shrapnel contained in the rockets fired by the Cobras, the pompous blowhard deflated and shut up. General Zais gave Proctor a thumbs-up and a little smile.

When Burnell's team and the radio relay were finally extracted and returned to Camp Eagle a few days later, they returned to a sad and sorely depleted company. Of the whole heavy team that had been with Contreros, only Billy Walkabout was back in the Lurp company area—and he was there in defiance of all respectable medical advice, but under the immediate care of the only medical authority that mattered to him, Doc Proctor. Word was that Linderer and Sours would probably be coming back to the company, but for all the rest of the wounded except them and Walkabout—and amazingly, Riley Cox—the war was over.

# Chapter Twenty

At the end of the most gloomy month in its short history, F Company, 58th Infantry (Long Range Patrol) received a new first sergeant—a big, hearty, cheerful fellow named Farrington. First Sergeant Farrington arrived about a week after First Sergeant Walker rotated back to the States, and his arrival was most definitely a positive morale factor for a unit that sorely needed one. Farrington had all the military background expected of a long-range patrol company first sergeant—which, because it was expected, didn't particularly impress anyone one way or another. But Farrington also had quite an impressive football career behind him, and this impressed everyone, even the two or three Lurps who shared a contempt for the football heroes in the sports pages of *Pacific Stars and Stripes* on the grounds that they were draft-dodging pussies. Within a day or two of his arrival in the company, Farrington was already both popular and respected—which is not an easy combination to establish in such a short time, and in the eyes of such people as the Lurps.

One of the things that made Farrington popular and won him respect was that he made a point of talking with every man in the unit. Of course, there weren't that many people in the unit at this juncture. F Company, 58th Infantry (LRP) was about the size of a platoon, not a company, and would have been hard-pressed to field three experienced teams from the combined personnel of both patrol platoons and the commo platoon.

It didn't bother First Sergeant Farrington that one of the acting platoon sergeants was a mere spec four, nor that this spec four had staff sergeants and buck sergeants in his platoon. In the Lurps, platoon sergeant was an administrative position, and the few remaining E-5s and E-6s were all team leaders and didn't want to be bothered keeping a duty roster—particularly not at a time like this. The 17th Cav was now demanding that the Lurps send KPs to the Cav mess. The Cav didn't seem to care that F/58's morning reports showed a platoon-size population. The Lurps were still expected to contribute a full company's share of E-3 and E-4 KPs every day. The fact that the Lurps generally preferred to stay in their own compound, living off C rations, Lurp rations, and indigenous rations, to mixing with the Cav troopers for meals didn't impress the powers that be at 2/17th Cav—and neither did the fact that Lurps were supposed to be elite and privileged characters, even the lowest of them at least the social equal and moral equivalent of the average E-7. The Lurps were so understrength they weren't running many missions, and the 17th Cav seemed determined to take advantage of their weaknesses by putting them on KP. Even Sp4 Billy Walkabout, who was up for the Medal of Honor, would have been expected to pull KP if he hadn't been on a profile for the wounds on his hands and arms. It helped to have an E-4 platoon sergeant who was willing to take his own place on the duty roster. And it also helped to have a company commander like Captain Eklund, and a "First Pig" like First Sergeant Farrington, both of whom just laughed when the Cav mess sergeant complained that the Lurps weren't doing a lick of work on KP and half the time couldn't even be found. As Captain Eklund explained to a sympathetic officer the Cav sent to complain, Lurps were supposed to be hard to find.

The waste of a whole heavy team had finally shaken some medals loose for the Lurps, which would probably have delighted Al Contreros if he'd been alive to enjoy his Purple Heart and DSC, and the other guys on his team had still been around to enjoy their medals. Unfortunately, the only one around the unit to enjoy his medals was Walkabout. And unfortunately, Walkabout didn't seem to be taking too well to his new hero status. November 4 and November 20 were over, but his buddies could see that he was having a hard time putting them behind him. And nothing in his training or experience had prepared him for dealing with generals—or for having men from other units staring at him and whispering, or coming up to shake hands when he wore a uniform with nametape outside the Camp Eagle Lurp compound.

In one very terrible day, F/58th had become one of the most highly decorated companies in the history of the 101st Airborne Division, but Lurps were traditionally cynical about medals, since it was rank, not medals, that made a man immune to degrading bullshit like pulling KP at the Cav mess. Unfortunately, the Shepherd Incident freeze still seemed to be in effect when it came to enlisted promotions. What the Lurps needed was promotions for the old guys, and then replacements for them to train up and teach the trade to. Instead, what division initially sent the Lurps was a crop of young junior NCOs who hadn't specifically volunteered for the job and had been chosen only because someone in Personnel had noticed that F/58th had recently lost some NCOs to rotation and other causes, and because they were Airborne qualified in a division now being filled up with legs. More than half of these young NCOs chose to stay, and those who chose to stay were invariably those who didn't mind deferring to men a pay grade or two below them. When at last the company started getting some new E-3s and E-4s, they tended to be naive young paratroopers who'd volunteered for Lurps in P-training back at Bien Hoa out of disgust on discovering that, except for the Lurps and the Pathfinders, the rest of the 101st Airborne Division was now in the process of going leg. Once they got a whiff of the game and the in-unit training, most of the enlisted swine decided to stay.

Two or three times during the last week of November and the first week of December, the Lurp company sent teams out on fairly uneventful recon missions. These were ad hoc teams, thrown together for the missions at hand and manned by the few experienced Lurps left in the company—many of whom were set to rotate back to the States or go on extension leave within a few days or a few weeks.

Training for the new men continued at a somewhat too leisurely pace. There were classes in the company area, rappelling and McQuire rig drills, and team classes when the new guys were put on teams. Almost every night, the Lurps were ordered to send ambush patrols outside the Camp Eagle perimeter, and these almost invariably fruitless ambushes were welcome training exercises. Slowly, rather reluctantly, the experienced Lurps began taking some of the new guys out on long-range patrols, one or two cherries on a team, and, with a few exceptions who were soon sent on to more conventional units, the cherries were quick learners and did well.

Not all of these missions were uneventful. On his first mission as team leader, Joe Bielesch gave the cherries on his team the chance to put some of their company training with the helicopters to use during a ladder extraction from a mission out near Leech Island. Being the biggest, heaviest, strongest man on his team, as well as the team leader, J.B. was the last man on the ladder, holding down at the base for the others to clamber up into the hovering helicopter. He was moving up the ladder himself when two North Vietnamese soldiers came running out of the trees so suddenly the door gunners didn't get off a round at them. Rushing the ladder, they tried to pull J.B. off it and take him prisoner. The ladder was swinging, the extraction ship was lifting out, and J.B. held on to the rung above him with both hands and kicked back at the NVA soldiers, then lifted his knees high, clipped onto the ladder with the D-ring snap link on his harness suspender, and rode free of his would-be captors.

Back in the rear, J.B. made light of this close call, saying something about how this only proved that the North Vietnamese army had a few guys with true Lurp initiative, and that his cherries better never get so cocky they started underestimating the enemy. He'd been vulnerable as hell, and if he'd slipped when he was kicking, they would have had him for sure.

Shortly before Christmas Sergeant Zoschak came back to the Lurp company and Mr. Poley returned to the Kingsmen. Their return was the cause of rejoicing among the Lurps who knew them. But the rejoicing on their return was nothing compared to the rejoicing when, shortly before Christmas, Gary Linderer returned to the company—on a very restrictive physical profile, and against the better judgment of rear echelon medical authorities who didn't understand how much he missed his brother Lurps.

Linderer's wounds were still draining, still breaking

open and bleeding from time to time, and still rendering him incapable of doing a proper job as a field Lurp. But his strong, optimistic, humorous good spirits were an inspiration to everyone, from the newly returned and deeply shocked Zoschak to the newest cherry in the company.

Zo was shocked to learn what had happened on November 20. He said he couldn't help feeling responsible, since it wouldn't have been that rash fool Contreros in charge of the team if he'd been there—it would have been *him*. And by God, if it had been him, the whole team would have been there, and not a one of them on profile from wounds! Zo didn't feel up to questioning Linderer and Walkabout too closely, but he talked to Captain Eklund, he talked to Meachum and Grant, he talked to Burnell, and he talked to Miller, who'd been carrying the radio for Lieutenant Williams and heard most of the radio traffic.

Under normal circumstances, Zoschak was not exactly a guilt-ridden liberal. But one night, in a long talk with Miller down by the bunker line, he positively wallowed in guilt and shamelessly lorded it over poor Miller. All Miller had to feel guilty about was being on R&R in Hong Kong when Teddy Bear Gaskell got shot in the ass and having the sense to go out with Burnell instead of Contreros on November 19. Though it was clear enough to Miller, Zo refused to see what good it would have done if he'd been with either Teddy Bear or Contreros. So what if the guy taking his place when Teddy Bear got shot went catatonic? It didn't make any difference, did it? And what difference would it have made if Miller had been out there with Contreros? Zo had heard from both Walkabout and Linderer that after the ambush, Contreros had been in no mood even to listen to Venable's suggestions that they book on out of there. If he wouldn't listen to Venable, there was no way he would have listened to Miller. Sure,

Miller himself would have gotten killed instead of Her-ringhausen, or Reiff, or whoever it was. But he couldn't have changed the whole operation. He couldn't have done a damn thing to make it turn out differently. Zo, on the other hand, would have been TL of the heavy team—and if he had been, none of those guys would have gotten fucked up. Zo was sure of it—and he was probably right.

During the Lurp company's period of rebuilding, at least one long-range patrol mission came down every week, all of them recon missions and most of them into familiar RZs. Sometimes, two teams might be out on recon missions and the rest of the company involved in ambush patrols.

Sergeant "Honest John" Burford led a recon patrol into the general area where he'd pulled a couple of memorable missions with SSG Byron. On his return, he sold Captain Eklund on the idea of a few offensive operations in the area, and Captain Eklund sold the idea to "Higher."

Working with the likes of Snuffy Smith, John Looney, John Meszaros, "Mother" Rucker, Larry Chambers, Larry Saenz, Ken Munoz, Kenn Miller, and the pick of the new guys, Burford led a succession of heavy team missions into the area the Lurps came to call "The Game Preserve." The name sprang from the fact that this was one place the Lurps were having more fun popping Uncle Ho's NVA than Robin Hood's Merry Men used to have poaching King John's deer in Sherwood Forest. The Game Preserve was a transitional sort of area, both geo-graphically and politically. To the west, there was forest that led gradually into hills, and those hills led gradually into mountains that a man could follow into Tibet without ever coming within two klicks of sea level. To the east, there was a tree-studded savannah of grassy, rolling hills that led to the coastal farmlands. It was within a hundred meters of the woodline, along the most prominent trail, that the transition from NVA to southern Viet Cong authority seemed to take place, and it was in this area, usually along this same trail, that the Lurps pulled a series of very successful ambushes.

In theory at least, each time Burford took one of his heavy teams into the Game Preserve it was more dangerous than the time before, for surely the enemy was bound to wise up eventually. But Burford was still planning outrages against the serenity of the Game Preserve when his DEROS date came through, and it was time for him to go back to the rear, then back to the States.

The Lurps were looking lucky again. But then another stroke of bad luck hit the company. First Sergeant Farrington suffered a sudden heart attack and had to be evacuated. He was replaced by First Sergeant Cardin, who made almost as bad an initial impression as Farrington had made a good one. Cardin had graduated from damn near every high-speed infantry and special operations course available to a U.S. Army paratrooper, and he made a big point of alternating his fatigue jackets so that everyone could see all the tabs and badges and patches he'd earned in his career. Standing in front of his first few company formations with all that full-colored embroidery on his "flower power" camouflage jackets, he looked like a Christmas tree—and that became one of his nicknames. He'd come to the 101st to get his first-sergeant ticket punched with an American troop unit, and he made no secret of the fact that he was then either going back to a Special Forces office job or on to the Sergeant Major's Academy. For a man who took such pride in the SF combat patch on his right shoulder, he had a definite attitude problem when it came to the young SOG troopers from FOB 1 who occasionally dropped by with their Nungs to visit Zo and some of the other guys.

Cardin tried to kick one group out of the compound for wearing tiger fatigues with no rank on them, but one of the SOG troopers showed him an ID card proving he was a first lieutenant and he had to back off and content himself with grumbling that these SOG troopers weren't *real* SF.

First Sergeant Cardin wasn't nearly as obnoxious an SF refugee as Captain Shepherd had been—although after one experience of rappelling into a mission with Cardin flying bellyman, "Mother" Rucker, at least, had good reason to think that Cardin was damn near as dangerous as Shepherd. Zoschak, Miller, and a few other Lurps eventually came to sort of like Cardin, for the man wasn't quite as stupid as he seemed. But for most of the company, Cardin's only solid positive achievement was bringing Sergeant First Class Milton "Davy Crockett" Lockett to the company as a platoon sergeant. A stocky, cheerful, easygoing black man, SFC Lockett was the veteran of a previous tour with the 1st Infantry Division's Lurp detachment. He was also one of the army's premier hand-to-hand combat demonstrators and a longtime Fort Benning Ranger instructor who had friends everywhere and about as much informal political pull as the average sergeant major when it came to getting things for the troops and keeping them out of trouble.

One sunny day, shortly after Sergeant Burford left, and shortly before SFC Willie Champion went home, Larry Chambers, Larry Saenz, Jim Schwartz, John Meszaros, Gary Linderer, and Kenn Miller were lazing around on postmission stand-down, listening to a tape of Marty Robbins gunfighter songs, cleaning weapons, writing letters, and just kicking back, batting the breeze and shooting the shit, when word came from the orderly room that there was an interesting set of orders posted on the new company bulletin board that Miller had painted glossy red and talked a couple of the Nungs from FOB 1 into decorating with bloodthirsty anti-Communist curses in gold Chinese characters. The Lurps loafed a little longer, then wandered by the bulletin board to take a look.

The orders were from the Department of the Army, and they were orders formally disbanding all of the TOE Lurp units in the Republic of Vietnam and, without any stated change in personnel or mission, redesignating them lettered companies of the 75th Infantry Regiment (Ranger), under the colors and heritage of the 5307th Composite Group—the legendary Merrill's Marauders of World War Two fame.

"May-Zeus" Meszaros said something flip and irreverent, like "That's cool," and tried not to act overly impressed. But May-Zeus had read a book about the Marauders, and he knew it really *was* cool that the army figured the Lurps had earned so respectable a lineage.

Gary Linderer said something along the lines that, these being formal orders that looked like they'd been written by a computer programmed by lawyers, there was no telling just yet what they really meant.

Kenn Miller growled and made it clear that he did not agree. That "Ranger" designation was going to make an impressive return address, but he wasn't too sure it was a good thing. He had seen things deteriorate from long-range *reconnaissance* patrol to long-range patrol, and he reminded everyone that this change from LRRP to LRP had only led to more denials of extraction and more orders to stick around and "develop the situation" when it was time to get the hell out. He said something gloomy about how conventional commanders back in World War Two and Korea had misused and wasted the Rangers, and predicted that this name change was going to bring the company almost nothing but misuse, bad luck, and what his first team leader, the wise and great Teddy Bear Gaskell, used to call "pork chops."

Miller had no special moral authority, having been lucky enough to have seen far less actual combat in his tour and first extension than Gary Linderer had seen in the month of November. But he was the longest-serving Lurp at the bulletin board, and the only one who had been a LRRP before becoming a LRP, and if he took this as an ominous sign of upcoming command abuse and misuse, upcoming "pork chops and bearfucks" like November 20, the others at least respected his pessimism by falling silent for a thoughtful moment themselves.

Larry Chambers bent forward and looked at the orders more closely, and then stepped back with a grave, but brave and determined, look on his face. "Well, I guess that's it," he said. "It looks like we're going to be Rangers now, and you know what that means, don't you?"

"No," said Meszaros, squinting cynically. Like Chambers, Linderer, and about half the Lurps in the company, Meszaros had put a few years of college behind him before he ran out of money and decided it might be interesting to go Airborne with a war on. He was usually the first guy to catch the drift when Chambers was into some gamesmanship, and he enjoyed playing the straight man. "No, Chambers," he said. "You tell us what it means."

"Well," said Chambers, fixing Miller, and then Linderer and Saenz, with a serious look. "If we're going to be Rangers, I guess that means we've got to start wearing Big Irons on our hips."

When the other Lurps stared at him, Chambers hastily explained that he was thinking in terms of the song lyrics—"He might have gone on livin', but he made one fatal slip, when he tried to match the Ranger with the Big Iron on his hip."

Gary Linderer sighed. This name change was already having a bad effect on the infamous Chambers sense of humor, and it was a sad thing to see Chambers back down and have to explain a joke.

That evening, down at the company shower, Captain Eklund was damn near floating on air.

"Hey, Champ," he gloated to SFC Champion, who'd worn the green beret but not the Fort Benning Ranger tab. "How do you think they're going to like our name change over in Group? They've still got the hat, but we've got the better name now!"

SFC Champion shrugged and said he didn't expect that the Lurps becoming Rangers was going to upset anyone over in Special Forces, if they noticed the name change at all.

When word came down—very forcefully—that Ranger status did not confer the right to wear the U.S. Army Ranger tab, for that right belonged only to those awarded the tab on completion of the Ranger School at Fort Benning, the Lurps didn't take serious offense, because they now had a red, black, and white Airborne Ranger scroll of their own to wear over the Screaming Eagle patch. The fact that the new scroll didn't fit as comfortably over an Airborne tab as the old Lurp scrolls didn't bother the Lurps too much. The 101st was pretty much a leg division now anyway. Let the legs wear the old Airborne tab over their Screaming Eagle patches. The Lurps had the words "Airborne" and "Ranger" on their new scrolls, and they figured the standard tabs would now be redundant anyway.

When word came that the traditional black beret of the U.S. Army Ranger was not yet authorized, and wouldn't

be worn in the 101st until it was, no matter what the other
Lurp units were doing, the general consensus was
remarkably indifferent. And when word came down that
the 101st Recondo patch on the black baseball caps the
Lurps wore was to be replaced with the old Merrill's
Marauders patch, there was no mad rush to the Korean
contract tailor's shop to make the changeover. And when
it came to wearing six-guns on their hips, the Rangers
pretty much passed on that, too. There weren't any
Walker Colts down at supply, and if a man wanted a
handgun, he could always take an M-1911.

The Department of the Army had declared them
Rangers, and the Lurps had no quarrel with the aptness of
the title. But for the most part, those who had been Lurps
before they were Rangers continued to think of themselves
as Lurps. Ranger was a fine title, the oldest and most illus-
trious of all American special operations designations,
going back to the French and Indian War, when George
Washington was still a mere company grade officer in the
service of the English king. The Ranger name had been
burnished over two hundred years of American history, and
the Lurps were certainly proud to bear it. But to those
Rangers who had been Lurps first, "Lurp" remained an
even more exalted name than "Ranger" because it was a
name that they'd made for themselves.

Fittingly enough, it was Ray Zoschak who put things
in perspective when he observed that "Ranger" had been
just a school name for too long, and as he still had almost
a full six-month extension ahead of him, he was willing
to do his part to make the designation respectable again.

It didn't really matter what other people called him, Zo
said. What mattered was that they still got to pull missions and kill gooks. Zoschak figured there'd be a lot of
that ahead for the Rangers—and, as usual, Zo was right.

# Lessons Learned

Gary Linderer and Rey Martinez, my teammates on this project, which was originally to be published as one long book instead of three shorter ones, noticed that this was the shortest of the three and suggested that I flesh it out with a "Lessons Learned" section. One of the reasons active-duty military personnel read books about previous wars is to benefit from the experience of those who went before them, and perhaps learn a few lessons the easy way, by reading them, rather than experiencing them in field training or in combat.

I'm not really sure that there is much I can offer in this regard. Current members of the U.S. military who are tasked with missions similar to those pulled by F Company, 58th Infantry (LRP) are much better trained and educated than we were. They are equipped with much better radios than we had, somewhat better weapons, and a whole array of tools, ranging from night-vision optics to global-positioning units and laser-sighting devices, that we could not have imagined in our wildest fantasies. Of course, most of our wildest fantasies were not about military equipment, but that's beside the point.

The basics for this type of work were laid out even before the establishment of the United States of America. Every army Ranger, whether he serves in the Ranger

Battalions, the Long Range Surveillance units, or in some other capacity, is familiar with Rogers' Rangers' Standing Orders. Some of the specific instructions might seem a little anachronistic, reflecting their origin in the French and Indian War, but the basic tenets make as much sense now as they did 250 years ago.

### Standing Orders, Rogers' Rangers

1. Don't forget nothing.
2. Have your musket clean as a whistle, hatchet scoured, sixty rounds of powder and ball, and be ready to move at a moment's warning.
3. When you're on the march, act the way you would if you were sneaking up on a deer; see the enemy first.
4. Tell the truth about what you see and what you do. There is an Army depending on us for correct information. You can lie all you please when you tell other folks about the Rangers. But never lie to an Officer or Ranger.
5. Don't never take a chance you don't have to.
6. When we're on the march, we march single file, far enough apart so that one shot can't go through two men.
7. If we strike swamp or soft ground, we spread out abreast so it's hard to track us.
8. When we march, we keep moving until dark, so as to give the enemy the least possible chance at us.
9. When we camp, half the party stays awake while the other half sleeps.
10. If we take prisoners, we keep 'em separate till we have time to examine them, so they can't cook up a story between them.
11. Don't ever march home the same way. Take a different route so you won't be ambushed.

12. No matter whether we travel in big parties or little ones, each party has to keep a scout 20 yards ahead, 20 yards on each flank, and 20 yards in the rear, so the main party can't be surprised and wiped out.

13. Every night you'll be told where to meet if surrounded by a superior force.

14. Don't sit down or eat without posting sentries.

15. Don't sleep beyond dawn; dawn's when the French and Indians attack.

16. Don't cross a river by a regular ford.

17. If somebody's tailing you, make a circle, come back on your own tracks, and ambush the folks that aim to ambush you.

18. Don't stand up when the enemy's coming against you. Kneel down, lie down, hide behind a tree.

19. Let the enemy come until he's close enough to touch. Then let him have it and jump out and finish him with your hatchet.

Now obviously, in this era of automatic weapons, sixty rounds is not adequate, and if you have to finish anyone off, there are better tools than a hatchet—although, come to think of it, a hatchet would do nicely if you happen to have one.

The twenty-yard rule for point, flank, and rear security (#12) is obviously not ironclad. A six-man recon team moving through thick jungle isn't going to be able to move in single file (#6) and maintain unit integrity with four of those men twenty yards away on security. But the point remains valid that any element should try to have 360-degree security. The way to do this with a small team is for each man to cover his own zone of responsibility as the unit moves and when the unit is halted.

Since any Indians an American soldier is likely to

encounter in combat these days are likely to be fellow American soldiers (and likely to be in elite infantry or special-operations units), and since the French are at least nominally our friends and allies, standing order #15 seems a little dated in its specifics. But the fact that the enemy is likely to attack at dawn or just before dawn remains as true today as it was in the French and Indian War, or in Vietnam.

Standing order #8 needs a little expansion. It was SOP during the Vietnam War for recon teams to move their night-halt position after settling in. In actual fact, this SOP was not always followed—but it should have been. Establishing one night-halt position as a decoy, then shifting to another saved more than one team from mortar and ground attacks.

It should be obvious that a small team cannot always circle back and ambush those on their trail (#17). If a small team is being tracked or chased by a much larger enemy element, this could be a suicidally stupid maneuver. The plain fact is that sometimes there is little choice but to just haul ass.

All in all, Rogers' Rangers' Standing Orders still offer about the best guide there is. There are, however, a few more standing orders that should be added to the original nineteen. The most obvious among them is to *always* have alternative plans of action. In war, as in normal life, it is wise to count on things going wrong. Another thing Rogers might have mentioned, but didn't, is to never initiate an attack without some idea of what you're attacking. Those four enemy soldiers bopping down the trail might offer a tempting target, but if there is any indication that they might be the point element of a unit much bigger than your own, it is wise to let them pass.

As a general rule, recon teams on reconnaissance missions are not out there to kill the enemy with the team's own organic weapons. The temptation to do so can be strong—and all too often during the Vietnam War, recon troops yielded to it. Doing so was not always disastrous, and not always a mistake. Sometimes it made good sense to take advantage of such opportunities, and during the Vietnam War, a lot of good information was gathered from the papers and equipment carried by enemy troops. But just as often, initiating contact compromised missions before they could be carried to completion.

Rogers and his Rangers didn't have radios and supporting firepower on call, and said nothing of their employment. A truism is a cliché that is true, and it is a truism that a special-operations troop's best friend is its radio. I am not even remotely qualified to offer any advice to present-day soldiers when it comes to communications equipment because the gear available to them now surpasses what we had by a couple orders of magnitude. Still, it's probably safe to say that even the best communications equipment will fail sometimes and in inexplicable ways. In this book, there is a story about a mission in which Sergeant John Burford's team found itself without radio communications with the relay teams and even with helicopters almost directly overhead, *despite the fact that all the radios and batteries had been tested before the mission.* Even fresh batteries did not help. I don't know if there is any scientific explanation for "dead zones" where electronic communications don't work, but I do know that, for whatever reason, such areas do seem to exist. Beyond "dead zones," there are many other factors that can interfere with good communication—and I am sure that even modern radios are not immune. I'm not sure what particular lesson can be learned from this sort of experience, other than to take the standard precautions and to expect that sometimes decidedly nonstandard problems will occur.

My first team leader, Sergeant Alan "Teddy Bear" Gaskell, used to say that a Lurp should earn his Combat Infantry Badge before becoming a Lurp, because, in theory at least, the only time a recon trooper gets shot at is when someone screws up. Of course, Teddy Bear knew that in the real world luck plays a part, and sometimes the luck is running in the enemy's favor. And he also knew that in the real world, reconnaissance troops are not exclusively employed in what the army somewhat strangely refers to as "passive" reconnaissance, for he'd pulled his share of raids and other such missions in which the enemy managed to get a few rounds off without the Lurps having screwed up or the luck of the occasion running in the enemy's favor. Ideally, of course, a recon team should do its job without the enemy ever knowing it is in the area. But this is not an ideal world.

Veterans of the 101st Airborne Division's Vietnam War Lurp units—1/101 LRRP; F Company, 58th LRP; and L Company, 75th Ranger—have regular reunions. Sometimes we join other Lurp/Ranger units at big reunions with one or another of the active-duty Ranger Battalions, and sometimes we have company reunions with the current 101st Airborne's Long Range Surveillance detachment. At reunions where we mingle with Battalion Rangers, we often hear young Rangers complain that—except for the Ranger Regiment's recon detachment—there is too little emphasis placed on the small-team sneaky-pete sort of missions we used to pull. When we have reunions with LRS Rangers, we hear complaints that the army seems to take this "passive" reconnaissance role a little too dogmatically and refuses to take seriously the idea that they might be called upon to actually kill enemy soldiers. We understand that the traditional Ranger missions of raids and reconnaissance are currently being assigned to two different sorts of Ranger units, and we don't mind that the battalions concentrate on raids and airfield seizures and such, while the LRSU concentrates on recon and covert surveillance. But it bothers all of us that the army doesn't seem to have learned one of the most obvious lessons all of us learned in Vietnam.

During Desert Storm, Lurp teams from the 101st Airborne's Long Range Surveillance detachment were sent on what can only be considered strategic missions deep behind enemy lines—and performed these missions without being allowed to carry the weapons and ammunition they would need for effective self-defence if things turned very bad for them. On the grounds that they had a "passive" role to play, teams going into Iraq were not allowed to carry full loads of ammunition, nor such "offensive" weapons as light machine guns and grenade launchers. During that same war, only one company from the 75th Ranger Regiment was deployed to the theater, and it does not appear to have done much in the way of small-unit operations behind enemy lines. Those of us who fought in a war a good deal longer than Desert Storm know something the army seems to have forgotten. In any ground war that lasts much longer than two weeks, current army doctrine is almost certain to fray at the seams, and both sorts of Ranger units will find themselves tasked with whatever Ranger missions the situation might demand.

It seems to me that the Long Range Surveillance units should be officially brought into the Ranger family. Personnel crossover between the LRS and Ranger Battalions doesn't seem to be much of a problem. Rangers in both sorts of Ranger unit these days often seem more interested in serving in the other sort when they leave their present assignments than they do in going to non-Delta Special Forces. These young Rangers know their full heritage as American Rangers better than the army brass seems to know it. At a recent reunion of the Vietnam-era Ranger Association at Fort Lewis, we old Lurp/Rangers were shocked to hear that the fine show they put on for us and the party we threw for them that night were about the only times in recent memory that the local Long Range Surveillance detachment and the local Ranger Battalion had done *anything* together—and neither one of them seemed to train quite enough with the local Special Forces Group. Come the next long and serious war, the mission overlap between them all will almost certainly become as apparent to the brass as it is to us old farts and the young troops, and we hope it isn't too costly a lesson for the brass to learn, because the brass won't be doing the dying.

I think it's the LRS that we worry about the most. The Long Range Surveillance detachments do not belong to any special-operations command. When it comes to command and control, they belong to Military Intelligence, Aviation, or Air Cav units under a conventional division or corps. The LRSU assigned to the 82nd Airborne Division and the 101st Airborne Division have helpful Special Forces units close at hand and access to training their parent units aren't always willing or able to give them. It is especially gratifying to us old 101st Lurp MACV Recondo School graduates to hear that good old 5th Special Forces Group is still looking out for our boys when the division won't. But it is less gratifying to visit Fort Campbell and hear Desert Storm veterans of both 5th SF Group and the 101st LRSU compare the equipment and support and level of prior training they received for what were often the same level of reconnaissance missions. The Long Range Surveillance detachments must be brought at least partially under the special-operations command, and the logical way to do this is to officially designate them Rangers, tighten up training and selection, and task them with at least a few of the strategic reconnaissance missions now assigned to Special Forces.

Command and control of Lurp and Ranger units is a worry, born from lessons learned in Vietnam. Changing the order of battle and command structure will not guarantee against an occasional incompetent or egomaniacal unit commander. But what about the 17th Cav's squadron commander who came up with the brilliant idea of inserting recon teams with smoke trailing from the helicopter skids and cavalry bugle charges blaring from loudspeakers? Or all the succession of field-grade outsiders who tried to grab command from Captain Eklund on November 20, 1968? And if you read this book, you certainly remember General Barsanti, who seemed to hold his Lurps back as a Praetorian Guard for fear of his own troops, and then neglected them when they showed their true nature. Anyone who truly believes that, come a long war, the Long Range Surveillance detachments won't be horribly or stupidly misused by a conventional commander—or even worse, one who resents elite enlisted men—does not know history.

Those are all lessons out of a long-ago war. I think there are equally important lessons to be learned from more recent military actions. With one exception, I am not qualified, knowledgeable enough, or cleared to comment on any mission that members of the 75th Rangers have performed in support of Special Forces Operational Detachment Delta, including Desert One. The same thing

is true of Desert Storm. From what I understand, anything major that went wrong for the 75th Rangers in
Grenada or Panama wasn't their own fault, and wasn't
anything they were trained to adapt to.

Mogadishu was different. All this media talk about
"Task Force Ranger," eighteen dead Rangers, and American Rangers dragged through the streets on a rope is
something of a smokescreen. The raids to capture the war-
lord whose ex-Marine son now claims to rule Somalia
were a Delta operation as much as a Ranger operation, and
all sorts of other people were involved—representatives
of almost the entire American special-operations commu-
nity. But Mogadishu stands out as a horrible and tragic
misuse of Rangers, as well as a lot of other people. The
raids were based on poor intelligence and too hastily conceived. Reaction forces were clearly inadequate. There are
lessons to be learned there, but it seems to me that the
most important lesson to be learned from Mogadishu—a
lesson that somewhat parallels the ultimate lesson to be
learned from Vietnam—is that even the United States of
America can't save the whole damn world, and even the
most humanitarian and idealistic of international motivations can get our country nothing more than lost prestige,
wasted tax dollars, general cynicism, and too many Purple
Hearts and body bags. Every damn time we go messing
around in the civil wars of people truly determined to kill
their neighbors, this seems to be the outcome.

This is a political lesson. It is also perhaps the most
important lesson that the sort of mainstream American
people, whose sons and daughters and brothers and sis-
ters do military service, have learned in the course of a
twentieth-century devoted to saving foreigners from each
other all over the world. Unfortunately, our political

leaders remain so enamored of fancying themselves world leaders, they haven't yet caught on to this lesson.

As Teddy Bear Gaskell well knew when he said that in an ideal world a Lurp should have his Combat Infantry Badge before becoming a Lurp, this is not an ideal world. There is no way around the sad fact that, in the next century, young Americans will continue to die in military service. It is up to us, those old enough to vote and old enough to have already learned a few lessons in life, to make sure that those who wear our country's uniform and put their lives on the line are putting their lives on the line in the true and best interests of their country and ours.

I hate to agree with Ronald Reagan, but Vietnam was, indeed, a noble cause. But the sad lesson remains that, noble as it might have been at conception, Vietnam was not our cause. Some of us had a lot of fun, some of us suffered horribly, and too many of us died. I am convinced now that the only benefit America got from her involvement in Vietnam was the lesson that we can't save all of the world every time we try, and unless our direct national interest or the decent survival of mankind at large is at stake, we shouldn't even try.

The bloody history of the 101st LRP/Rangers
by one of its own.

**SIX SILENT MEN**
**Book One**
**by Reynel Martinez**

In 1965, the 1st Brigade of the 101st Airborne Division
was detached from the division and assigned to
Vietnam. Reynel Martinez provides a personal account
of the first faltering steps of the brigade's provisional
LRRP unit as the men learn how to battle the VC and
NVA while surviving the more pernicious orders of their
own, occasionally thoughtless, high-level commanders.
SIX SILENT MEN: Book One provides an often bloody
but always honorable chronicle of courage under fire.

**SIX SILENT MEN**
**Book One**
**By Reynel Martinez**

Published by Ballantine Books.
Available in your local bookstore.

The bloody history of the 101st LRP/Rangers
by one of its own.


**SIX SILENT MEN**
**Book Three**
**by Gary A. Linderer**


By 1969, the NVA had grown more experienced at coun-
tering the tactics of the long-range patrols, and SIX
SILENT MEN: *Book Three* describes some of the fiercest
fighting Lurps saw during the war. Based on his own
experiences and extensive interviews with other combat
vets of the 101st's Lurp companies, Gary Linderer writes
this final, heroic chapter in the seven bloody years that
Lurps served God and country in Vietnam. These tough
young warriors—grossly outnumbered and deep in
enemy territory—fought with the guts, intensity, and
courage that have made them legends in the 101st.


**SIX SILENT MEN**
**Book Three**
**By Gary Linderer**

Published by Ballantine Books.
Available in your local bookstore.